Human Values

Human Values

New Essays on Ethics and Natural Law

Edited by

David S. Oderberg

and

Timothy Chappell

First published 2004 by
PALGRAVE MACMILLAN
Houndmills, Basingstoke, Hampshire RG21 6XS and
175 Fifth Avenue, New York, N.Y. 10010
Companies and representatives throughout the world

PALGRAVE MACMILLAN is the global academic imprint of the Palgrave
Macmillan division of St. Martin's Press, LLC and of Palgrave Macmillan Ltd.
Macmillan® is a registered trademark in the United States, United Kingdom
and other countries. Palgrave is a registered trademark in the European
Union and other countries.

ISBN 1–4039–1810–4

This book is printed on paper suitable for recycling and made from fully
managed and sustained forest sources.

A catalogue record for this book is available from the British Library.

Library of Congress Cataloging-in-Publication Data
Human values : new essays on ethics and natural law / edited by David S.
    Oderberg and Timothy Chappell.
        p.   cm.
    Includes bibliographical references and index.
    ISBN 1–4039–1810–4 (cloth)
    1. Christian ethics—Catholic authors.   2. Natural law—Religious
    aspects—Catholic Chruch.   3. Ethics.   4. Natural law.   I. Oderberg,
    David S.   II. Chappell, T.D.J. (Timothy D.J.)

    BJ1249.H79 2004
    171′.2—dc22

                                                        2004051682

10   9   8   7   6   5   4   3   2   1
13   12   11   10   09   08   07   06   05   04

Printed and bound in Great Britain by
Antony Rowe Ltd, Chippenham and Eastbourne

Contents

Notes on Contributors

Timothy Chappell is Senior Lecturer in Philosophy at the University of Dundee. He is the author of *Understanding Human Goods* (1998), *Aristotle and Augustine on Freedom* (1995), and editor of *The Plato Reader* (1996), and *Philosophy of the Environment* (1997). His forthcoming books are *Reading Plato's Theaetetus* and *The Inescapable Self.*

John Cottingham is Professor of Philosophy at the University of Reading. He has published seven books as sole author, including *Descartes*, *The Rationalists*, and *Philosophy and the Good Life*, and has also produced many editions, translations, and edited collections. He is co-editor and translator of the three-volume Cambridge edition of *The Philosophical Writings of Descartes*, and editor of *Ratio*, the international journal of analytic philosophy. He has also published numerous articles on moral philosophy, and on the history of philosophy. His most recent book *On the Meaning of Life* (2002) deals with central themes in the philosophy of religion. He is currently Stanton Lecturer in the Philosophy of Religion at the University of Cambridge, and his *The Spiritual Dimension: Religion, Science, and Human Value* is to be published by Cambridge University Press.

Gerard J. Hughes was for many years chairman of the department of philosophy at Heythrop College, University of London, and is now Master of Campion Hall, University of Oxford. He has published articles on a variety of topics in moral philosophy, as well as *The Nature of God* and, most recently, *Aristotle on Ethics.*

Jacqueline A. Laing is Senior Lecturer in Law at London Metropolitan University, where she teaches jurisprudence and criminal law. She has also taught moral philosophy at the Universities of Oxford and Melbourne. She is co-editor (with David S. Oderberg) of *Human Lives: Critical Essays on Consequentialist Bioethics* and has published articles in legal and philosophical journals. Her current research interests focus on issues in biotechnology, especially human cloning and artificial reproduction.

Christopher Martin is a lecturer at the University of St Thomas, Houston. He has previously taught at the Universities of Glasgow, Navarre, and Oxford. He has written on medieval philosophy, especially on St Thomas Aquinas, as well as on ethics, particularly Aristotelian ethics, and on related themes (e.g. moral psychology). His most recent book is *Thomas Aquinas: God and Explanations* (1997).

Mark C. Murphy is Professor of Philosophy at Georgetown University. His main work is on natural law theory, both in its historical manifestations and as a live option for ethics, politics, and jurisprudence. He is the author of *Natural Law and Practical Rationality* (2001) and *An Essay on Divine Authority* (2002), and is the editor of *Alasdair MacIntyre* (2003). He is currently at work on *Natural Law in Jurisprudence and Politics*.

David S. Oderberg is Professor of Philosophy at the University of Reading, England. He is the author of many articles in metaphysics, ethics, philosophical logic and other subjects. Among other books he is the author of *Moral Theory: A Non-Consequentialist Approach* (2000) and *Applied Ethics: A Non-Consequentialist Approach* (2000), as well as co-editor with Jacqueline A. Laing of *Human Lives: Critical Essays on Consequentialist Bioethics* (1997).

Henry S. Richardson is Professor of Philosophy at Georgetown University. He is the author of *Practical Reasoning about Final Ends* (1994); *Democratic Autonomy* (2002); 'Desire and the Good in *De Anima*', in *Essays on Aristotle's 'De Anima'*, ed. M. Nussbaum and A.O. Rorty (1992); and 'Thinking about Conflicts of Desires', in *Practical Conflicts: New Philosophical Essays*, ed. P. Baumann and M. Betzler (2004).

Christopher Tollefsen is an Associate Professor of Philosophy at the University of South Carolina. He works on issues in meta-ethics and ethical theory, as well as applied, and especially medical ethics. Recent work has appeared in *The Journal of Value Inquiry, Ethical Theory and Moral Practice*, and the *Journal of Medicine and Philosophy*, and volumes such as Ana Iltis (ed.), *Institutional Integrity in Health Care* (2003) and William Alston (ed.), *Realism and Antirealism* (2002). In 2004–2005, he will be a James Madison Fellow at Princeton University.

Suzanne Uniacke is Reader in Applied Ethics at the University of Hull, England. She has published widely in ethics, applied ethics, and philosophy of law. Her publications include *Permissible Killing: The Self-Defence Justification of Homicide* (1994), articles in edited collections and journals, and the entry on the 'Principle of Double Effect' in the *Routledge Encyclopedia of Philosophy*. Her current research addresses issues of responsibility and moral obligation, and rights as permissions and constraints.

Helen Watt is Director of the Linacre Centre for Healthcare Ethics, London. She is the author of *Life and Death in Healthcare Ethics: A Short Introduction* (2000), and of various articles on bioethical issues, including reproductive ethics and end-of-life decisions. She is currently editing a book on the topic of cooperation in evil.

Introduction

Natural law theory says that humans can only live well if they recognise the goods that are natural for humans and understand how those goods generate the obligations and the permissions that together characterise the system of practical guidance that we call morality. Natural law – for the source of the name see Aquinas, *Summa Theologiae* Ia IIae q. 94 – is a long-established and flourishing ethical tradition, with roots in Plato, Aristotle, and Aquinas, and it is increasingly recognised as a worthy competitor to Kantianism, utilitarianism, and virtue ethics. The chapters in this book reflect the growing influence, sophistication, and importance of natural law theory within contemporary ethical debate. And they demonstrate by example how much vitality there is in natural law – how much rich and as-yet-unrealised theoretical potential that ancient tradition of ethical thinking still holds today.

More than one of the chapters focus, in effect, on the provocative phrase with which we began the last paragraph – 'the goods that are natural for humans'. What does it mean to describe goods as *natural* for humans? And which goods are 'natural' in this sense, anyway? In the light of modern evolutionary theory, can we reasonably describe any moral goods as natural?

This is one of the questions raised by John Cottingham, in the first chapter of the book, ' "Our natural guide...": Conscience, "Nature", and Moral Experience'. Cottingham examines the influential contemporary doctrine known as ethical naturalism, which he portrays as part of an empiricist tradition in moral philosophy that has its origins in the Enlightenment. As he notes, this doctrine is no less fraught with ambiguities than opposing doctrines are: terms such as 'nature' and 'natural' are among the most ambiguous in the philosophical vocabulary. The chapter begins by exploring some of these ambiguities, taking its cue from the insightful analysis provided by Joseph Butler in the eighteenth century. Having clarified the ambiguities, Cottingham is able to recover what he sees as the traditional normative notion of the 'natural' – the one that held sway before the term was appropriated by the empirical 'naturalisers': 'the "natural" can have two quite distinct senses as applied to our species: it can refer to the properties (inclinations, dispositions) that we as a matter of fact happen to possess; or it can refer to authoritative principles that are "inscribed in our hearts" '.

This distinction sets the stage for a possible rehabilitation of the ancient notion of *conscience* – a notion that the 'naturalising' tendencies (in the modern sense) have tended to squeeze out. Although the idea of conscience is a distinctly unfashionable one in contemporary moral philosophy, Cottingham's chapter aims to show that it is a notion that resonates with many aspects of our human experience. He also argues, however, that our understanding of conscience as (in one sense) a 'natural' guide to action needs to be enriched well beyond what most philosophers have been prepared to contemplate, if we are to achieve a proper grasp of its role in our moral development. And this leads him, finally, to make connections between the concept of conscience as 'natural guide' and the traditional theory of 'natural law'. His suggestion is that the metaphysics underpinning natural law theory may well offer a sounder basis than its 'naturalistic' modern rival for providing a satisfying account of human moral experience.

In the second chapter, 'Basic Goods, Practical Insight, and External Reasons', Christopher Tollefsen focuses on another issue that is raised by natural law theory's appeal to nature. This is the very understandable question: If something is a natural good, does that mean that all humans will automatically (be motivated to or have reason to) pursue it? As Tollefsen notes, many natural law theorists start by giving an account of the basic or natural goods. And they are typically committed to the following two claims: first (*universalism*), that all genuine agents have some practical grasp of the basic human goods; and second (*eudai-monism*), that the point of human action for the sake of the basic goods is human flourishing, a point which, again, all agents in some sense understand.

The conjunction of these two claims, Tollefsen points out, seems to result in a blurring of the internalism/externalism distinction as famously drawn by Bernard Williams. This is a distinction between those 'internal' reasons that arise only from an agent's antecedently existing desires and beliefs, and the 'external' reasons that, on some Kantian views, are supposed to be capable of influencing any agent, 'from the outside' so to speak, no matter what his antecedently existing desires and beliefs may be. The blurring that Tollefsen notes is this. Since the starting points of correct deliberation are shared by all, it is true that there is a motivational path from where an agent is to what an agent ought to do. But since basic goods are objectively good, the subjectivism that externalist views oppose is not in play. The resulting position is not straightforwardly internalist in the way Williams describes, for it is not subjectivist; but it is not straightforwardly externalist either, because there exists a motivational path for all agents towards what is morally required.

In his chapter, Tollefsen argues that there is more to the appeal of externalism than objectivity. The picture above remains too indebted to Williams in its account of correct deliberation. What is common to subjectivist accounts, and to internalist views based on such accounts, is that no more can emerge from practical reasoning than goes in, even on Williams's rather sophisticated account of deliberation. Practical reasoning is at worst merely technical, but at best only specificatory. Against this view, Tollefsen insists that basic goods theories should, and in most cases do, leave room for practical reason also to bring to light new aspects of reasons that are not means or specifications of reasons we already are aware of. While our new reasons have an intelligible relationship to the reasons of which we were previously aware, we are capable of practical insight into what was previously opaque to us.

This means, Tollefsen suggests, that a basic goods theory can respect three related intuitions. The first is the intuition behind John McDowell's claim that the idea of moral conversion is 'the idea of an intelligible shift in motivation that is exactly *not* effected by inducing a person to discover, by practical reasoning controlled by existing motivations, some internal reasons that he did not previously realize he had'. Second, such a theory can respect Aristotle's insight into the importance of character formation and the difficulty of reformation, without making such reformation impossible or unintelligible. And third, basic goods theories will be able to make sense of the thought that a moral crisis is often the event that precipitates moral conversion or reformation.

Tollefsen concludes by specifying three ways, consonant with universalism and eudaimonism, in which practical reasoning is insightful about reasons that are not purely internal. These involve reasoning and awareness about the nature and depth of the basic goods, about the shape of a human life, and about the scope of the goodness of the goods across agents. Reasoning about these aspects of reasons for action is not narrowly controlled by existing motivations; it is neither technical nor specificatory; nor, on the other hand, is it entirely cut off from an agent's practical awareness of the basic goods and her desire to flourish.

In his chapter on 'The Fact/Value Distinction', Christopher Martin takes up a different question about 'the natural' and 'the non-natural'. Martin's project is to dispute the existence of any such distinction, despite the fact that, since at least the time of Moore's *Principia Ethica* in 1903, it has been a distinguishing feature of English-speaking moral philosophy to maintain some kind of strong fact/value distinction. Martin objects that the very variety and inconsistency of the arguments given for this distinction, and the theories used to support it, may make us suspicious, particularly when we notice that the distinction is not so obvious to people of other cultures.

One argument for the distinction is based on the claim that people disagree about value judgements, while they agree about factual judgements. Martin comments that it is difficult to enumerate all the different ways in which this claim is either false or irrelevant to the fact/value distinction.

A second argument is that value judgements, if they referred to such alleged objective entities as 'values', would contain reference to metaphysically or epistemologically 'queer' entities, and that these should be rejected. To this Martin responds that the argument is only plausible if one is *a priori* committed to materialism and empiricism and mistakes the logical category of words such as 'good': they are not absolute expressions, but relative ones.

A third argument is that value judgements commit the one who judges whereas factual judgements do not. This, on Martin's reading, turns out to be true, but only because of trivial facts of psychology and logic, such as that one can speak to oneself in the second person.

If the distinction thus lacks a logical basis, what – Martin asks – impels people to believe in it? His response is that, since those who believe it are overwhelmingly from an English-speaking cultural background, cultural explanations may be sought. English-speaking cultures are Protestant, therefore more prone to voluntarism in ethics; they have common-law systems, which distinguish between judges of law and judges of fact; and linguistically they have the strongly alliterative, aesthetically attractive pair 'right and wrong', which seems to mean more than 'good and bad' and to be more detached from facts.

As its title suggests, a central concern of Henry S. Richardson's chapter, 'Incommensurability and Basic Goods: A Tension in the New Natural Law Theory', is with the question of how the different goods recognised by natural law theory are to be evaluated relative to each other. In a critical examination of work by Germain Grisez, John Finnis, Mark C. Murphy, and Alfonso Gómez-Lobo, Richardson notes that while these theorists maintain that there are *conceptual links between* the basic goods and human nature, there is a clear sense in which they seek to avoid *deriving* the basic goods directly *from* human nature. Accordingly, they cast the basic goods as sources of value, holding that, necessarily, all reasons for action derive entirely from them. At the same time, partly in order to help secure the 'Pauline Principle' – that evil not be done that good may come of it – which might otherwise be threatened within a good-based view, these theorists also affirm that goods are thoroughly incommensurable, both across and within categories of basic goodness. Richardson argues that these two central commitments of the new natural law theory – to the basic goods as sources of value and to thorough incommensurability – are mutually inconsistent. The incommensurability claim, in his view, undercuts the claim that a small, finite list of basic goods can rightly be seen as the source of all reasons for action. Hence his attitude to the programme of natural law theory is that of an interested but critical spectator.

Timothy Chappell's chapter, 'The Polymorphy of Practical Reason', is written as a survey of a number of different issues concerning natural law theory. Chappell shares Richardson's interest in incommensurability, and to some extent shares his critical attitude to natural law. Unlike Richardson, however, Chappell does not doubt the overall viability of the programme of natural law theory, as becomes clear from his articulation of the notions of 'respecting' and 'pursuing' goods, and from the argument at the beginning of his chapter that there is something deeply wrong with the very idea of consequentialist 'maximisation'.

On the other hand, Chappell does have some specific criticisms of the natural law programme as it is most usually developed. He is dubious, for example, about the kind of eudaimonism that Tollefsen develops in the second chapter and Oderberg in the sixth: the view that all the goods that motivate human action are *human* goods, 'aspects of integral human fulfilment', to use a well-known phrase of Grisez. Chappell's complaint is that this 'anthropocentric account of what it is to be a good seems to get the order of explanation back to front': 'If the goods were all defined as aspects of human flourishing, that would simply raise the familiar question why *human* flourishing, particularly, was such a good thing. Why not a moral focus on cockroach flourishing, or on Martian *eudaimonia*?'

Chappell suggests that this Aristotelian anthropocentrism might usefully be replaced by a more Platonist approach, on which – to echo the *Euthyphro* – the goods are not good because they are good for humans, but are goods for humans because they are good. For Chappell, the goods are not by definition aspects of human flourishing; rather, they are 'ideal standards that apply in different normative dimensions'; and it is this fact that explains how the goods, or some of them, can function as aspects of human flourishing. Chappell is well aware that this approach to the metaphysics of value runs straight into John Mackie's famous 'argument from queerness' against the objectivity of ethics; but in Chappell's view that is no bad thing, since he, unlike Martin in Chapter 3, and unlike a fair number of other natural law theorists, is happy to endorse a metaphysically deep distinction between the normative and the non-normative.

David S. Oderberg's chapter, 'The Structure and Content of the Good', focuses like those by Chappell, Tollefsen, and Richardson, on the notion of the human goods. Oderberg begins by contrasting two methodologically distinct but complementary ways of approaching natural law theory (NLT). One is a mainly agent-centred approach, centring on practical reasoning and the intelligibility of action, paying attention to human tendencies and inclinations. The other, more traditional and mainly world-centred approach, focuses on the metaphysics of the good by means of an analysis of human nature and human faculties, and of the way in which the good must be structured for it to be an object of human pursuit or, more specifically, a foundation for moral decision-making.

In his chapter Oderberg takes a primarily world-centred approach to fundamental questions of content and structure. First, looking at some typical examples from NL theorists of lists of the basic goods, he analyses various members that they have proposed to see what the correct list must contain. Next, he looks at questions concerning how the natural law must be structured, in particular, whether the list of basic goods is finite (here Oderberg criticises Chappell's suggestion in *Understanding Human Goods* (1998) that the list might be indefinitely long), whether there is a supreme or superordinate good, and what kinds of hierarchical relations within and across goods must exist in order for the basic goods to serve as a foundation for practical reasoning about morality. The two main conclusions that Oderberg draws are, first, that ontology must be taken seriously, and miscategorisation avoided, when identifying basic goods; second, that the structure of the good requires a system of *principles* enabling various kinds of comparative judgement within and across goods, in order for NLT to serve as a basis for guiding concrete moral decisions.

One very important question that frequently comes up for moral decision is this: In what circumstances is it justified to inflict harm upon other people? Within the terms of natural law theory, when can someone be harmed without any good being violated? Or more broadly, exactly what kinds of action are there that pursue some good(s) without violating any?

This broad question has already been broached in, for instance, Chappell's remarks at the end of his chapter on the well-known 'principle of double effect'. In one way or another, the question is focal for all of the last five chapters in the book.

Thus Suzanne Uniacke, in her 'Harming and Wronging: The Importance of Normative Context', highlights the importance of the distinction between *harming* someone (injuring or damaging her interests or welfare) and *wronging* her (treating her unjustly, violating her rights) to non-consequentialist moral theory and to practical ethics. Uniacke examines the ethics of retaliation, considering, in particular, hostile acts that aim to inflict harm on others. About such acts, her claim is that context is crucial. Unless we consider the normative context in which any particular act of harm is done, there can be no reasoned answer to the question whether or not there is a moral presumption against it. In the light of this argument, Uniacke rejects both of two widely accepted views: first, that there is a general moral constraint against aiming to inflict harm on other persons; and second, that there is a general corresponding right against harmful interference by other persons *qua* persons.

Rather differently, Jacqueline A. Laing's chapter 'Law, Liberalism, and the Common Good' criticises the idea, pervasive in contemporary Western thought, that if consenting adults want to do something, then unless it causes immediate harm or offence to others, the law has no business intervening. This rationale, called the principle of modern liberal autonomy (MLA), is commonly used to urge permissive laws concerning private recreational drug use, pornography, and reproductive and sexual liberty. By considering the implications of genuine reproductive liberty, Laing argues that we cannot regard sex, family, and reproduction as purely private matters immune from legal regulation deriving from consideration of the common good. At stake are the interests of children, of future generations, and indeed of the very identity, race, and culture of the community involved.

Laing finds that there is in the natural law tradition an understanding of the common good that is instructive in this regard. In that tradition, the common good may be regarded as a mean between two extremes – the self-destructiveness of modern liberal autonomy and that of totalitarianism. It is in this equilibrium, to be found between the two excesses considered, that we begin to understand how necessary is a proper understanding of both common and individual flourishing to establishing exactly which concrete actions involve or do not involve the violation of the human goods.

The last three chapters in the book all bring us back to the principle of double effect (PDE). Gerard J. Hughes is critical of the principle (in his '"Double Effect" or Practical Wisdom?'). He characterises it as an attempt to explain why an action which might at first sight appear to contravene a moral principle does not do so, and is therefore permissible. This result is achieved in part by a particular view of intention, and in part by an account of what is the action in itself that is intended. There is also a proportionality clause. Hughes argues that there are serious problems with each of these three elements which can be solved only at the cost of making PDE unable to do what it was set up to do. Hughes proposes a replacement for PDE: his view is that in both Aristotle and Aquinas there is an account of practical wisdom that would make PDE unnecessary. The cost of this manoeuvre would be a changed view of the role of principles in moral reasoning (moving us, perhaps, rather in the direction of particularism); but according to Hughes, this cost is worth bearing and is in any event inevitable.

Helen Watt and Mark C. Murphy are more sanguine about the prospects for PDE. In a sense, though, Watt's 'Beyond Double Effect: Side-Effects and Bodily Harm' argues that PDE alone does not capture everything of moral importance in the area. She thinks that the relationship between intentions and side-effects needs some further thought: for while it is commonplace for defenders of PDE to point out that it does not give *carte blanche* for causing side-effects that are disproportionately harmful, it is less often noted that there are side-effects which, while remaining unintended, nonetheless have a central role in the description of certain kinds of act. Rather than being just a factor to be weighed against the good effects at which we are aiming, bad side-effects can generate an independent moral conclusion, in conjunction with the long- or short-term intentions with which they are connected.

Watt's chapter considers side-effects of this morally conclusive kind. She focuses on side-effects of serious bodily harm caused by an action intended to affect, if not to harm, the individual concerned. An example would be the retrieval of a heart from a donor who is still alive which need not involve the intention to kill or harm, since death or injury to the donor will not itself promote the surgeon's goals. Watt argues that to intend to affect a person's body internally (as opposed to the body's location) in a way foreseen to do that person no good, but only serious and permanent harm, is sufficient for a serious wrong to the person so affected. The side-effect of harm is not a 'mere' side-effect which good effects for others could in principle outweigh.

In the final part of her chapter, Watt applies these principles to the case of pregnancy in general, and maternal–foetal conflicts in particular. She argues that while the proscription of lethal bodily invasions of the foetus, or of the mother, applies equally in the context of pregnancy, there is a stronger argument against deliberate 'relocations' of the foetus that do not involve the aim to kill or to affect internally in a lethal/harmful way.

Mark C. Murphy's chapter 'Intention, Foresight, and Success' neither criticises PDE (like Hughes) nor goes beyond it (like Watt): his chapter is a full-blown defence of PDE. He begins by noting that PDE presupposes that there is a practically relevant distinction between actions in which evil is intended and actions from which evil results can merely be foreseen. His thesis is that this distinction is practically relevant on account of the way that intention defines the success of one's action: because what is intended sets the success conditions for one's action, intending evil makes it the case that one's action can be a success only if evil results, and one can thus have reason to regret, as such, the absence of evil. Further, inasmuch as one's good is constituted at least in part by the successful achievement of one's objectives, when one intends evil, one's good comes to be constituted at least in part by evil states of affairs. This is intrinsically bad, both with respect to the agent's integrity and with respect to the agent's relationship to other rational beings. Murphy's chapter thus gives us an account of *why* it is wrong to intend evil, but not to foresee it, that fits in appealingly with commonplace pre-philosophical intuitions.

The editors hope that with this new and diverse collection of chapters on ethics and natural law theory, a wider audience will come to see that the tradition expounded and discussed here continues as a vibrant research programme engaged with contemporary thinking. They also hope that the book will give further impetus to placing natural law theory alongside the other ethical positions standardly presented in the textbooks and curriculum.

One editor (DSO) wishes to thank the Leverhulme Trust for their generous support in the form of a research fellowship, during the period of which the work on this book was done. He would also like to thank his co-editor Timothy Chappell for the sort of collaboration that made

working on this book such a pleasure. For a number of very helpful discussions on natural law and related topics during the period of this
book's preparation, the other editor (TDJC) is grateful to, among others,
Antony Duff, Christopher Martin, Mark C. Murphy, Mark Nelson,
Christine Swanton, Christopher Tollefsen – and David S. Oderberg.

The Editors
March 2004

1

'Our Natural Guide…': Conscience, 'Nature', and Moral Experience

John Cottingham

1 Introduction: The empiricist appropriation of the 'natural'

The term 'natural', together with its cognates, is among the most problematic in the philosophical vocabulary, and in any discussion involving the term it is very important to be aware of the way in which its traditional meaning has been all but erased in current philosophical usage. In contemporary philosophical debate, the word 'natural' is most frequently associated with the programme known as 'naturalism', which has become something of a default agenda in modern analytic philosophy. Though it is often not precisely defined, it signals, very roughly, a determination to account for everything there is without any appeal to supernatural (often pejoratively called 'spooky') or other metaphysically charged explanations. In the sphere of moral philosophy, the programme aims to explain the realm of the normative (including the domain of moral obligation) in broadly empirical terms – as somehow part of, continuous with, or in some sense derivable from, the ordinary natural phenomenal world around us.

This 'empirical naturalist' programme, to use a phrase coined by Stephen Darwall, has origins that stretch back to the early-modern period: in the sphere of moral philosophy it includes such figures as Hobbes, Cumberland, Hutcheson, and Hume, all of whom were, as Darwall puts it, 'driven primarily by the desire to account for normativity in a way consistent with an empiricist epistemology and naturalist metaphysics'.[1] One strand in this early-modern or Enlightenment agenda was the attempt to reduce ethics to psychology – for example, to explain the obligations we are under, or feel ourselves to be under, by reference to internal sentiments, drives, impulses, motives, or propensities.

David Hume perhaps represents the summit of this psychologising agenda (partly anticipating what Kant was later to call his Copernican revolution – the relocating of supposedly objective realities as properties or preconditions of subjective experience). Just as causal necessity (at least on one standard interpretation of Hume[2]) dissolves away as an objective power and boils down to no more than a habituated internal expectation in the observer, so in the same way Hume tells us that if we examine wilful murder 'in all lights', we will be unable to detect anything in the action itself that can be called *vice*: 'the vice entirely escapes you as long as you consider the object. You can never find it, till you turn your reflexion into your own breast, and find a sentiment of disapprobation, which arises in you....'[3] The supposed advantage of such a programme, for many of these early naturalisers, as for their modern successors, was that it purportedly allowed morality to be explained in terms of perfectly ordinary occurrences – the sentiments and inclinations we find arising naturally within us. Hence the domain of morality was in principle no more 'special' or discontinuous with ordinary natural phenomena than any other psychological state we experience, such as a feeling of fear or an appetite for food. Of course, a supplementary 'error theory' was needed to explain why so many people had hitherto mistakenly viewed morality as something objective and supra-personal. Here again one could try to play the 'Copernican' or projectivist card, citing the mind's propensity (as Hume graphically put it) to 'spread itself on external objects'.[4]

Although by no means all the empirical-naturalist moralists took so radical a line as Hume, the general tendency of this movement was to attempt to make moral philosophy into a branch of natural science; in the words of Richard Cumberland, writing at the end of the seventeenth century, the aim was to 'resolve [t]he Whole of *moral Philosophy* into *natural Observations* known by the Experience of all men, or into Conclusions of true *Natural Philosophy*'.[5] Hunger and thirst were natural phenomena – in principle, perfectly proper subjects for experiential science. Very well, in the same way your feeling that you should return the money you borrowed yesterday, or your abhorrence for cruelty, or your willingness on occasion to sacrifice selfish gain for the common good – all, it was supposed, could in principle be traced to the natural impulses arising within the human breast. (Incidentally, though many of the naturalisers stressed the importance of internal feelings or sentiments, this did not commit them to saying there was no place for reason in ethics. Nevertheless, they tended to relegate reason to the essentially instrumental role of calculating what means were conducive to furthering the ends that our *natural* impulses motivated us to pursue.)[6]

In this kind of climate, Joseph Butler, one of the more reflective moral thinkers of the eighteenth century, deserves the credit for putting some serious philosophical pressure on the slippery concepts of 'nature' and 'the natural'. For Butler was one of the first to realise just how easily these terms, which may seem harmless enough in ordinary parlance, can become infected with systematic ambiguity. The 'nature' that the Stoics appealed to, when they told us to 'live in accordance with nature',[7] was very different from the 'nature' that was the focus of the new, empirically inspired moral theorists.

My first task in this chapter (in section 2) will be to examine some of these ambiguities, taking my cue in part from Butler's insightful analysis. Getting clear about the ambiguities will clear the way for recovering the traditional normative notion of the 'natural' – the one that held sway before the term was appropriated by the empirical 'naturalisers'. This will in turn set the stage (in section 3) for a possible rehabilitation of the ancient notion of *conscience* – a notion that the naturalising tendencies (in the modern sense) have tended to squeeze out. Although the idea of conscience is a distinctly unfashionable one in contemporary moral philosophy, I hope it will emerge that it is a notion that resonates with many aspects of our human experience. But I shall go on to suggest (in section 4) that our understanding of conscience as a 'natural' (in one sense) guide to action needs to be considerably enriched, beyond what most philosophers have been prepared to provide, if we are to achieve a proper grasp of its role in our moral development. Finally, in the fifth and last section, I shall relate the concept of conscience as 'natural guide' to the traditional theory of 'natural law', and suggest that the metaphysics underpinning this theory may well offer a sounder basis than its naturalistic modern rival for providing a satisfying account of human moral experience.

2 Two senses of 'natural'

In the second of his *Fifteen Sermons* (1726), Butler at first appears to be taking an empirical psychologising approach, talking of various 'natural principles' in man. 'Principles', in this sense, were simply motives or springs of action, such as, for example, impulses towards friendship or self-love. And alongside these there is, Butler observes, another natural principle, namely that whereby 'man approves or disapproves his heart, temper and actions': this is *conscience*. But now comes the crucial distinction. 'By nature', Butler observes, 'is often meant no more than some principle in man without regard either to the kind or degree of it. Thus the passion of anger and the affection of parents to their children, would be called equally *natural*.'[8] This is, if you like, the straightforward empirical sense of the term. And different in degree, but still firmly empirical, Butler goes on to note, is the sense that allowed St Paul to suggest (in the letter to the Ephesians) that mankind is vicious by nature – 'we are by nature the children of wrath'[9] – here meaning no more than that certain human impulses, for example, the impulse to anger, are often extremely powerful and tend to predominate.

Yet alongside these empirical senses, Butler insists, is a quite different sense of 'natural'. St Paul observed in the second chapter of his letter to the Romans that the Gentiles, though not possessing the Law, 'do *by nature* (*physei*) the things contained in the law ... which show the work of the law written in their hearts, their conscience also bearing witness'.[10] Now, if this use of 'nature' were just the same as the previously noted ones, Butler acutely points out, in no way would it license talk of a *law* written in the heart:

> [S]ince other passions ... which lead us ... astray, are themselves in a degree *equally natural*, and often most prevalent ... it is plain the former [good impulses] considered merely as natural, good and right as they are, can no more be a law to us than the latter ... But there is a superior principle of reflection or conscience in every man ... which pronounces some actions to be in themselves just, right, good; others to be in themselves evil, wrong, unjust ... It is by this faculty, *natural to man*, that he is a moral agent ...: by this faculty, I say, not to be considered merely as a principle in his heart, which is to have some influence as well as others; but considered as a faculty in kind and in nature supreme over all others, and which *bears its own authority* of being so.[11]

So the 'natural' can have two quite distinct senses as applied to our species: it can refer to the properties (inclinations, dispositions) that we as a matter of fact happen to possess; or it can refer to authoritative principles that are 'inscribed in our hearts'. In some sense the latter are just as 'natural' as the former – that is, they are a characteristic part of what it is to be a human being. But only the latter possess what Butler calls 'natural authority', or what current philosophical fashion calls 'normativity'.

The distinction that Butler is teasing out here is sorely needed, since the use of the term 'nature' has a long record of causing trouble in the history of philosophy. *Physis* in Aristotle is the world of physical nature, which in some respects can be explained in purely factual, mechanical terms: Aristotle never denies the importance of the raw material and efficient causality on which his empiricist predecessors such as Democritus had entirely relied. But *physis* is more often, indeed most often in Aristotle, an inescapably normative term, one which links into his teleological vision of the cosmos: nature, in this sense, 'does nothing in vain', as Aristotle frequently and famously asserts.[12] Or as Leibniz put it, reviving and indeed radically updating Aristotelian naturalism to fit a Christian context, the 'divine and infinitely marvellous artifice of the Author of nature [ensures]...there is nothing waste, nothing sterile, nothing dead in the universe; no chaos, no confusions, save in appearance'.[13]

To take another important example, Descartes, normally thought of as poles apart from Aristotle and Leibniz in taking a distinctly non-normative and mechanistic view of the natural world, often uses 'nature' in just such a strongly normative sense. The closing section of his *Meditations* contains three successive paragraphs all beginning with the magisterial phrase, *Natura docet* – 'nature teaches'.[14] The things that nature teaches us turn out *not* to be the things we are often spontaneously inclined to believe – such as that the stars are very small, or that the earth is immobile and flat; these, Descartes insists, are only the *apparent* teachings of nature, rash beliefs that were acquired by the 'natural' (in one sense) human habit of jumping to conclusions. But the teachings of nature invoked at the close of the *Meditations* refer to Nature in a much grander sense: 'I understand by the term none other than God himself, or the order and disposition established by God in created things,...[or, in the case of my own nature] the totality of things bestowed on me by God.'[15] What we are 'naturally' inclined to believe, in the mundane empirical sense of 'natural', has no authority at all – indeed it is a major purpose of the Cartesian programme to rid ourselves of the preconceived opinions to which the weakness of our human nature so often inclines us. But what we are inclined, indeed impelled, to believe when the 'light of nature', the *lumen naturale*, illumines our minds is none other than the deliverances of the divinely bestowed faculty of reason, the *lux rationis*. Descartes's conception of nature here is as normative as could be; to parody Alexander Pope, he is proclaiming, in effect, 'God said: "Let Nature be!" and all was light.'[16]

Though Descartes, when he talks of the natural light, is thinking primarily of the clearly and distinctly perceived truths of logic and mathematics, he does also include moral principles: when the mind is irradiated with 'reasons of truth *or of goodness*' (note the inclusion of the second disjunct), then we are made irresistibly aware of what we should believe (in the case of theoretical truths), or of what we should choose to do (in the case of practical principles).[17] The visual metaphor of light, and its application to moral as well as purely theoretical ideas, is of course an ancient notion with roots going back to Augustine and through him right back to Plato.[18] The natural light, one might say, puts us in touch with the two principal domains of normativity – logico-mathematical necessity on the one hand, and moral obligatoriness on the other. And what was 'natural' for Descartes, in this strong normative sense, is 'natural' for Butler in just the same way; the faculty of conscience, which Butler describes as 'natural to man', has precisely the function of Descartes' natural light – that of revealing what is right and so providing an authoritative guide to right action.

3   The natural and the normative: two problems

The picture so far presented puts Butler's views on conscience in line with a long tradition, running from Classical times through the Christian fathers of the Middle Ages and right down to the early-modern period – a tradition that invokes the concept of the natural in a resoundingly authoritative and normative way. But what we also see in Butler is what happens when this long tradition collides with the more sceptical and empiricist elements of the Enlightenment worldview. Although Butler had carefully distinguished his normative sense of 'natural' from the more factual and empirical one, he was all too aware that in the latter sense 'man has dispositions and principles within, which lead him to do evil...as well as good', and that many of his philosophical critics were likely to insist that 'the nature of man is...to be judged... by what appears in the common world, in the bulk of mankind'.[19] Underlying these remarks is a certain implied anxiety about whether the traditional concept of conscience would be able to hold its ground in an increasingly 'naturalistic' philosophical climate. Despite Butler's valiant efforts, the onslaught he feared is one whose aftershock is still with us today – so much so that the great bulk of current work in moral theory now avoids the term 'conscience' altogether. It would be a very bold philosopher today who invoked the idea that we are endowed by 'nature' (in the traditional normative sense) with a faculty that guides us to right action.

The first serious obstacle to talking this way nowadays has to do with what Bernard Williams called the 'radical contingency of the ethical'.[20] Granted that many people have strong intuitions that cruelty, say, or rampant selfishness, is wrong, the dire history of the last hundred years (to look no further) nevertheless suggests that many others apparently have such feelings only weakly or not at all. And, at a more general and even more disorienting level, it seems quite possible that, had the evolution or the socio-historical development of the human race taken a slightly different path, then the powerful ethical intuitions to which traditional moralists have so confidently appealed might have been altogether different. Once we raise the thought that the structure of the ethical beliefs and practices we happen to have could so easily have been otherwise, then (so runs this line of argument) talk of eternal laws of morality grafted in all human hearts begins to look like something of a fantasy.

The second worry, threatening to be no less subversive of traditional ideas of conscience, comes from a more theoretical quarter, namely from the famous Humean thesis about the impossibility of bridging the gap from *is* to *ought*. The faculty of conscience, as we have seen, is for Butler not just one of the (empirical) 'principles' or springs of action within us, but is 'in kind and in principle supreme over all others'. Whence this supremacy? Indeed, Butler himself raises this question: 'allowing that mankind hath the rule of right within himself, yet it may be asked, What obligations are we under to attend to and follow it?'[21] Some of Butler's phrases suggest that conscience is somehow 'self-authorizing': it 'bears its own authority of being [supreme]'. Well, perhaps anyone troubled by the pangs of conscience is automatically, as it were, disposed to grant it a certain normative authority. But this simply raises the question of what it is that *gives* conscience this supposed authority. As a typical modern critic puts it:

> Perhaps we cannot have conscience without some tendency to believe that it has authority, but we may still query this very belief; we may ask whether it has the authority it claims, and, if so, what that authority derives from.[22]

What might Butler's own answer to this challenge have been? The commentator to whom I have already referred more than once, Stephen Darwall, ends up attributing to Butler a proto-Kantian position, which he calls 'autonomous internalism', namely that the authority of conscience is a condition of the very possibility of an agent's having reasons to act at all, since only a being who has the capacity for maintaining a self-regulated constitutional order can have reasons for acting, and this capacity depends on the agent's taking her conscience to be authoritative.[23] Whether or not such a view can plausibly be laid at Butler's door, it does not seem to me a particularly attractive one. For the notion of conscience implies not just that I am in touch with certain reasons for acting, but that these reasons have a peculiar conclusive or binding force; and it is not clear (to me at any rate) how the mere possibility of autonomous rational agency presupposes this kind of conclusiveness.[24]

Butler's own position, however, seems to me likely to have been far less complex than this contorted Kantian line, and much more overtly theistic. In the Third Sermon he argues very straightforwardly as follows:

> But allowing that mankind hath the rule of right within himself, yet it may be asked 'What obligations are we under to attend to and follow it?' I answer:...Conscience does not only offer itself to show us the way we should walk in, but it likewise carries its own authority with it, that it is our *natural guide*; the *guide assigned us by the Author of our nature*: it therefore belongs to our condition of being, it is our duty, to walk in that path and follow this guide without looking about to see whether we may not possibly forsake [it] with impunity.[25]

Conscience is our 'natural', that is to say, God-given, guide. The theological metaphysics presupposed may (to say the least) now be more disputed than it was in Butler's day, but the idea itself is very simple, and fits in with many other aspects of the theistic worldview. Descartes' theory of clear and distinct perception was premised on the idea that (as he put it to a questioner) 'a reliable mind was God's gift to me'.[26] Just as God bestows on man the faculty of intellectual vision, so that the human mind becomes in a sense a mirror (albeit a finite one) of the divine, giving us limited but accurate access to the domain of logic and mathematics, so, on what I take to be Butler's picture, the conscience is a divinely bestowed faculty of moral judgement, giving us access to the domain of the moral law.[27]

For reasons which stem from what philosophers know as the 'Euthyphro dilemma', the principles of this moral law 'written in our hearts' cannot be a series of *arbitrary* divine commands.[28] The law written in our hearts is that provided by a *providential* 'author of nature', that is, a God who cares for the welfare of his creatures. Virtue, or obeying the moral law (and this is a theme shared by Butler and many of his contemporaries) is 'beyond all contradiction...naturally the interest, and vice the misery of such a creature as man, placed in the circumstances which we are in this world'.[29] As Butler puts it:

> man cannot be considered as a creature *left by his maker* to act at random, and live at large up to the extent of his natural power, as passion, humour, wilfulness happen to carry him; which is the condition brute creatures are in...He hath the rule of right within: what is wanting is only that he honestly attend to it.[30]

This seems to give the basis for an answer to those who complain (like Stephen Darwall) that 'no facts about providence can solve the is/ought gap, or give conscience the right kind of normative supremacy'.[31] Of course, one may question the existence of a providential order – in which case the Bernard Williams worry about radical contingency will come into play. Ethical rules will simply turn out to be a contingent set of evolving social codes, and there will be no warrant for allowing the 'morality system', as Williams calls it, its pretensions to command our allegiance. But if a theistic worldview *is* adopted, and if conscience is, like Descartes' light of reason, a God-given gift, then the normativity becomes about as manifest as can be. Finite creatures are necessarily going to be imperfect in many respects, and if they also have genuine two-way freedom, they will necessarily have the power to go astray (to turn away from the deliverances of the natural light).[32] But if there are objective reasons, grounded in the possibility of our ultimate human fulfilment, for us to take a certain path, and if we have a natural, divinely bestowed faculty guiding us towards that path, then the deliverances of conscience will have as much normative authority as could be desired. There may be epistemic worries about how we could know that any of the elements of this theistic worldview are correct, or about how we can know that a given insight represents the authentic voice of conscience; but these are quite different kinds of worry – quite different from claiming there are logical or conceptual difficulties about how the necessary normativity can obtain. The 'natural law' inscribed in our hearts embodies reasons that are to be respected by humans because they direct us along the path towards the ultimate fulfilment of our nature – the goal that a being of the utmost benevolence and compassion has created us to achieve.

4 Nature as guide

To shed a little more light on this notion of 'nature as guide', it may be helpful to draw some comparisons with the work of a later eighteenth-century writer for whom the idea of a 'natural guide' for mankind had a considerable fascination – the poet William Wordsworth. Nature, for Wordsworth, meant in the first place external nature – the 'meadows and...woods and mountains' that he loved,[33] and which his poetry so splendidly celebrates. But although a common caricature portrays Words-worth as a kind of cheery pantheistic pagan, the vision which nature inspires in him is a deeply moral one: significantly, he describes nature as 'The guide, the guardian of my heart, and soul / *Of all my moral being.*'[34] The natural world is for Wordsworth one that calls forth in us vital responses, both aesthetic ones (to use a rather inadequate term) – responses of exaltation and joy – and also moral ones – responses of human sympathy and fellow-feeling. In the *Lines written a few miles above Tintern Abbey* (composed in 1798, some seventy years after Butler penned his *Sermons*), the notion of nature as a leader or guide is particularly prominent:

> Nature never did betray
> The heart that loved her;'tis her privilege
> Through all the years of this our life, to lead
> From joy to joy...[35]

Nature here has a specific role – to guide us throughout the allotted span of our mortal lives to experiences which will put us in touch with a deeper moral and aesthetic reality that infuses the world around us. To say that this is Nature's 'privilege' is a remarkable idea, and one which I think has to be taken seriously. Wordsworth is not just referring to an effect that, at the purely empirical level, the natural environment has upon us; rather, this is a role that is *assigned* to nature in the overall providential scheme of things. The language here is inescapably teleological: though Wordsworth does not make it explicit, Nature is in this sense the 'handmaid' of the Author of Nature – she has been given a privileged job to do, to attend to the development of the moral sensibility of humankind.[36] And the results of nature's guidance are vividly expressed by Wordsworth in some famous lines earlier on in *Tintern Abbey*:

> I have learned
> To look on nature not as in the hour

Of thoughtless youth, but hearing oftentimes
The still, sad music of humanity,
Nor harsh, nor grating, though of ample power
To chasten and subdue. And I have felt
A presence that disturbs me with the sense
Of elevated thoughts; a sense sublime
Of something far more deeply interfused
Whose dwelling is the light of setting suns,
And the round ocean, and the living air
And the blue sky, and in the mind of man...[37]

It is probably fruitless to raise the question of whether we should give an 'immanent' or a 'transcendent' interpretation to the divine presence with which the poet here feels himself in touch. The key point is that the language is unmistakably theistic – that is to say, it does not merely, in pantheistic fashion, acknowledge a multitude of vibrant suprahuman forces in nature, nor in deistic fashion merely invoke a vast impersonal power behind the universe, but clearly recognises the goodness and beauty of the cosmos in a way that intimately relates it to human concerns. The vision, once glimpsed, says Wordsworth a few lines later, gives us something that no subsequent pain or distress can entirely erase, a 'cheerful faith that all which we behold/Is full of *blessings*'.[38]

An obvious point of contrast between Butler's and Wordsworth's conceptions of 'nature as guide' is that Butler is thinking of an internal voice within us, while Wordsworth is talking about the natural world around us. But despite this superficial difference there is, I think, a clear underlying similarity. For what Wordsworth feels himself to be guided by is not simply an ensemble of external objects, but the inner response that they evoke in his heart. So both thinkers have a picture in which what we are 'guided by' has a dual aspect – an objective created order, and a human faculty that is naturally responsive to that order. Conscience for Butler, the poetic vision for Wordsworth, are sure natural guides that put us in touch with objective domains of beauty and goodness.

The Wordsworthian model, however, seems to me to provide us with further, and deeper, illumination about the nature of our moral and aesthetic experience. For what emerges in Wordsworth is that the very dichotomy between objective external reality and personal subjective response is in a certain sense misleading: what happens is that the perception of the poet responds to the guidance of nature in such a way that he is enabled to see it in a radically transformed way. There is a natural harmony, an answering resonance, as the child of nature wanders through 'the meadows and the woods/And mountains and...all that we behold/From this green earth'.[39] He is made aware of 'all the mighty world/Of eye and ear, both what they half-create, /And what perceive'.[40] And the result is that what is experienced is not merely a certain kind of environment, but a morally significant world – a world that is 'full of blessings'.

This interpretative or transformative aspect to our human experience provides, it seems to me, an important supplement to what can seem the rather dry and over-intellectualistic accounts of moral awareness often provided by philosophers and theologians. The natural guide that thinkers like Samuel Clarke and Joseph Butler appeal to is an inner faculty that enables us to do something like what the geometers do in their study – to work out general principles and their application to particular cases (except that we are dealing with principles of right action rather than principles of abstract theoretical truth). This approach has antecedents that go right back to Aquinas, who asserts that we have the faculty of *synderesis*, which gives us knowledge of the first principles of moral action, and *conscientia*, which applies it to particular cases.[41] But if one turns instead to the way in which moral teaching is conveyed for example in the Gospels, the picture is very different. There the main emphasis is on what the Greeks called *metanoia* – a radical shift in our moral outlook; and what principally engenders such a shift is not exposure to particular moral assessments or general principles, but, above all, devices such as the parables – stories embedded in concrete experience with a specific emotional impact, which are designed to work a fundamental change in the way we perceive the world.

This connects, finally, with another significant element of the Wordsworthian picture, his stress on moral development and *learning*. The poet has '*learned*/to look on nature not as in the hour/of thoughtless youth, but hearing oftentimes/the still sad music of humanity'. The process of growth and transformation is a crucial part of what it is to be a developed human moral agent: our moral lives are a *journey* in a much deeper sense than applies to many parts of our intellectual lives (e.g. our accumulating knowledge of geography or natural history). Now philosophers such as Thomas Aquinas did not of course overlook the idea of *learning* in the moral sphere. Aquinas was well aware of the Aristotelian stress on the importance of training and habituation in ethics, and he himself spoke of habits of virtue, and described conscience in terms of habits of will, as well as of practical reasoning (albeit insisting on an innate, divinely implanted component in all this).[42] But the human moral journey as described in the works of the great spiritual writers (Augustine is perhaps the paradigm case, though there are many others) is radically different in its outlines – radically different from what one might call the 'classroom' model, a model of careful, progressive moulding of habits based on innate capacities of practical intellect and will. All such 'normal' apparatus no doubt has its place, but, if anything like the religious worldview is correct, there is something more dynamic and more dramatic typically at work in the human spirit. As moral beings, we do not just start from a reliable innate deposit, and then accumulate information and become more skilled in processing it; rather, we gradually, laboriously, stimulated by examples, moved by parables, humbled by error, purged by suffering, begin to change. The faculty enabling us to respond in this way may be innate, and in that sense 'natural', but it also requires our being open to the possibility of transformation – in Pauline language, to putting off the old nature and taking on the new, or in the language of the fourth Gospel, to the possibility of rebirth.[43]

In this sense the ideas of conscience are very unlike the 'innate ideas' so crudely caricatured by Locke (as if they were lying in the open book of the mind waiting to be read); nor are they, as Locke's own empiricist ideology would have us suppose, merely gradually accumulated and rearranged data of the senses, which simply have to be 'received' via observation. If the traditional idea of conscience stretching from Aquinas down to Butler and beyond is right, there must be an element of 'natural' innate inner guidance we can rely on. But if we add to this the crucial idea of a journey of growth and development, then the 'ideas' of conscience will be 'natural' or innate in humankind more in the fashion conceived by Leibniz – as veined or seamed shapes hidden within the marble, waiting for all the painful labour of the sculptor's hammer blows to reveal them.[44]

The upshot, if this religious vision of our place in the cosmos is accepted, is that we humans are endowed with a natural power to see the moral and aesthetic significance of the world around us, to see the natural world as 'charged with the grandeur of God', as Gerard Manley Hopkins so memorably puts it;[45] and to see the suffering human world as calling for responses of compassion and love. Some elements of this experience will be available to us quite unproblematically and spontaneously, as simple delight and joy at the world's beauty; other elements, the more complex moral responses, may require a deeper inner transformation; though both, on the theistic picture, will be seen as dependent on something beyond ourselves, perhaps on something like what the theologians call 'grace'. To put it another way, nothing in the empirical facts dispassionately analysed can automatically yield the kind of interpretation that sees the natural world as 'full of blessings' or the suffering human world as having the power to 'chasten and subdue' our selfish impulses. Such a vision will be available only if we follow our 'natural guide' – where 'natural' is construed not of course in the empirical sense, but in the richer normative (and ultimately religious) sense I have been exploring.

5   Nature and natural law

Let us draw some threads together. One principal point that I hope has by now emerged is that how we interpret the concept of 'nature' turns out to be crucial for how we understand the domain of morality and how we locate it within the rest of our worldview. The 'empirical-naturalist' conception, which has been steadily gathering support since the Enlightenment, construes nature as, roughly, the sum total of empirically determinable contingent facts or states of affairs (including biological and psychological facts about human beings and their prefer-ences), and then attempts to show how morality can be derived from, or in some sense shown to be continuous with, these facts. But such an approach (unless it is prepared to explain away all morality as an illusion arising from the projection outwards of purely subjective inclinations) will run into serious problems in explaining how some of our 'natural' preferences can be supposed to have normative force. How can the right kind of moral authority stem from mere contingent facts about the inclinations we happen to have evolved to possess? By contrast, there is an older (yet, I would argue, still viable) tradition that construes Nature very differently – as an inherently normative domain. On this view, it is from the way in which the natural world (including our own human nature) is divinely ordered that there arise those objective values which our moral judgements (if sound) reflect. So in making our moral judgements we are responding to something objective – the goals and constraints that determine the possibility of a worthwhile human life, independently of our transitory inclinations and preferences.

There is here a partial, but significant, parallel with aesthetic judge-ment. On the Wordsworthian picture that we have been looking at, the natural world is seen not as a mere collection of material particles in random motion, but as a *cosmos* – a harmonious, ordered whole, shot through with harmony and rhythm and symmetry; and our aesthetic judgements about the beauty of the natural world are, when sound, responsive to these objective properties. In somewhat the same way, the human world – the world that consists of the unfolding of our lives – is seen not merely as a contingently evolving series of interactions between members of a certain species, but as a teleological story, the story of a struggle to achieve those objective goods that it is in our nature to reach after. And the moral judgements we make about our own lives and those of our fellow humans will, when they are sound, be responsive to those objective goods – the goods we need to be oriented towards if our lives are to have meaning and value.

The picture just sketched is, of course, a highly metaphysical one: 'nature' sheds its modern pretensions to be a neutral scientific term, and reverts to its traditional role – the role it arguably has in Aristotle, and certainly has in Aquinas and Descartes and Leibniz and Butler – as the lynchpin of a theistic worldview. Together with this metaphysical picture of morality, moreover, goes a certain kind of moral epistemology – the theory of conscience as a 'natural guide' which, when properly cultivated, works within us to help us orient ourselves towards the objective goods that we are meant to pursue. But linking the metaphysical picture with the epistemic picture in this way brings us to a final question of some importance – a question whose relevance may be underlined by the fact that the name of Aquinas has surfaced several times in our discussion so far. How does the account of conscience as our 'natural guide' relate to the idea of morality as grounded in 'natural law' – perhaps the most famous legacy of the Thomistic system of ethics?

Aquinas' notion of conscience, as already noted, can seem rather intellectualistic, in so far as he sees moral awareness as a matter of the intuition of moral axioms and their application to particular cases. The idea of natural law is introduced by Aquinas very much in this kind of context, so that natural law is seen in terms of the fundamental rational principles underlying all morality:

> the precepts of natural law are to practical reasoning what the first principles of demonstrations are to theoretical reasoning...All things to be done or to be avoided pertain to the precepts of natural law, which practical reasoning apprehends naturally as being human goods.[46]

Rationality is crucially involved in all this: indeed, the 'light of reason', later famously invoked in Cartesian philosophy, is of course an idea that Descartes would principally have been acquainted with, via his Jesuit teachers, from the writings of Aquinas.[47] According to Aquinas, human beings, in virtue of the faculty of reason, have a share in the eternal reason of God; but the way in which they participate in this eternal rational order is by an endowment of human nature, the 'light of reason' which enables us to perceive good and evil.[48]

This rationalistic picture is, however, modified to an important extent when Aquinas discusses the ways in which conformity to the eternal moral law actually occurs. One way is by knowledge – presumably this involves the deductive application of the rational principles of right action to individual cases. But there is another way, namely by means of an 'inward principle', which moves us to act.[49] In a subtle account of the psychology of moral action, Aquinas allows for a complex interplay of intellect and will at every level of attention, reflection, and conduct. To intuit something as good is only the first stage in a complex process leading to eventual right action, and in that process the mind must not just apprehend an object intellectually, but must dwell on it in such a way as to generate a firm appetitive disposition towards the object in question.[50] The upshot is that the Thomist story of the moral life is far more complex than the formal unravelling of a deductive process based on rational intuition. At every stage there is a co-operation between the intellect and the will, and the need to cultivate supporting habits of desire and inclination. So despite its rationalistic overtones, the natural law theory seems perfectly compatible with a 'Wordsworthian' stress on how certain kinds of experience open our minds and hearts so that we are morally responsive in the right way.[51] Indeed, Aquinas himself, in his account of divine grace, allows for just such an 'opening process', one that respects our human freedom, but at the same time enables the will to move from a state of resistance or quiescence to one of loving acceptance and co-operation, and hence allows for the possibility of our achieving goods that we could not attain by our own unaided efforts.[52] We are not superhuman beings whose intellects are permanently fixed on the good and whose wills are always diligently attentive; hence in any plausible account of human development, there will be an indispensable role for something 'not ourselves which makes for right-eousness'.[53] To acknowledge this is to recognise what it is to be a creature of dependent and limited rationality, and of a nature that is good but corruptible.

Irrespective of any psychological appeal it may have, many philosophers of course will be disposed to reject this kind of metaphysical picture out of hand, on the grounds that any worldview that takes us beyond the domain of the natural (empirical, phenomenal) world fails the standards for knowledge laid down by the Enlightenment. And this brings us back full circle to the theme with which we began, the ruling modern dogma of 'naturalism', with its insistence on the wholesale elimination of the 'spooky'. The prospects for contemporary naturalism (and whether it can provide a viable alternative account of normativity) cannot be evaluated here; but perhaps it is just worth noting that in its modern dogmatic form it goes considerably beyond the classic Enlightenment position. For Kant at least was clear that what lay beyond the reach of empirical knowledge could still be a proper object of faith – the 'cheerful faith' (as Wordsworth termed it) that is allowed to emerge when the limits of knowledge have been defined, and transcended.[54] Yet, whatever its epistemic status, there is one central element in the metaphysical picture running from Aquinas down to Butler and Wordsworth, and beyond, that I suspect few who honestly consult their experience would be comfortable about dismissing out of hand: that when we learn to listen attentively to the voice of that 'natural guide' within us, it becomes possible to glimpse the world (the world of our natural environment and the world of human existence) as irradiated with beauty and with value. We then experience the world not as an aggregate of 'natural facts', but as a cosmos, a natural *order* – that is to say, as something which, for all its flaws, reflects that good towards which, as Aristotle and Aquinas insisted, all things naturally tend.[55]

Notes

1. Stephen Darwall, *The British Moralists and the Internal 'Ought' 1640–1740* (Cambridge: Cambridge University Press, 1995): 14.
2. There is, however, a very plausible alternative view of Hume as not denying the existence of causal necessity but merely being sceptical about the possibility of our ever having knowledge of it. Cf. John Wright, *The Sceptical Realism of David Hume* (Cambridge: Cambridge University Press, 1983); followed by Galen Strawson in *The Secret Connexion* (Oxford: Clarendon, 1989).
3. David Hume, *A Treatise of Human Nature* (1739–40): Book III, Part 1, Section i, penultimate paragraph.
4. Hume, *Treatise*: Book I, Part 3, Section xiv.
5. Richard Cumberland, *A Treatise of the Laws of Nature* (*De Legibus Naturae Disquisitio Philosophica*, 1672), trans. J. Maxwell (1727) (repr. New York: Garland, 1978): 41. Cited in Darwall, *British Moralists*: 15.
6. This at least is the line taken by Hume; cf. *A Treatise of Human Nature* (1739–40): Book II, Part iii, Section 3.
7. This slogan (*homologoumenôs tê physei zên*), advanced by the followers of Zeno of Citium, the founder of Stoicism, is preserved in the compilations of the anthologist Stobaeus (early 5th century AD); see A.A. Long and D.N. Sedley

(eds), *The Hellenistic Philosopher* (Cambridge: Cambridge University Press, 1987), no. 63A and B.

8. Joseph Butler, *Fifteen Sermons* (1726): Sermon II, §5, in J.B. Schneewind (ed.), *Moral Philosophy from Montaigne to Kant* (Cambridge: Cambridge University Press, 1990), Vol. II: 531. Also in D.D. Raphael (ed.), *British Moralists 1650–1800* (Oxford: Clarendon, 1969): §398.

9. Ephesians, 2:3.

10. Butler, Sermon II, §5. The phrase within inverted commas is from the Authorized Version (1611), as quoted by Butler. The New Revised Standard Version (1989) horribly mangles the original Greek text: 'do *instinctively* what the law requires'.

11. Butler, Sermon II, §8: Schneewind (ed.), *Moral Philosophy*: 532 and in Raphael (ed.), *British Moralists*: §399. Compare the following: 'If by following nature were meant only acting as we please, it would indeed be ridiculous to speak of nature as any guide in morals ... [T]hat every man is naturally a law to himself, that every one may find within himself the rule of right, and obligations to follow it ... this St Paul affirms in the words of the text [Romans 2:14]': Sermon II, Raphael (ed.): §397.

12. For example in *de Caelo*: I, 4; *de Partibus Animalium*: II, 13. For more on this theme in Aristotle, see R.J. Hankinson, 'Philosophy of Science', in J. Barnes (ed.), *The Cambridge Companion to Aristotle* (Cambridge: Cambridge University Press, 1995): ch. 4.

13. G.W. Leibniz, *Monadology* (1714): §§65, 69; trans. in G.H.R. Parkinson (ed.), *Leibniz: Philosophical Writings* (London: Dent, 1973): 190.

14. For more on this, see J. Cottingham, 'Descartes' Sixth Meditation: The External World, "Nature" and Human Experience', *Philosophy*, Supp. Vol. 20 (1986): 73–89; repr. in V. Chappell (ed.), *Descartes's Meditations: Critical Essays* (Lanham, MD: Rowman & Littlefield, 1997): ch. 10.

15. *Meditationes* (1641), Sixth Meditation, AT VII, 80; CSM II, 56. 'AT' refers to the standard Franco-Latin edition of Descartes by C. Adam and P. Tannery, *Œuvres de Descartes* (12 vols, revised edn, Paris: Vrin/CNRS, 1964–76); 'CSM' refers to the English translation by J. Cottingham, R. Stoothoff and D. Murdoch, *The Philosophical Writings of Descartes*, Vols I and II (Cambridge: Cambridge University Press, 1985), and 'CSMK' to Vol. III, *The Correspondence*, by the same translators plus A. Kenny (Cambridge University Press, 1991).

16. The notion of the *lux rationis* or 'light of reason' found in the *Regulae* (c. 1628) (AT X, 368; CSM I, 14) becomes in the *Meditations* the *lumen naturale*, the 'natural light' (e.g. AT VII, 40; CSM II, 28).

17. 'The more I incline [towards one of two alternatives] either because I clearly understand that reasons of truth and goodness point that way, or because of a divinely produced disposition of my inmost thoughts, the freer is my choice.' Fourth Meditation, AT VII, 57–8; CSM II, 40.

18. Cf. Plato, *Republic* (c. 380 BC): 514–18; Augustine of Hippo, *De Trinitate* (c. 410): XII. xv. 24. There are complex links between Plato and Augustine, of which the most prominent is the Gospel according to John (c. AD 100), 1:9.

19. Sermon I, in Raphael (ed.), *British Moralists*: §§392, 393.

20. See Bernard Williams, *Truth and Truthfulness* (Princeton: Princeton University Press, 2002): 20.
21. Sermon III, 5; quoted in Darwall, *The British Moralists*: 254.
22. Darwall: 271.
23. Ibid: 274–82. Darwall canvasses another view, namely a kind of argument from design – 'that conscience gives us conclusive reasons because we are *designed* to be guided by its directives, and we function properly only when we are so' (Darwall: 247). But he casts doubt on whether this argument can work: 'Parts or principles of a functional system can have a kind of ordering, but not one of relative *authority*... There might be a well-designed system adapted to quite different purposes than those for which our design fits us, one whose makeup included conscience and appetites, but in which these played different functional roles – in which it was not part of the design that conscience, despite its (intrinsic) superintendent pretensions, should actually superintend' (262).
24. Compare the following: 'By saying that conscience has supreme authority, Butler means that we regard the pronouncements of conscience, not simply as interesting or uninteresting statements of fact, and not simply as reasons to be balanced against others but as *conclusive* reasons for or against doing the actions about which it pronounces' (C.D. Broad, *Five Types of Ethical Theory* [1930], cited in Darwall: 247).
25. *Fifteen Sermons*: Sermon III, 5, in Raphael (ed.), §407; Schneewind (ed.): 536 (emphasis added).
26. '*Rectum ingenium a Deo accepi*': Descartes, *Conversation with Burman* (1648), AT V, 148; CSMK: 334.
27. This puts Butler close to an intuitionist position similar to that of Samuel Clarke, who argued that the realm of 'eternal and necessary relations' included a 'natural and unalterable difference between good and evil' which our human reason unmistakably perceives. (Samuel Clarke, *A Discourse Concerning the Unchangeable Obligations of Natural Religion* [1706], in Raphael (ed.): §§225, 227.) Stephen Darwall insists on seeing Butler's view as radically different from Clarke's – though admitting the 'puzzling' fact that he did express approval of Clarke's view (Darwall: 283n). Darwall lays great weight on Butler's announcement in the Preface to his *Fifteen Sermons* that he does not propose to follow Clarke's method, because rather than inquiring, *a priori*, into the 'abstract relations of things', he prefers to start from 'matters of fact', namely from 'the particular nature of man, its several parts, their economy or constitution' (Preface to *Sermons*: §7, in Raphael (ed.): §374). However, this appears to be a point about *heuristic methodology*, not metaphysics, and seems entirely compatible with the interpretation that the *Sermons* will *eventually* endorse the idea of a objective normative realm revealed by conscience. Butler himself makes it clear that the Clarkean *a priori* method and his own methodology in the *Sermons* 'strengthen and support each other' (Preface to *Sermons*: §7).
28. The dilemma (derived from a question raised by Socrates in Plato's *Euthyphro* [c. 390 BC]) is whether things are right simply because they are commanded by God, or whether on the other hand they are commanded by God because they are right. Opting for the first horn of the dilemma seems morally unsatisfactory since it appears to make morality dependent on the arbitrary will of

God (while the second option has been regarded as theologically unsatisfactory since it appears to allow that rightness is independent of or prior to God).

29. Shaftesbury's view, cited by Butler in the Preface to the *Sermons*: Raphael (ed.): §380.

30. Sermon III, in Raphael (ed.): §405. Note that at the start of the passage quoted, Butler adds the qualifier 'Exclusive of revelation...', thereby allowing for direct intervention by the deity into human affairs, to supplement the ordinary operation of the divinely bestowed faculty of conscience. The concluding phrase about the need to attend to the deliverances of conscience follows a standard line in mainstream Christian theology, designed to safeguard the freedom of the human will; compare Descartes' Fourth Meditation, and see note 32.

31. Darwall: 271.

32. Compare J. Cottingham, 'Descartes and the Voluntariness of Belief', *The Monist*, 85 (2002): 343–60.

33. *Lines written a few miles above Tintern Abbey* (1798), in S. Gill (ed.), *William Wordsworth: A Critical Edition of the Major Works* (Oxford: Oxford University Press, 1984): lines 103–5.

34. *Tintern Abbey*: lines 111–12 (emphasis added).

35. Ibid: lines 123–6.

36. It is interesting (though I would not venture to claim a Wordsworthian influence) to note that the poet Gerard Manley Hopkins on several occasions compares the Virgin Mary (the archetypal 'Handmaid of the Lord') to the natural world; see 'The Blessed Virgin compared to the Air we Breathe', from *Poems (1876–1889)*, no. 37, repr. in W.H. Gardner (ed.), *Poems and Prose of Gerard Manley Hopkins* (Harmondsworth: Penguin, 1953): 54; and cf. also 'The May Magnificat', no. 19 (p. 37).

37. *Tintern Abbey*: lines 89–100.

38. Ibid: lines 135–6 (emphasis added).

39. Ibid: lines 104–6.

40. Ibid: lines 106–8.

41. 'Synderesis' (also 'synteresis') appears to have come into philosophical terminology via a corruption of *syneidesis*, St Paul's word for conscience. Aquinas distinguishes, however, the general faculty of *synderesis* from *conscientia*, which latter involves applying principles to particular cases so as to evaluate what one should now do and what one has done in the past. See *Quaestiones Disputatae de Veritate* (1256–9): 17; cf. Eleonore Stump, *Aquinas* (London: Routledge, 2003): 89.

42. Cf. *Summa Theologiae* (1266–73) Ia IIae, q. 94 aa. 3 and 6. See also Stump, *Aquinas*: 89.

43. Cf. Ephesians, 4:20–4; John, 3:3.

44. Cf. G.W. Leibniz, *Nouvaux essais sur l'entendement humain* (1704), Preface, in P. Remnant and J. Bennett (eds), *New Essays on Human Understanding* (Cambridge: Cambridge University Press, 1981): 52. Contrast John Locke, An *Essay Concerning Human Understanding* (1690): Book I, ch. 2, §5. Contrast also the more 'static' picture presented by Butler: see quotation flagged at note 30.

45. Hopkins, 'God's Grandeur', from *Poems (1876–1889)*, no. 8 (ed. Gardner, p. 27).

46. *Summa Theologiae,* Ia IIae, q. 94 a. 2. Note that the Thomist conception involves not just the idea of goods to be pursued but also the idea of constraints – 'things to be avoided'. Both the *prosequenda* (the things to be pursued) and the *fugienda* (the things to be avoided) derive from 'eternal laws', or 'the very nature of the governance of things on the part of God as ruler of the Universe' (*Summa Theologiae,* Ia IIae, q. 91 a. 1). Cf. Stump, *Aquinas:* 26.
47. Descartes attended the Jesuit college at La Flèche in Anjou as a boarding pupil from around 1606 to 1614.
48. *Summa Theologiae,* Ia IIae, q. 91 a. 2. Cf. Stump, *Aquinas:* 88. Compare the following: 'The natural law is nothing other than the light of understanding placed in us by God; through it we know what we must do and what we must avoid. God has given this light or law at the creation' (*Collationes in Decem Praecepta* [1273], I).
49. *Summa Theologiae,* Ia IIae, q. 93 a. 6.
50. See further Ralph McInerny, 'Ethics', in N. Kretzmann and E. Stump (eds), *The Cambridge Companion to Aquinas* (Cambridge: CUP, 1993): 206–7.
51. This fusion of intellect and emotions is clearly acknowledged in contemporary views of the doctrine of natural law that clearly follow the broad outlines of the Thomist tradition. Compare the following: 'In the depths of his conscience, man detects a law which he does not impose upon himself, but which holds him to obedience. Always summoning him to love good and avoid evil, the voice of conscience when necessary *speaks to his heart*: do this, shun that' (Second Vatican Council, *Gaudium et Spes* [1965]: 16; emphasis added).
52. For an excellent discussion of Aquinas's account of grace, see Stump, *Aquinas:* 394.
53. 'The real germ of religious consciousness, of out which sprang Israel's name for God, to which the records of history adapted themselves, and which came to be clothed upon, in time, with a mighty growth of poetry and tradition, was a consciousness of *the not ourselves which makes for righteousness.*' Matthew Arnold, *Literature and Dogma* (1873): ch. I, §5, repr. in Matthew Arnold, *Dissent and Dogma* (Ann Arbor: University of Michigan Press, 1968): 189.
54. Immanuel Kant, *Critique of Pure Reason* (*Kritik der Reinen Vernunft,* 1781, 1787), B xxx (trans. N. Kemp Smith [New York: St Martin's Press, 1965]), p. 29: 'I have found it necessary to deny knowledge in order to make room for faith'. Kant's term (prefiguring Hegel) is *aufheben,* implying not so much that one has to 'deny' knowledge in order to make room for faith (as Kemp Smith's translation misleadingly has it) as that one has to transcend it. Cf. H. Kaygill, *A Kant Dictionary* (Oxford: Blackwell, 1995), entry 'faith'.
55. Aristotle, *Nicomachean Ethics* (325 BC), I: 1. Aquinas, *Summa Theologiae,* I, q. 59 a. 1; cf. *Summa Contra Gentiles* (1259–65): II, 47.

2

Basic Goods, Practical Insight, and External Reasons

Christopher Tollefsen

1

Many basic goods theories hold the following two claims. First, the foundation of human action is in the practical grasp that all genuine agents have of the basic human goods, that is, in their grasp of basic opportunities for human flourishing.[1] Different goods theories give somewhat different accounts of what these basic goods are, but the lists generally include human life and health, knowledge, excellence at work and play, friendship, integrity and practical reasonableness. The claim is thus that in some sense or other *all* agents have an awareness of these goods as to be pursued; such knowledge is not merely for the few, but is part and parcel of ordinary human agency.

The second claim is related to the first. The basic goods are deemed desirable by agents because they offer the promise of human well-being; agents have a practical understanding that they would be better off for participating in the basic goods. Goods-based theories are thus, as Germain Grisez says, 'based upon the ordering of human actions to human fulfillment.'[2] The notion of happiness, flourishing, well-being, in fact seems to enter into basic goods views in two ways. First, well-being or happiness is the reason any of the basic goods appeals to us; but second, well-being or happiness emerges as an ideal description of the point of pursuing all the goods in a reasonable fashion. That is to say, fully reasonable agents recognize that the goods cannot be pursued in a piecemeal or random or self-stultifying fashion, if human agents are to benefit in satisfactory ways from these pursuits. 'Happiness' or 'well-being' or 'the ideal of integral human fulfillment' thus emerges as a description of the point of fully reasonable action. So, basic goods views are eudaimonistic.

But again, that well-being is the overall point of human action is something agents are universally thought to recognize.

The two claims, then, are that the foundational principles of human action are apprehended by all agents as basic goods, and that human flourishing or well-being is also universally recognized, and desired, as the point of pursuing basic goods. Thus the first task of a basic goods theory is to provide a moral principle that, again quoting Grisez, 'provide[s] the basis for guiding choices toward overall human fulfillment.'[3]

The conjunction of these claims seems to result, however, in a blurring of the well-known internalism/externalism distinction as drawn by Bernard Williams. In 'Internal and External Reasons,' Williams argues that an action possibility can only be a reason for action for an agent if there is a deliberative path which can be charted from some existing motivation of the agent to the relevant possibility.[4] But Williams further claims that all existing motivations for agents are best characterized as desires of a Humean sort. The resulting picture has struck many philosophers as deeply, and disconcertingly, subjective; all reasons for action are such, on this picture, only because of their connection to the contingent desire set of some particular agent.

Williams therefore denies the existence of external reasons – reasons unconnected to the subjective motivational set of an agent. In doing so, he seems to some to be denying the existence of objective reasons, reasons not grounded in merely contingent desires. But basic goods views seem to cut through the two distinctions of internal/external reasons and subjective/objective reasons, in a way not envisaged by Williams in that article. Since the starting points of correct deliberation are shared by all agents – the basic goods, plus the recognition of well-being as the point of action – it seems true that there is a deliberative path from where any agent is to what that agent ought to do, taking deliberation to be concerned, as Aristotle suggests, with means and not with ends. But since basic goods are objectively good, not grounded in contingent desires, the subjectivism of Williams's view seems to be undercut. The resulting picture is not straightforwardly internalist in the way Williams describes, for it is not subjectivist; but it is not straightforwardly externalist either, because there exists a motivational and deliberative path for all agents towards what is morally required.

2

Nonetheless, stated so baldly, the resulting picture seems unsatisfactory in two related ways, both of which have been recognized in recent work on practical reason. First, deliberation risks seeming, on this picture, to be overly instrumental. If reason moves, in deliberation, from resources that are already fully present to a conclusion, then, as in Williams's picture, it seems as if no more can emerge from practical reasoning than goes into it. This threatens to make practical reasoning an overly technical affair.

Second, the resulting picture seems not to do justice to the appeal of external reasons. We want to say, of some agents in some circumstances, that there is a reason for them to do something, even as we believe that there is something quite opaque about this reason to the agent in question, something that makes it impossible for that agent to move *straightforwardly* from what she already desires to the reason itself. The denial of external reasons threatens to force a denial of the possibility that there is discovery in practical reason, rather than simply a working out of what is already at practical reason's disposal.

John McDowell has given voice to some of these concerns in his article 'Might There Be External Reasons?' The key to seeing that there might be is in cutting the connection between an agent's coming to discover that a possibility offers her a reason to act, and deliberatively arriving at that conclusion. Deliberation does indeed need to start somewhere, and so seems to depend for its resources on what was available to it from within the agent's set of subjective mental states. But the idea of a moral conversion, McDowell writes, is 'the idea of an intelligible shift in motivation that is exactly *not* effected by inducing a person to discover, by practical reasoning controlled by existing motivations, some internal reasons that he did not previously realize he had.'[5]

McDowell's idea of conversion has, however, something of a 'bolt from the blue' quality to it, as Elijah Millgram has pointed out.[6] Millgram has attempted to provide an account that is more plausible, because more worked-out and attentive to the reality of agents' lives, of how an agent can come to see that she has all along had a reason for doing something, even though she was not in a position to deliberate to a recognition of that reason. The account draws on a parallel with theoretical reason: sometimes there is a reason for an agent to come to believe some proposition, even though she cannot get, by a process of reasoning, to that proposition from where she is cognitively, because sometimes it is available to knowers to turn to the fact itself, as it were, and see that it is the case. Where the fact is sufficiently proximate that the agent could so turn, but nevertheless not something already within the agent's cognitive economy, then there is a kind of external reason for belief.

Similarly, where an agent could come to understand some possibility as providing a reason for action not through deliberation from her available motivations, but only through experiencing the relevant possibility, the agent can be described as discovering that she has a reason which she did not previously recognize as such. In Millgram's example, an agent cannot deliberate from her enjoyment of light verse to an understanding that she has a reason to read more serious poetry, but she can recognize the truth of this after having had the relevant experience.

It would, of course, be available to the internalist to object that the agent comes to have a reason, but that she did not previously have this reason, and in a sense this must be granted. We must distinguish, therefore, between two kinds of reason attributions. We say occasionally that such and such is a reason *for* some agent, meaning that the reason is currently within the scope of her deliberative awareness. But we also say that *there is a reason* for so-and-so to do such-and-such, without taking it as necessary that the agent should currently be able to recognize this. 'She would love poetry if she just gave it a chance,' we say, gesturing towards such reasons. But here Williams's arguments exert their pull: what sense is there in saying that there is a reason, if there is no possibility of it becoming, through deliberation, a reason for the agent in question? McDowell and Millgram may be taken to be answering precisely this question, McDowell with his suggestions about conversion, Millgram with his argument about experience.

3

Seen in this light, it seems crucially important to this picture that Millgram's agent had, for example, the initial interest in light verse. Two extremes need to be avoided: the radically instrumentalist picture, on which one could infer one's way to the unrecognized reason from the appeal of, in this case, light verse, and the radically externalist picture, on which one's real reasons are potentially entirely unrelated to what one actually recognizes as a reason. The middle possibility is one that acknowledges 'the possibility that reasons may be rooted in an agent's subjective motivational set without being directed toward the satisfaction of elements of that set.'[7]

This raises the question of whether the 'rooted in but not controlled by' picture can be extended and more deeply explained; can some systematicity be brought to the domain of non-deliberative practical insight, such as McDowell's 'conversion' and Millgram's 'experience'? McDowell's picture, for example, seems insufficiently intelligible as stated – it will seem a matter of luck that one experiences conversion, unless there is *some* way in which the conversion is 'rooted in' something that the agent already has a grasp of. In the remainder of this chapter I investigate three ways, consonant with the claims of basic goods theories, in which practical reason can become insightful about reasons for action that are not fully internal in Williams's sense but are not objectionably external either. These involve: insight into the nature of the basic goods, a nature characterized by incompletability, breadth, and depth; observations about the normative shape of a human life; and an understanding of the scope of the goodness of goods across agents, that is, that goods are good not simply for oneself but for all persons. Reason's grasp of reasons for action, in these areas, is not (always) narrowly controlled by existing motivations; it is not straightforwardly instrumental; and it is, on the other side, not completely cut off from an agent's practical awareness of the basic goods and her desire to flourish.

The resulting picture will respect three related considerations. First, McDowell's claim that the idea of a moral conversion which involves coming to see things aright is intelligible. Second, it respects an Aristotelian insight into the importance of character formation and the difficulty of reformation, without making such reformation impossible. Third, it will make sense of the thought that a moral crisis is often the event that precipitates moral conversion or reformation, an idea congenial, I shall argue, to Millgram's account of the role of experience.

4

It is essential and universal to those theories here characterized as basic goods theories, that basic human goods are not states of affairs. Rather, they are essentially open-ended possibilities for action, which cannot be exhausted by the pursuit of any, or all, agents. The goods, we could say, have both breadth and depth, and may not, any of them, come to completion in an agent's, or all agents', lifetime.

Consider a good such as human life and health. The image of breadth helps us to recognize that this good is not to be pursued in one privileged way; doctors, for example, do not have the only, or the superior, mode of pursuit of this good. Rather, every agent may potentially pursue this complex good in more than one way, and in ways that differ from every other agent. Even within the field of medicine, a profession dedicated to the good of life and health, there is an overwhelming variety of ways of practicing it – specific forms of service to this particular good. But beyond the practice of medicine, the good of life is pursued whenever an agent goes to the gym to work out, brushes her teeth, cares for her children, donates money to Oxfam, and so on.

The breadth of the goods emerges from a feature of basic goods that will be important later in this chapter, so it is worth noting now: basic goods are fundamentally impersonal and intelligible. They are not agent-relative, and they are not particulars, as, for example, the objects of sensible inclinations, considered as motivating, are. When an agent sensibly desires some state of affairs, this state of affairs, considered precisely as such, is a reason, or a quasi-reason, only for the agent with the particular desire. But basic goods are intelligibly good for all agents and provide the same basic reasons for action for all agents.

As Thomas Nagel pointed out in *The Possibility of Altruism*, this means that there will be a variety of descriptions of action which may be embraced under a more general description that refers to that good.[8] So breadth emerges from the impersonality of goods as reasons for action.

Goods also have depth. This too is related to the denial that goods are essentially states of affairs. John Dewey believed that all final ends were final in the sense of being completable, but this is false.[9] The goods of life and health, or knowledge, or friendship are never completed. There always remain new possibilities for pursuit of these goods, many of which are only made available to agents by their already having pursued the goods to some extent or other.[10]

Moreover, this incompletability underwrites the possibility of excellence and creativity in the pursuit of goods, both in an individual's life and across the lives of generations: medicine today is vastly more advanced than medicine two thousand years ago, but it is neither finished nor finishable. When a medical tradition flourishes, the advances of previous generations are built on by the current generation, which will be sure to provide resources to future generations so that the progress may continue. Similarly, in an individual's life, a successful pursuit of knowledge or friendship, for example, is one that opens up new possibilities previously unseen, and allows the agent to develop new excellences previously unimagined.

By contrast, if basic goods were states of affairs, then, as Dewey says, virtues would be narrowly technical skills, and the meaningfulness of the pursuit of the goods would be threatened precisely by the possibility of completion of the pursuit. For, having 'accomplished' a good, an agent would be left with nothing further to do; and if, on the other hand, the agent did not accomplish the good, then the pursuit would have been meaningless because it would have failed to achieve its end. Basic goods, by contrast, are achieved in their pursuit, which pursuit, if done well, always opens up a new horizon of pursuit, rather than bringing us closer to a shutting door.

5

It is surely possible, however, for an agent to have sufficient grasp of a good – say, aesthetic experience – to be able to recognize it as giving reasons to act, but to have failed to understand, perhaps radically, the phenomena of breadth and depth of that good. This is compatible with many of the aims of education: parents and teachers are responsible for much of the introduction of a pupil to the basic goods, even though the pupil will have already felt the inclinations to knowledge or aesthetic enjoyment. One of the crucial tasks of education, however, is to bring the pupil to the insight that the good in question is not something that can be uniquely and finally accomplished; to the insight that there is not one privileged mode of its pursuit; and to the insight that there is always a more satisfactory avenue of pursuit, and a greater degree of excellence to be had in the pursuit of the good, than the pupil is currently aware of.

This description is, in fact, a very MacIntyrean one, consistent with much that Alasdair MacIntyre says about the role of authority in the initiation of agents into practices.[11] But the description establishes, as MacIntyre has certainly seen, that an agent's grasp of the good can be deformed through failure to recognize these points. The agent who fails to recognize the breadth of the good of aesthetic experience will dismiss as illusions or frauds forms of that experience other than those she has acquaintance with. The agent who fails to recognize depth will typically be shallow, refusing the challenge of more difficult work and settling for the least common denominator in, say, artistic merit. And in those cases in which the denial of depth is accompanied by the belief in completability, the mistake will result in an overly technical and instrumentalist approach – the approach of the mountain climber who thinks life will be meaningless if he does not reach the summit, and who instrumentalizes everything in pursuit of this narrowly conceived goal.

Millgram's admirer of light verse perhaps suffers from some of these failings: she does not recognize other avenues to poetic enjoyment, nor does she recognize the limits of the avenue with which she is familiar, and the ways in which a richer pursuit could be possible. Similarly, an agent whose idea of friendship was largely based on the idea of utility or pleasure, or an agent whose idea of life and health was limited to that of 'feeling good,' would be blocked from the appreciation of the depth and breadth of these goods.

Of such agents, it seems that the external reason claim – there is a reason for her to read Shakespeare; or for him to exercise, rather than merely to take diet supplements, and so on – is true. But the path to such reasons is neither, on the one hand, deliberative, nor, on the other, entirely unrooted in current motivations. It is not deliberative because the externality of the reasons comes precisely from an inadequacy in the agent's current subjective motivational set. The agent does not have enough of a grasp of the goods in question to deliberate from that grasp to the new insight. But the agent who, while subject to unreasonable limitations in her understanding of the good available through light verse, nonetheless has *that* appreciation, is in a different state altogether from an agent who, ex hypothesi, has no appreciation of the arts. There is hope for such an agent to see things aright.

6

There is a problem, however, which should not be overlooked. First, Millgram's description of experience as the key turning point, while promising, is problematic. For the agent's understanding and appreciation of experience will itself be shaped by her understanding and appreciation of the goods at stake in experience. This is why agents weaned on a steady diet of vulgar music, art, and literature do not find their first experience of Homer eye-opening, but *painful*. Similarly, as pointed out, McDowell's description of conversion is also problematic: little seems possible by way of explanation of the conversion. Hence Millgram's suggestion that McDowell's conversion experience has a sort of 'bolt from the blue' quality to it.[12]

The key, in this and in the next two types of cases discussed below, is the intrinsically unsatisfactory nature of the agent's present grasp, a grasp that in some cases, at least, may be such as to precipitate a moral crisis from which the agent emerges with new practical insight.

The sense of crisis I intend here should be taken as least analogous to Thomas Kuhn's notion of a crisis in science, although I shall attempt to make the transition from crisis to new paradigm somewhat more intelligible than does Kuhn. In Kuhn's classic account, in *The Structure of Scientific Revolutions*, scientists operate within a paradigm which provides the conceptual framework of normal science.[13] From within that framework, a fair number of anomalies may be written off as unproblematic, but eventually some anomaly or set of anomalies generates a crisis in normal science, a crisis that can only be overcome by a paradigm shift – a radical change in the framework through which the data and method of science are intelligible.

Rather notoriously, Kuhn's account flirts with a deeply anti-realist view of knowledge – when the scientist internalizes a new paradigm, she comes to inhabit a new world. This is at least *prima facie* in tension with a conception of theoretical reason as responsive to the way the world is, rather than constitutive of it. But a constitutive role for reason would be less problematic in the domain of the practical, where, as Boyle writes, 'the idea is that we can understand as interesting, worth pursuing, or good some possible futures of ourselves to which we can contribute by acting.'[14]

My suggestion, then, is that the world which can be projected by practical reason guided by a deficient understanding of the goods, an understanding that fails to appreciate their breadth or depth, plays a role for an agent analogous to that of a paradigm for a scientist for whom a crisis is looming. For the world projected by such an agent is intrinsically and ultimately radically unsatisfactory, judged in terms of the very general point of practical reason. A world in which goods are understood as completable states of affairs, for instance, is one to which the Deweyan critique above applies.

Because the practical paradigm shapes the agent's awareness, this will not be immediately, or necessarily, apparent to a deficient agent. But to the extent that the projected world is unsatisfactory, this should result in the continuous generation of practical anomalies – ways in which the agent comes into conflict or frustration with and in the world to which she contributes by acting. The mountain climber will find, as do many agents who wrongly make goods into goals, that the success does not provide the satisfaction sought. The agent who enters marriage thinking of it as a means to a set of harmonious experiences, rather than an essentially incompletable good requiring constant labor and creativity, will find, as do so many, that the experiences eventually run dry, and that not much else suffices to keep the relationship together. The agent immersed in light verse, and with a blind eye to all else, will eventually find it boring.

These crises, some minor, some more significant, seem largely crises of depth. But crises can emerge from failures to recognize breadth as well: the agent who has belittled or derided others' pursuits of goods she too pursues will find herself cut off from the resources and fulfillments made available by those alternative pursuits. Seeking to experience more of the good of life, or knowledge, or aesthetic experience, she will find her opportunities stunted. Moreover, she will find that the possibility of mutual pursuit of valued goods, and shared appreciation of those goods, will likewise be blocked. Consider, for example, the snobbery of some practitioners of professional philosophy who do not simply avoid going in for the style of philosophy of others, but do not consider it philosophy at all. As recent advances along the border of analytic and continental philosophy, or historical and systematic philosophy, for example, have indicated, such philosophers have in some cases cut themselves off from significant resources, and have blocked fellowship with other agents essentially committed to the same goods.

7

The agent in practical crisis is thus, like Kuhn's scientist, in need of a new paradigm – it is not a matter of reasoning from the old paradigm to what is wanting, any more than Kuhn's scientist can continue to reason from within the framework of normal science. But the paradigm shift will be ultimately unintelligible if it does not respond precisely to the deficiencies that generate the need in the first place. This is where, in the practical sphere, the basic goods approach, with its two central theses, is at a distinct conceptual advantage.

Recall that all agents have some, if only minimal, grasp of the basic goods, and that flourishing is taken by basic goods approaches to be the point, both narrowly and broadly, of intelligible human action. These two facts establish the possibility of an intelligible practical crisis. The crisis emerges in the first place because the understanding of the goods had by a deficient agent cannot deliver on what it promises: in other words, the agent's projected world brings him to a point of frustration judged in terms of what the projected world promises. But that promise itself is based upon the same resources – inadequately grasped – on which the new, more adequate projected world will be based as well – the attraction of the basic goods, and the hope that their reasonable pursuit through time will offer human fulfillment.

The new future is made possible, that is, by a conjunction of insights: the recognition that the goods pursued give meaning and value to our actions; and the recognition that as currently understood, those goods cannot deliver on their promise. The specific deficiencies of the agent's practical understanding must be understood, in light of the crisis, to be a consequence of an unwarranted limiting of the goods. The agent thus comes to see, in a way rooted in, but not controlled by, her previous appreciation of the goods, a new depth and breadth, accompanied by an essential incompletability, of the sources of values in action.

The role that experience plays in revealing new reasons is thus rather nuanced, and continuous with the nature of conversion. Experience of what is in itself more satisfactory is not sufficient, at least initially, for the agent to recognize the superior nature of what is experienced. For the very character flaws that prevent the agent from recognizing in the absence of new experience a reason for action can reshape that experience in a way that renders its relevance to reasons opaque to that agent. The agent who attempts to read something better than the cheap trash he usually indulges in will often at first find the experience painful. This will likewise be the case for the lazy agent who attempts to introduce discipline into his life, or the dissolute agent who attempts to honor a vow of marital chastity. What is essential is this: any life, or projected future, that is not lived in a way fully and reasonably responsive to the basic goods is a life whose promise will eventually run dry. A fully reasonable approach to the goods is a necessary condition for flourishing, which all agents desire. A false picture, and unreasonable projected future, thus contains the seeds of its own destruction.[15]

8

The image of practical crisis, and the way in which it can generate a new practical insight, repeats itself in other areas. I will consider two more, then turn to a further investigation of the nature of the insight itself. The multiplicity of goods raises what Timothy Chappell has called the problem of reconciliation.[16] Given that maximization is precluded by the nature of the goods as incommensurable and as not being states of affairs, what constitutes a reasonable pursuit of the goods? One significant aspect of a full answer to this question, an aspect recognized by a number of philosophers, is that the reasonable point of view on the pursuit of the multiplicity of goods requires a degree of detachment from an agent's particular temporal location, in favor of a more holistic view, that is, a view of the agent's life as a potential whole. This atemporal perspective provides the standpoint from which the importance and organization of the temporal parts of one's life should be assessed.

Consider, for example, the agent who writes poetry on Tuesday, plays with his children on Wednesday, does philosophy on Thursday, and so on. This agent will never pursue any of the goods well; to write decent poetry, for example, requires sustained effort over time, and a willingness to forego the pursuit of various other goods for the sake of commitment to poetry. Moreover, such an agent's life, organized only in the most minimal way according to an arbitrary calendar schedule, threatens much in the way of conflict and strain. When the agent's children wish to play on Monday, what resources are there for the agent reasonably to deal with the conflict?[17]

Goods-based theories have in common, as it were, a commitment to commitment. All, without apparent exception, stress the need for agents to introduce order into their lives by giving some pursuits priority over others and allowing those pursuits to shape the agents' lives, by easing conflict, and by creating opportunities for sustained devotion to the goods. A rational plan of life, in John Rawls's words, is called for by reason as one part, at least, of a solution to the problem of reconciliation.[18]

Recognition of this – not as a philosophically articulated view, but a simple practical recognition – is thus necessary for all agents. But this recognition can be blocked by an agent's temporal bias. An agent can and does arbitrarily privilege her 'present self,' or see her life as largely discrete segments, dividing it up diachronically – childhood, college, grown-up, and old – and synchronically – work, home, and church – in ways that fail to recognize the need for unity in and through a life. The projected futures of such agents are too temporally minimal and partial. Of such agents, we want to say that there are reasons for them to take a longer view, or a more holistic approach, to their lives. There are reasons for them to do so, because they would be better off if they did.

The notion of a point of view here is helpful: what such agents essentially need is a new perspective from which they may view their lives, given that they are accustomed to viewing it from some more narrow point of view. John Finnis draws attention, for example, to the way in which one can view her life from the standpoint of her own death.[19] Recent emphasis on narrative seems likewise to reflect awareness of the way in which the temporality of one's life and the multiplicity of goods together require that one's life be viewed as a kind of whole, with the appropriately introduced organization. Such images seem consonant with the nature of reason itself, which seems to have a fundamental concern for the whole.[20]

What deficient practical reasoners grasp, however, are parts only – the importance of the agent's life now, of pursuing goods here and now, and so on. But from the part, there is no deliberative path to the whole; one cannot deliberate from recognition of the present importance of goods to the need to view one's life from the standpoint of one's death. Nonetheless, the problem of reconciliation is not just a theoretical problem of moral philosophy: it has the potential to emerge, for deficient agents, as the practical clash of the goods in a life that is disorganized or temporally biased. The conflicts between the demands of the goods can be actually experienced in the lives of such agents.

Again, of course, it is the case that blindness affects interpretation: aware only of the importance of living for the moment, an agent can rationalize conflict as 'valuable experience,' or fail even to recognize conflict. But the important point is that such conflicts are genuinely disruptive of an agent's well-being, and well-being is what all agents want. Agents with a deficient grasp of the need for structure and commitment have within themselves the origins of a practical crisis, the upshot of which can be the forced recognition of the larger standpoint. Again, experience can play a role: the agent who comes close to death takes a forced form of the point of view from the end of his life. Or agents can recognize in other agents, suddenly, that their structured commitments are a large part of why those agents' lives are more successful. Consider, for example, the agent who decries marriage (and children) as an unwanted and constraining limitation – the *Sex and the City* agent. Surely some such agents can be jolted by the recognition that the stability and so-called 'limitation' of a well-married couple's life together are actually richer and more perfective than is the constant search for new sexual partners.

9

This same need for a more holistic view of the scope of the goods applies to an agent's practical awareness of other agents and of their relation to the basic goods. As specified earlier, basic goods are impersonally and intelligibly good – they provide agent-neutral reasons for action. Thus, the goods of human life are as good for any other agent as they are for me. Smith has the same reason for action, in considering the value of life, as Jones, and can see that in some circumstances she should act for the sake of that value in relation to Jones rather than herself. Similarly, agents can co-operate in the pursuit of goods only because of the impersonality of those goods.

The pursuit of the basic goods in a fully reasonable way, a way that acknowledges the reality of those goods, must thus acknowledge them as goods for others, and the participation in them by others as intrinsically valuable. As fully understood, the ideal pursued in human action is maximally inclusive of agents, and includes the participation of all agents in the goods – it is an ideal of a community of friendship.

Again, though, agents can fail to recognize this in ways that are structurally parallel to the failure to recognize the whole of one's life as the relevant area over which one acts.

An agent's awareness of the goods – of life, or play, or knowledge, for example – can be arbitrarily limited to the bearing of those goods on the agent herself. This can be a result of education, of poor philosophical theory, or of rationalization due to the sway of desires that, unlike the goods, are essentially personal and particular. It is certainly true that some agents are aware of the impersonality of the goods, and the value of community in the goods, but choose to act to satisfy their own desires, or for some limited personal sharing in the good. But for some agents, it is the practical awareness itself that is deficient, and even for those agents initially aware of the unreasonableness of their choices, by habituation and rationalization they can come to a new lack of awareness of what they once recognized.

The conversion of an agent from the practical solipsism involved in recognizing only the relation of the goods to himself, to a full awareness of the goods in relation to the 'other,' has been a theme of recent philosophical writing, especially in the continental tradition. Martin Buber, Emmanuel Levinas, and Karol Wojtyla, for example, have all made this a central concern of their work.[21] But there is, again, no reason to think that this wider and more inclusive awareness is a result of deliberation from what the agent is already aware of. And yet agents raised in a context in which they were encouraged only to see the goods as they related to themselves (or their 'group') occasionally describe a sudden awareness of the wider practical universe which includes all other rational agents, a form of awareness that seems to be a form of non-deliberative practical insight.

This insight would be utterly unintelligible were it not for the fact that a life of practical solipsism is deeply unsatisfactory. Agents flourish by attention to the fullness of the goods, and that fullness requires unavoidable reference to other agents. This may be via pursuit of goods that require other agents, such as friendship or religion, or because other goods such as knowledge and life are pursued effectively only in common with other agents. Or it may be because the goods themselves are seen and appreciated only partially if they are understood as bearing solely on oneself. The practically solipsistic life, like the temporally partial life, is inevitably frustrating and unsatisfactory, full of conflict with others, and unable to penetrate significantly into the depth of the goods or to appreciate their breadth. It would seem, in fact, reasonable to expect that the three sorts of failings discussed in this chapter, practical solipsism, temporal bias, and a failure to appreciate the depth and breadth of the basic goods, will often go together in mutually reinforcing ways.

10

The theory of the goods and of the path to ethics from the goods, articulated by Grisez, Boyle, and Finnis, has a particular structure. (Other basic goods theories have generally similar structures, although there are occasionally significant differences.[22]) Beginning with the first principle of practical reason, that good is to be done and pursued, and evil avoided, as a principle for intelligible action, and with a practical awareness of the basic goods, Grisez *et al.* go on to defend a first principle of morality: 'In voluntarily acting for human goods and avoiding what is opposed to them, one ought to choose and otherwise will those and only those possibilities whose willing is compatible with a will toward integral human fulfillment.'[23] They then go on to derive a number of intermediate principles – modes of responsibility – from this principle, all of which specify ways of acting that would violate this will to integral human fulfillment.

These modes of responsibility, such as, 'One should not be deterred by felt inertia from acting for intelligible goods,' or 'One should not be pressed by felt enthusiasm or impatience to act individualistically for intelligible goods,' are themselves the source of derivation of specific moral norms, some of which are familiar from traditional sources such as the Ten Commandments. To follow the moral norms is to adhere to his eight modes of responsibility, and, as Grisez writes, these 'guide action positively toward integral human fulfillment.'[24]

Where, in this structure, is there room for the three practical insights I have described, into the breadth and depth of the goods, the necessity of a structured pursuit of those goods over a life, and the scope of the goods over all agents? These are the insights that underlie conversion experiences and emerge, at least in some agents, not from deliberation, but in response to practical crises. In some works, Finnis, for example, has listed among the modes of responsibility a norm directing agents to form a rational plan of life.[25] But if that mode of responsibility is derived from the first principle of morality, then this would militate against my interpretation of the awareness of this need as a practical insight not achieved by deliberation. And in the articulation of the modes of responsibility found in Grisez's *Christian Moral Principles*, this norm is not to be found, although there are related norms.

A more auspicious location to look for something like these three forms of practical awareness seems to me to be within the first principles of the theory. These include the basic apprehension of the goods and the first principle of morality itself, a principle that specifies a certain understanding of what is generally grasped by practical reasoners as the point of human action – fulfillment. This ideal of fulfillment, with the goods taken as its constituents, guides human action. Yet practical reasoners may have more or less deficient or acceptable understandings of the concept both of the goods and of fulfillment, as Aristotle and Aquinas make clear in their discussions of, for example, the lives of honor, pleasure, and money-making.

We could thus see the three practical insights as insights into the nature of the goods and of the fulfillment that should guide all human action. Again, in Grisez's formulation, the principle is: 'In voluntarily acting for human goods and avoiding what is opposed to them, one ought to choose and otherwise will those and only those possibilities whose willing is compatible with a will toward integral human fulfillment.'[26] Grisez then goes on to specify that 'integral human fulfillment' must be understood as an ideal, not a realizable state of affairs: 'The ideal of integral human fulfillment is that of a single system in which all the goods of human persons would contribute to the fulfillment of the whole community of persons.'[27]

11

It seems clear that not all agents recognize and appreciate the full truth of this principle, nor the full nature of the goods that contribute to the fulfillment referred to in it. But acknowledging this does not seem to call into question the claim that all agents desire fulfillment, nor that the fulfillment actually sought by all agents inevitably makes reference to the basic goods. The *de facto* pursuit of fulfillment by everyday agents is compatible with various misunderstandings of the fulfillment that it is reasonable to desire. Agents who, because they have failed to recognize the depth, breadth, and incompletability of the basic goods, for example, will misconceive the fulfillment which is the root of morality as the fulfillment to be found in states of affairs and discrete goals. Agents might further fail to recognize the role that the word 'integral' should play in their understanding of human fulfillment: they might understand that fulfillment in a partial, temporally or personally biased way, and thus pursue the goods disjointedly or egoistically.

The three insights discussed in this chapter are thus, as it were, three aspects of the intelligibility of the notions of fulfillment and of the basic goods that must be grasped by any practical agent who is to have such a sufficient understanding of fulfillment that it can reasonably govern his practical life and deliberations. But the intelligibility of a concept is itself not something to be reasoned to on the basis of premises, unless the concept is itself in some way derivative or constructed from other concepts. The concept of 'the ideal of integral human fulfillment,' although complex, and making reference to the basic goods, does not seem either derivative or constructed, but rather basic; it must, like the concepts of the goods themselves, be understood practically in itself.

Agents who have a sound practical understanding of these concepts thus obtain such understanding through practical insight. Grisez, Finnis, and Boyle have often stressed that the practical insight into the nature and desirability of the various goods is not independent of, though also not inferred from, experience or instruction. The same seems true of the concept at the heart of the first principle of morality. For many agents – those well brought up – their (often inarticulate, implicit) understanding of the concept of integral human fulfillment is a result of their education, particularly in the home, and their experience in the home of the way order and harmony in and between persons, in the pursuit of goods, is more satisfactory than other modes of behavior. But for agents who have rejected that early teaching and experience, or who have never been fortunate enough to receive it, a correct understanding of integral human fulfillment may be the painful result of experience, that experience of the radical insufficiency of partial and otherwise deficient understandings of the goods and of the nature of fulfillment. The crisis that such experience can generate may point these agents towards a richer awareness of the end of human action.

12

It is not clear that other moral theories can accommodate in an intelligible way the form of insight that crisis brings on and that culminates in conversion. Consequentialism can make little sense of the claim that the goods to be pursued are not states of affairs; and the view put forth by Henry Sidgwick, that there is a profound dualism to practical reason, makes it utterly unintelligible why an agent would pursue the overall good, rather than his own overall good.[28]

Kant claims that agents who act immorally act heteronomously, and thus from a fundamentally different motive than autonomous agents.

Moreover, the motive from which they act is one incompatible with rational freedom.[29] It is thus difficult to see how, from the standpoint of a heteronomous agent, one could ever come to see the desirability of acting autonomously, much less be capable of so acting. The gap between the immoral and the moral seems too large to bridge intelligibly.

Recent revivals of realism are subtle and often attentive in profound ways to certain phenomenological characteristics of our approach to morally fraught circumstances. Nonetheless, they seem to give no reason why one would be interested, deeply, in moral properties that are supposed to be perceived in something like the way secondary qualities are.[30] Eudaimonism is insufficiently brought into play in such theories. But eudaimonism is necessary to explain why a conversion gives an agent something worth pursuing from that agent's practical point of view. Believers are irrational or unreasonable when they fail to see or acknowledge what is right before their eyes. But it is not clear how agents are irrational or unreasonable when they fail to take an interest in moral properties, if those properties are insufficiently tied to what agents need or want, or to what makes those agents better off. The eudaimonism of basic goods theories, by contrast, can make clear what was lacking before the conversion, and what the conversion promises.

Utilitarianism, Kantianism, and McDowellian realism all seem to me to present a picture on which some reasons are indeed external. McDowell, of course, explicitly argues this. For a Kantian agent who is acting heteronomously, the demands of autonomy are external reasons; similarly, for an agent pursuing her individual good, the good from the point of view of the universe seems equally external. Such theories, indeed, seem to be the primary targets of Williams's early essay. But basic goods views, I have argued, can respect something that external reason theories recognize – that for some agents there is a sense of discovery where reasons are concerned. As the hymn says, echoing John 9:25, 'I was blind, but now I see.'

Basic goods views can honor this by recognizing deficiencies in the practical understanding that some (perhaps most) agents have of the basic goods and of the notion of fulfillment, the core concepts from which all other practical reasons emerge. Agents can be deficient in their appreciation of the depth and breadth of the basic goods. They can confuse completable projects with the goods themselves. Agents can further fail to recognize that the pursuit of flourishing is the pursuit of *integral* human flourishing – flourishing over time, and across the multiplicity of agents. There seems little hope of moving an agent to an appreciation of the value of knowledge if he has no such appreciation at all, or of moving an agent with no desire for fulfillment to a recognition of the need reasonably to structure his life, or to pursue community with others. But from deficient appreciations in these areas, conjoined with an awareness that these (deficient) appreciations result in frustration, conflict, or lack of meaning, some agents may move rationally, but non-deliberatively, to a deeper awareness of what there was reason for them to do and pursue, but which was not yet for them a reason.

Notes

1. Timothy Chappell, however, is an exception to this welfarist conception of the basic goods. See his contribution to this book.
2. Germain Grisez, *The Way of the Lord Jesus*, Vol. One: *Christian Moral Principles* (Chicago: Franciscan Herald Press, 1983): 197.
3. Ibid: 184.
4. Bernard Williams, 'Internal and External Reasons', in his *Moral Luck* (Cambridge: Cambridge University Press, 1981): 101–2.
5. John McDowell, 'Might There Be External Reasons?', in J.E.J. Altham and R. Harrison (eds), *Mind, World, and Ethics* (Cambridge: Cambridge University Press, 1995): 68–85; quotation at 74.
6. Elijah Millgram, 'Williams' Argument Against External Reasons', *Noûs* 30 (1996): 197–220.
7. Ibid: 211.
8. Thomas Nagel, *The Possibility of Altruism* (Princeton: Princeton University Press, 1977): 90.
9. See, for example, John Dewey, 'Theory of Valuation', in Jo Ann Boydston (ed.), *The Later Works, 1925–1953* (Carbondale: Southern Illinois University Press, 1988): 3–90. See also Henry S. Richardson's criticism of Dewey's views on this matter in Richardson, *Practical Reasoning about Final Ends* (Cambridge: Cambridge University Press, 1994): 159–65.
10. Of course, the pursuit of goods requires the pursuit of specific good-oriented projects. These projects are often completable. The mistake is to confuse projects and the goods that make these projects worthwhile.
11. See Alasdair MacIntyre, *After Virtue* (Notre Dame: University of Notre Dame Press, 1984): ch. 14.
12. See note 6.
13. Thomas Kuhn, *The Structure of Scientific Revolutions* (Chicago: University of Chicago Press, 1970).
14. Joseph Boyle, 'Reasons for Action: Evaluative Cognitions that Underlie Motivations', *The American Journal of Jurisprudence* 46 (2001): 177–97, at 191.
15. This essentially Platonic thought seems to me to be the guiding insight of much of the *Republic*; see also the second of Marx's *Theses on Feuerbach*.
16. Timothy Chappell, *Understanding Human Goods* (Edinburgh: University of Edinburgh Press, 1998): 7.
17. See Richardson, *Practical Reasoning about Final Ends*, for an extensive discussion of such issues.

18. See John Rawls, *A Theory of Justice* (Cambridge, MA: Harvard University Press, 1974).
19. John Finnis, *Natural Law and Natural Rights* (Oxford: Clarendon Press, 1980).
20. See Christopher Tollefsen, 'Sidgwickian Objectivity and Ordinary Morality', *Journal of Value Inquiry* 33 (1997): 57–70.
21. See, for example, Martin Buber, *I and Thou* (New York: Free Press, 1971); Emmanuel Levinas, *Alterity and Transcendence* (New York: Columbia University Press, 2000); and Karol Wojtyla, *Love and Responsibility* (New York: Farrar Straus & Giroux, 1981).
22. For example, see the different interpretations of Aquinas's first principle of practical reason in the work of Grisez, 'The First Principle of Practical Reason: A Commentary on the *Summa Theologiae*, 1–2, Question 94, Article 2', *Natural Law Forum* 10 (1965): 168–201; and in Chappell, *Understanding Human Goods*: ch. 3.
23. Grisez, *Christian Moral Principles*: 184.
24. Ibid: 226.
25. Finnis, *Natural Law and Natural Rights*.
26. See note 23.
27. Grisez: 185.
28. Henry Sidgwick, *The Methods of Ethics* (Indiana: Hackett Press, 1981).
29. Immanuel Kant, *Critique of Practical Reason*, trans. Lewis White Beck (New York: MacMillan, 1985).
30. See, for example, John McDowell, 'Values as Secondary Qualities', in Ted Honderich (ed.), *Morality and Objectivity* (London: Routledge & Kegan Paul, 1985).

3
The Fact/Value Distinction

Christopher Martin

1 Introduction

I am writing this in 2003, the centenary of G.E. Moore's *Principia Ethica*. I do not wish to commemorate this book, but rather to help to bury a theme which it re-introduced to the English-speaking philosophical world: the fact/value distinction.[1]

Moore's own account of the distinction – in terms of a metaphysical gap between 'natural' and 'non-natural' properties – came to be rejected quite quickly and widely. Indeed it can be denied that he made a fact/value distinction at all, merely a distinction between two kinds of facts. But if there are two kinds of facts, very different from each other, and 'factual' judgements express one kind of fact while 'value' judgements express another, then we undoubtedly have a distinction between two kinds of judgement. Some distinction of this kind continued to be made, by author after author during the twentieth century, for a wide variety of alleged reasons. Roger Crisp, in his excellent article in the *Routledge Encyclopedia of Philosophy*,[2] says that 'the fact/value distinction was of great importance in twentieth century moral philosophy', but the past tense may have been premature. At the popular level, the distinction continues to be held: at least nine-tenths, I would say, of first-year undergraduates believe in it, even if confusedly, and even if they also hold other beliefs inconsistent with it. It is significant, too, that there is a popular and highly regarded textbook, J.L. Mackie's *Ethics: Inventing Right and Wrong*, which has been available for more than twenty-five years, and one of whose main attractions is that it gives a clear set of arguments for one version of the distinction.[3] Again, some would say here that since Mackie claims that 'there are no objective values',[4] this means that he does not recognise the distinction. His is an 'error-theory'. But this is to say that value judgements need to be accounted for by an error-theory, while other judgements do not, and hence a distinction is still made between value judgements and other judgements. The difference between this and a fact/value distinction is one I cannot discern.

I would like to bring together here some major arguments given for the fact/value distinction and to suggest that they are very weak. If there is little rational basis for the distinction, we must look for other explanations for its popularity. I hope to suggest that appropriate explanations relate to special features of English-speaking culture.

At a level of intellectual autobiography, I was introduced to the distinction as a matter of course, as undergraduates still were in British universities in those days – the late 1970s. (But I can also testify to its being taught to undergraduates as a matter of course as late as the 1990s.) I recognised it as something intuitively plausible, as one did, even if one also wanted to find ways to repudiate it. I was surprised, then, when teaching in Spain some years later, to find that none of my students were in the least inclined to accept the distinction. Still more, it was completely unknown to them, and only with great difficulty could I give them any idea of what it meant. I began then to suspect that the distinction was a parochial prejudice of English-speaking culture, dependent on contingent historical and cultural factors.

There is something curious about the distinction, in any case, as the number and variety of its upholders suggest. They all have this in common, that they believe in a 'fact/value distinction', but they do so for inconsistent reasons. Hume, perhaps, upholds the distinction because of a supposed inferential gap between 'is'-sentences and 'ought'-sentences. Moore gives no importance to this, but upholds the distinction because of a metaphysical difference between natural qualities and non-natural qualities. C.L. Stevenson rejects this, but upholds the distinction because of a logical and psychological difference: factual judgements relate to states of affairs in the world outside us, while value judgements are not really judgements at all, but expressions of our feelings. R.M. Hare rejects this in his turn, but upholds the distinction because of a difference between description, in the indicative mood, and prescription, in the imperative mood; and so on.

This history is a very curious one. Each upholder of the distinction seems to undermine or abandon precisely those theoretical grounds which seemed so important to his predecessor, but he then at once proceeds to give a new theory to justify the distinction – a theory that will probably soon be undermined or abandoned by his own successor. What seems never to be considered is the possibility of giving up the distinction altogether, though one would think that a series of apparent failures to justify it theoretically would make this a reasonable course of action. There appears to be something at work here that is more funda-mental than any of the detailed theories that purport to give a basis for the distinction.

It is in fact difficult to come by an independent account of what exactly the fact/value distinction is supposed to be – independent, I mean, of any of particular questionable theory that is supposed to justify it. The author who comes nearest, in my view, is Mackie.[5] But there is a threefold difference to observe here. We need: (1) an account or descrip-tion of the distinction; (2) an argument or set of arguments for it; and (3) a theoretical context. (1) and (2) should be common, with minor differences, to all upholders of the distinction, whilst (3) will vary. In fact we find that most give us their version of (3) and perhaps a very imperfect version of (2). Mackie gives us a good and full version of (2) that others could use if they pleased. No one, I think, gives us (1): they just take it for granted.

To try to establish the distinction, one might suggest that 'value' judgements are not truth-apt in the same way that 'factual' judgements are. But this would mean that Moore did not uphold the fact/value dis-tinction, which he certainly did. In any case this would still give us no content for 'fact' and 'value'. One might look for some light from Crisp. But he says: 'According to proponents of the fact/value distinction, no states of the world can be said to be values, and evaluative judgements are best understood not to be pure statements of fact.'[6] But while this gives the impression of helping us understand the distinction, it would not do so unless we *already* were ourselves inclined to believe in it. It is surely no use trying to introduce a distinction between x's and y's by saying, 'According to proponents of the x/y distinction, no states of the world can be said to be y's, and y-type judgements are best understood not to be pure statements of x.'

Perhaps we can fall back on paradigm cases: the paradigm cases of factual judgements seem to be the utterances of the sciences, and judge-ments that are immediately verifiable by empirical means. Paradigm cases of value judgements, on the other hand, are sometimes taken to be utterances with 'ought' as their copula, but since it is usually specified that this 'ought' must be the 'moral' ought, it looks as if this will be little help. One might do better by putting forward, as paradigm cases of value judgements, utterances about human good. But only if one already accepts the distinction will one find this characterisation an adequate way of stating it. Even on the most realist view of values there will be some differences between the two sets of paradigm cases:

utterances about human good will almost inevitably involve need, while very many utterances of science do not, and perhaps no immediate empirical observation will do so. But this is a distinction – broadly, between sentences that only involve actuality and those that must involve necessity – which can very well be investigated and often has been. It is not a great logical or metaphysical or psychological or epistemological gulf that no one can cross.[7]

One is tempted to suspect that we are facing here a false presupposition. A legend has it that Charles II posed a question to the Royal Society, as to why a quantity of water with a live fish in it should weigh no more than the same quantity of water without the fish. The question received a host of different answers from the assembled *savants* until someone, perhaps the king himself, proposed making the experiment and found out that it does not.

One might say that there is a smell of fish, not only about some of the theories used to justify the distinction, but even about the features that are supposed to mark it out. For example, it often used to be said that value judgements had some special 'universalisability' not possessed by factual judgements. The notion of 'universalisability', crudely, is that when we make a value judgement we are thereby committed to maintaining that the same judgement holds of anyone else in the same circumstances, or (more cautiously) in 'relevantly similar' circumstances.

But this idea of universalisability limps on both legs, not least because of the well-known objection by J.O. Urmson in 'Saints and Heroes', where he points out that people who perform what used to be called acts of supererogation think, on the one hand, that they very definitely ought to do them, but refuse to say that others ought to.[8] So it is not true that when one thinks 'I ought to do X' one must think that all others in identical, or 'relevantly similar' circumstances, ought to do X as well.

Moreover, even if it were true that value judgements are universalisable, it seems that very many factual judgements are as well. If I judge, 'I have put on weight since I came to America', must I not also maintain that the same is true of anyone in the same circumstances – someone, say, who came to America when I did, who weighed n lbs when he came to America, as I did, and who now weighs $n+m$ lbs, as I do? Or, indeed, of anyone in 'relevantly similar' circumstances: as, for example, that he or she came to America at some time, and then, for some number x, weighed x lbs, and who now, for some number y, weighs $x+y$ lbs?

It remains difficult, then, to obtain a general characterisation of what the fact/value distinction is. There are arguments offered for it, many of which directly presuppose the particular theoretical position the author adopts. Mackie, though, stands out as giving completely general arguments for the distinction in itself, independent of his own theoretical account of it.[9] I shall try to address them (unequally) here, calling them 'the argument from disagreement', 'the argument from queerness', and the 'argument from reason-giving force'.

2   The argument from disagreement

This first argument is the commonest, the least intellectually respectable, and perhaps the oldest – a version of it is to be found in Plato's *Euthyphro*[10] and a crude version is probably to be heard in most bars and in the first class of every moral philosophy course in the English-speaking world. It is to the effect that factual judgements must be very different from value judgements because people agree about factual judgements but disagree about value judgements.[11]

The claim, however, is not true; and if it were true, it would not be important. First, both halves of it are false. People disagree widely even on simple factual questions. The newspapers frequently report that the level of scientific literacy even in the richest Western countries is very low. If you stop a person in a shopping mall in Britain or the US and ask a couple of questions – 'Does the earth go around the sun or does the sun go round the earth?' and 'How long does it take for the earth to go around the sun?' – you have, on average, a slightly worse than even chance of getting a pair of right answers.[12] That is, careful surveys tell us that when two 'educated' people are asked a pair of questions, there is no more than a 50 per cent chance that they will answer the same way. This result cannot legitimately be called agreement.

The fundamental problem, though, is that upholders of the distinction will refuse to recognise the different answers as disagreement. It will be said that – unlike in the case of value questions – all those who give the correct answer are in agreement and all those who give the wrong answer are *ignorant*: thus there will be no disagreement. This move takes away all credibility from the opinion poll as a means to establish the distinction: it too obviously presupposes the validity of the distinction in the first place.

As Peter Geach points out in *The Virtues*, a poll is valueless unless comparable groups are being polled. We might add that it is likewise valueless in establishing different degrees of agreement unless comparable questions are being asked. In fact, what is usually done is to pre-select a fairly unified cultural group to be asked factual questions, and then to ask them easy ones. Then one polls a much larger group, often pre-selected precisely for its cultural variation, about difficult moral questions. Few seem to notice this, or to ask what 'difficulty' consists in here: it seems to be taken for granted that only easy factual questions are to be asked, and even then the results of the poll are fudged, as above, by refusing to call it disagreement when people give different answers. Meanwhile, the most difficult value questions may be asked; or perhaps it is presumed that all value questions are of their essence on a level of easiness with the easiest factual questions. If we compare the answers from a large, varied group on difficult value questions with the answers from a small, cohesive group on easy factual questions, any alleged difference in the amount of agreement shows precisely nothing.

It is amusing to notice, by the way, that if the poll had been taken in the seventeenth century there would have been wider disagreement, even among a definitely well-educated group, on whether the earth goes around the sun or the sun around the earth. But at the same time, there would have been wide agreement on the value judgement that conduct proscribed by the Ten Commandments was wrong. Had someone been inspired to invent the fact/value distinction in the seventeenth century, he would have inverted it.

It is also important to notice that for some reason one is allowed, as a matter of sociological *mores*, to admit that one is not an expert in science or history, and thus to say 'I don't know' to questions on these subjects. (One is allowed, in extreme cases, even to claim or admit to sense defects, and to be pitied rather than despised.) But one is made the object of scorn if one tries to refrain from giving an opinion on a value question, no matter how recondite it may be. Presumably the explanation for this difference has to do with the association of 'I don't know' with 'I don't care'. But it really is not surprising that in a field in which one is discouraged from expressing ignorance there should be more apparent disagreement than in a field in which expressing ignorance is tolerated.

One should perhaps remember, as well, that there may be reason to believe that value questions are *a priori* likely to be more difficult than, for example, simple factual questions – empirical questions, scientific questions, or even historical questions. For unlike the first two kinds of factual question, for instance, value questions involve the relationship between an individual and its context, and typically involve human behaviour, which is notoriously a relatively complex and difficult subject, by anyone's account of it. As for historical questions, since they are about the past, they are less likely to be influenced by current interests than judgements on ethical questions. In this way they are likely to be easier.

I maintain, then, that there is no relevant difference in agreement between factual and value questions, and that even if there were it would not matter: the difference would be attributable to the greater difficulty of value questions. Indeed, moral disagreement and factual disagreement often go together. Geach makes this point with regard to the Trobriand Islanders:[13] their sexual *mores* are (or were) extremely unusual, in that (famously) they had no taboo against father–daughter incest. But their disagreement from the rest of the world on this point rested on a factual disagreement, or at least a conceptual one. They did not recognise the *existence* of fathers, did not recognise the role of what we call 'fathers' in the production of children.

It is sometimes replied: 'We will grant that there is disagreement on some facts and agreement on some values, but this is merely contingent. What is important is that in factual matters there is an agreement on the procedure for reaching an answer, whereas in value judgements there is no such agreement.'[14]

This, I say, is yet another piece of assertion for which there is no evidence. There is agreement on procedure for the same reason that there is agreement on answers – because we refuse to recognise as disagreement any dissent either from our answers or from our procedures. We call it not 'disagreement', but 'ignorance'. There is no reason why a moral realist should not be equally entitled to call 'ignorant' someone who differs on moral questions, whether as to substance or procedure.

If the defender of the distinction makes a retreat from the claim about agreement on substance to a claim about agreement on procedure, we can challenge him as to what our usual procedure is. Our usual procedure is to trust authority, something Elizabeth Anscombe noticed:[15] most judgements, whether of value or of fact, are reached on the basis of another's authority. The bulk of what we believe, we believe because someone else has told us. This is our normal procedure in judging. Authority is a problematic notion, and Anscombe was right to draw attention to the degree to which this question has been neglected; but there is no radical distinction to be made between facts and values on this basis.

Moreover, this procedure, whether in the realm of value judgements or of factual judgements, unavoidably involves a value question. Beyond the very limited sphere of immediate empirical judgements, all judgements require that we should trust other people.[16] But who we should trust, and when, is not a purely factual question – it includes a prudential judgement. There are times when we should trust others (most times, probably) and times when we should not – but just because this value judgement is for most of us quick, instinctive, and unproblematic does not mean that it is not made.

3 The argument from queerness

I do not think that there is a better statement of the 'argument from queerness' than the one found in Mackie.[17] '[The argument] has two parts, one metaphysical, the other epistemological. If there were objective values, then they would have to be entities or qualities or relations of a very strange sort, utterly different from anything else in the universe. Correspondingly, if we were aware of them it would have to be by some special faculty of moral perception or intuition, utterly different from our ordinary ways of knowing everything else.'[18] To me, this seems to say little more than that values are not physical entities, qualities, or relations, and that they are not directly empirically accessible to us. I, for one, do not find this surprising.

Indeed, Mackie recognises this, saying that the best reply to the 'argument from queerness' is 'not to evade the issue, but to look for companions in guilt'.[19] He refers us to Richard Price (a mid-eighteenth-century critic of Locke) as teaching that 'it is not moral knowledge alone that such an empiricism as those of Locke and Hume is unable to account for, but also our knowledge and even our ideas of essence, number, identity, diversity, solidity, inertia, substance, [...] necessity and possibility in general, power and causation'.[20]

That is, if values are 'queer', then equally so are notions which we use every day without difficulty or question. The list could be extended to include numbers, the past and the future, the notion of sign *qua* sign, even time and space (which are not physical entities in that they do not themselves exist in time and space)[21] and perhaps many other notions. It is true that these 'queer' but everyday notions require elucidation, but that elucidation is what metaphysics and epistemology consist in. One is tempted to ask, when Mackie implies that notions such as these are 'very strange' and 'utterly different': is he doing more than making a profession of materialist and empiricist faith? To be sure, Mackie goes on to tell us that he believes he can 'on empiricist foundations, construct an account of the ideas and beliefs and knowledge of these matters'.[22] But this too is a profession of faith.

Some people, I believe, think that values are 'queer' because they mistake their logical category. They think, perhaps, that goodness is

'queer' because it does not relate in the way they expect to other properties, unlike a term such as 'human'. We can say that what is human is
animal, and that being animal is part of what makes a human to be
human: a human is human in virtue, in part, of the properties involved
in being an animal. By contrast, a good doughnut may be good precisely in virtue of properties that a good mole-wrench lacks, and a
good mole-wrench may be good in virtue of properties that a good
doughnut lacks.

The reply to this is an old story.[23] Geach draws attention to the difference between an attributive adjective and a predicative one, and Mackie
gives some recognition to Geach's account.[24] 'This is a Welsh mole-
wrench', where 'Welsh' is a predicative adjective, splits up into 'This is a
mole-wrench' and 'This is Welsh'; but 'This is a good mole-wrench' does
not split up into 'This is a mole-wrench' and 'This is good'. Everything
that is good, in this sense, is good *in some way*: in the way of being good
appropriate to the kind that it belongs to.

Mackie insists later on:[25] 'Contrary to what Geach claims, "good" is
not always attributive in the sense of needing some determinate noun
to lean upon. We often say "That was a good thing" meaning "a good
thing to happen", which can be paraphrased as "a welcome occurrence",
leaving to whom it is welcome undecided.' I simply deny this: to say
'that was a good thing to happen', unless we can understand from the
context just for whom it was a good thing, has no determinate meaning. It seems to me absurd to suppose that an occurrence is welcome,
'leaving to whom it is welcome undecided' – as absurd as saying that an
occurrence is long awaited, leaving by whom it is long awaited
undecided. Philippa Foot makes a similar point in 'Utilitarianism and
the Virtues'.[26]

Mackie is perhaps right to say that not all uses of 'good' follow
exactly the pattern Geach has drawn attention to, but it does not follow
that 'good' is ever free-floating. We might say that goodness is a relative
notion in at least two different ways: a thing, event, or action *a* can be
a good F, where 'F' stands for some real or artificial kind that *a* belongs
to, or it can be good for *b*'s needs, purposes, or interests. These relationships are not transparently clear. But we should not cease investigating
them merely because some authors have misconstrued 'goodness' as
standing for an absolute notion instead of a relative one.[27] It is true that
if goodness were absolute it would be very queer: but that is a good
reason to regard it as non-absolute, not to regard it as queer.

Necessity and possibility are, after all, pretty queer notions on anyone's account: but that is not a reason to suppose that there is an

unbridgeable gap between actuality on the one hand, and necessity and possibility on the other. Indeed, one of the queerest accounts of necessity is one of the most discussed – David Lewis's 'possible worlds' theory, which seems to make statements about modality to be disguisedly statements about some queer actuality.[28] (I think I have to call the alleged reality of possible worlds a 'queer actuality'. It is true that Lewis would not admit that modal utterances express actualities, nor that they are in any way queer, but these points would not by any means be granted by his critics.) It is a sad state of affairs when this kind of licence is permitted to one kind of philosopher and denied to another.

4 Action-guiding force

A third argument for the fact/value distinction rests on the claim that value judgements motivate, or afford reasons for acting in the way they prescribe, in some strong or unconditional way. Factual judgements, on the other hand, are supposed to motivate or give reasons for acting only conditionally – on, for instance, the desires and beliefs of the agent.

Answering this challenge has been at or near the core of Foot's work for many years, and I have always found her treatments of it clear and convincing. Her latest account is in the first half of her book *Natural Goodness*,[29] and I think that nothing positive could be added to what she says there. The view she has come to expound involves a quite different account of nature and reasonableness, and of the way they underlie one's reasons for acting, from that given by someone such as Mackie. In this view she is surely right.

But long ago she drew attention to a curious exaggeration about motivation sometimes found among upholders of the distinction:[30] 'If the Martians take the writings of moral philosophers as a guide to what goes on on this planet they will get a shock when they arrive.' I think this is correct, and that even if a fuller truth about reasonableness is to be found in the later Foot, she had valuable ideas in her older negative arguments. We can, for example, grant quite a lot to the supporter of the argument from action-guiding force without having to grant his conclusion. For example, we might grant, for the sake of argument, that if I say or believe 'I ought to do X' and in fact do not do X, without feeling any particular remorse about my omission, then the most appropriate explanation is that my utterance or belief was not sincere. In this sense there seems to be some kind of strong connection between my believing 'I ought to do X' and my doing X.[31]

Yet even if we grant that there may be some such strong, unconditional connection between 'I ought to do X' and doing X, it is important to notice that this applies only to sentences of the form '*I* ought to do X', not to sentences of the forms 'You/she/he/we/they ought to do X'. In Foot's earlier work she rightly drew attention to the fact that not all 'ought'-sentences are unconditionally action-guiding.[32] There was thus a gap between her and those she was criticising. They were concentrating (without noticing it) almost exclusively on the first-person case, for which the claim of action-guiding force could more plausibly be made. I claim that the gap in action-guiding force, if there is one, is not between 'is'-sentences on the one hand and 'ought'-sentences on the other, but between 'I ought'-sentences on the one hand and all other sentences on the other – 'is'-sentences, and 'you/he/she/we/they ought'-sentences, alike.

It is easy to see why this should be. 'Is'-sentences, people used to say, will move an agent to action only conditionally on his or her having (broadly speaking) certain needs, desires, beliefs about his or her needs, and so on. But the same is true of 'you ought'-sentences. When I tell you 'You ought to do X', this utterance will move you to act or give you a reason for acting only conditionally – only in so far as you have certain needs, and so on; concretely, conditionally on your having *the same* needs, and so on, that I have.

But even this distinction, between value judgements made using the first person and those using the second or the third person, ceases to have any importance when it is looked at carefully. For every time I say 'I must do X', I might equally well say *to myself* 'You must do X', addressing myself in the second person instead of talking about myself in the first person. Some people do this habitually, some not, but surely on any occasion anyone might do so. But we said above that 'You ought to do X' will give a motive or reason to the person addressed on the condition that he or she has the same needs, and so on, as the person speaking. However, when the person addressed is the same person as the person speaking, the two will unavoidably have the same needs, and so on, even if those needs, and so on, are inconsistent. The apparently magical or mesmeric[33] reason-giving or motivating force of value judgements seems, then, to depend jointly on the trivial psychological fact that one can talk to oneself in the second person, and on Leibniz's Law: it has nothing to do with ethics at all. The action-guiding force of 'I ought'-sentences turns out not to be unconditional, but just as conditional as the action-guiding force of 'you ought'-sentences. It is merely that the condition must always be fulfilled. To call the action-guiding force of 'I ought'-sentences unconditional simply because the condition that I am myself is always fulfilled is like saying that 'We're in for a storm, or I'm a Dutchman' is not a disjunctive sentence simply because I am not a Dutchman and hence the disjunctive sentence as used makes an assertoric statement.

5 Then why the attraction of the fact/value distinction?

I think that I have shown reason to believe that the arguments usually given for maintaining a fact/value distinction are quite inadequate. The question then arises, why do people believe in it? I want to suggest that there are cultural and historical explanations which make the distinction attractive, particularly in English-speaking countries, and particularly in our time. These ideas must remain at least a little vague and speculative.

Insistence on disagreement, for example, may be connected with a laudable desire to avoid totalitarianism, within the context of a pernicious acceptance of consequentialism. Consequentialism, of one form or another, has been accepted by the mainstream of English-speaking philosophers since Moore's time. Rejecting consequentialism put one outside the mainstream: there is a considerable coincidence between the heretics who opposed consequentialism and the heretics who opposed the fact/value distinction.[34] The reason for this is that consequentialism has been represented as supremely rational, or indeed equivalent to rationality.[35] (Though in fact, as Foot and Geach point out,[36] that rationality is illusory: neither the concept of 'goodness' nor the concept of 'consequences' required by consequentialism can be spelled out coherently.)

The last hundred years have also been the years of totalitarian governments. Totalitarian governments – though one might seek other descriptions – are crucially those that take a single, definite view of human good and apply it in a consequentialist way. If one is convinced that consequentialism is inescapable rationality, then it seems that the only way to avoid slipping into totalitarianism is to refuse to admit that there can be a single, definite, true view of human good – that is, to insist on the fact/value distinction, stressing plurality and disagreement. Thus people have been forced to accept the fact/value distinction by their own decency and by their misunderstanding of rationality.

Also relevant in encouraging people to believe in the fact/value distinction is the vague belief, shown in the argument from disagreement, that all value judgements ought be easy. (This belief must be there and be effective, or why should anyone be surprised that there is disagreement about value-judgements? One is not surprised, after all, to hear different answers to difficult questions on any other subject.[37])

At work here might be what is sometimes called 'the ghost of God': that is, a structural element in moral opinions which made sense when people believed in God, but which now makes no sense at all. An enormously important example of the 'ghost of God' in contemporary Western moral thought is the survival of legal or quasi-legal concepts such as sin, guilt, and merit. These stand between us and, say, a good understanding of Aristotle; but, more importantly, they stand between us and the very concept of a good life, conceived of as prior to and discoverable independently of such legalistic notions as meritorious action.[38]

It is easy to see how the 'ghost of God' makes people think that all value judgements must be easy. There is a relic of childish religion – even among those who have not had a religious upbringing – that sometimes make people think at the back of their minds that they may be punished for acting badly; also that it may be impossible to act well if one does not know what is good and what is bad; and, crucially, that it would not be fair for one to be punished for not knowing what is good unless it were easy to know what is good and what is bad.

But, in Heaven's name (one may apostrophise appropriately), if there is no belief in God or in rewards or punishments, what reason is there for thinking that life is fair, and that it must therefore be easy to know what is good and what is bad? In fact, someone as brave and as honest as Socrates seems to have spent his life sincerely trying to find out. But it is not absurd to maintain that he did not succeed, for all his sincerity, honesty, and courage.[39] This is at least *prima facie* evidence for value questions being difficult ones.

It is true that this aspect of the ghost of God is not confined to the English-speaking countries – though perhaps one might expect a childish belief that things ought to be fair to be more common in the countries that invented organised sport. What more particularly belongs to the culture of our language-group is the idea that because 'we' differ on value judgements, value judgements are subject to the will in a way that factual judgements are not. This is indirectly linked to the ghost of God as it appears in a special way in English-speaking countries. For English-speaking countries are in general traditionally Protestant counties, and since the rise of Protestantism, voluntarism in theological ethics has been commoner there than in Catholic countries. (Voluntarism in theological ethics is the idea that what is good and bad depends entirely on God's will, and that we might wake up tomorrow and find out that God now commanded us to hate him instead of loving him, and, if that were so, it would be good for us to hate God.) Voluntarism certainly had opposition among Protestants, but less clearly and definitely.[40]

If there is no God, but there is still a presumption that values are subject to the will, then they must be subject to human will. This is an unconscious belief, I think, that in some way underpins the fact/value distinction – an unconscious belief for which there is no rational explanation. In English-speaking countries, it makes value judgements appear peculiarly detached from all other judgements.

The connection between the argument from queerness and English-speaking philosophical culture is crucially important, but too obvious to require stating in more than a few words. The dominant philosophies of English-speaking countries during the last hundred years have been empiricist and metaphysically reductivist. It is enough, in Britain or the USA, or especially in Australia, to draw attention to the fact that values do not exist physically or cannot be directly sensed, for one's readers to suppose that they do not exist at all. The inference just is not so rapid in continental Europe. We face here a simple prejudice, in my view.

In the argument from action-guiding force, there may well be another 'ghost of God' prejudice tied up: 'I ought to do X' no doubt sometimes comes, in the minds of sincere believers in theological ethics, to be identified with 'I ought to do X or I will offend against God's law'. This gives a strong motivation or reason, whether one looks at it merely from the point of view of self-interest, or from the point of view of a desire to preserve the order of God's justice. It ought to be remembered that in the time of Hume, great figures in the transmission of traditional morals, such as Johnson, would insist that supernatural sanction was necessary for preserving moral order. Moreover, in Britain and the United States, the great unbelieving moralists of the following century spent a good deal of effort in insisting that Johnson was wrong. Thus moralists of all sorts came to insist on the importance of motivation, of various sorts, in moral utterances. That this did occur among English-speaking writers, I know; whether it was any different in other countries, I do not know. One suspects, from the accusation of hypocrisy often levelled at the British, particularly in the nineteenth century, that there might be a difference here.[41]

One feature that definitely distinguishes English-speaking countries from European countries is their respective legal systems. English-speaking countries have a common-law system, in which a clear distinction, not found outside it, is made between the judge of law and the judge of fact. As we have seen, since the adoption of Christianity throughout Europe, ethics has been thought of chiefly in legal terms – as an expression of the law of God, whether directly revealed or naturally available to the sincere seeker. Hence legal metaphors and concepts sank deep into ethical thought – far deeper than they had been in the thought of, say, Aristotle, in which they are rarely found.[42] Given the strength of legal concepts in ethics, and the importance of the fact/law distinction in common-law systems, it would be natural for some kind of fact/value distinction to arise and flourish there. The English fact/law distinction becomes a 'fact/God's law' distinction, and thus, after belief in God has faded, a fact/value distinction.

A last element of the distinctively English-speaking aspects that may underlie the fact/value distinction is not theological or philosophical, or strictly legal, but rather linguistic and aesthetic. The English language, unlike French, German, Italian, and Spanish, has not one but two pairs of opposed value-terms. The other languages have the equivalent of our 'good' and 'bad' but they do not have such strong or widely used terms as our 'right' and 'wrong'. This was brought to my attention first by seeing an otherwise perfectly competent Spanish translation of the *Principia Ethica* in which the two words 'right' and 'wrong' were translated by 'correcto' and 'incorrecto'. At first it looked like an error, or a satire on the once famous punctiliousness of the English gentleman, but a little reflection made me realise that there were not really any other words that the translator could have used.[43]

I do not think an English speaker would deny that 'right' and 'wrong' in modern usage extend to the whole field of human behaviour, and are perhaps stronger and more intuitively used in ethical contexts than 'good' and 'bad'. But they are words that go with actions, not with dispositions – that is, they fit with legal and theological conceptions such as 'crime' and 'sin'. They are, indeed, in their origins legal terms, meaning something like 'justice' and 'injustice'.[44] By being legal or quasi-legal notions they tie us back to the conception of ethics as a law imposed from without, thus strongly favouring the effects of the ghost of God on our thinking. They are very distant from the notions of human flourishing that someone like Aristotle or his followers would want to see in an account of the good life.

That the English language originally had these two words is, I suppose, a purely contingent matter. But that it has kept them and uses them in an ethically forceful way is probably owing to another fact, perhaps equally unimportant in itself: that pairs of alliterating short words sound good to an English-speaker's ear.[45]

Pairs like 'bed and board', 'chalk and cheese', 'dig and delve', 'hot as hell', 'Jack and Jill', 'life and limb', 'a man or a mouse', 'push and pull', 'rack and ruin', 'sticks and stones', 'time and tide', 'tit for tat' – all these are part of the now unavoidable aesthetics of our language – I was tempted to say, part of the warp and woof of our language. I believe that it is due to this piece of folk-aesthetics that we talk as much of 'right and wrong' as we do of 'good and bad', and that this keeps our thought on ethical questions tied to legal models, tied to the ghost of God, distant from evidence about human flourishing – tied, in short, to the fact/value distinction.

Notes

1. The major themes of this chapter are developed from a couple of pages of an article of mine, 'Virtues, Motivation, and the End of Life', in L. Gormally (ed.), *Moral Truth and Moral Tradition: Essays in Honour of Peter Geach and Elizabeth Anscombe* (Dublin: Four Courts Press, 1994): 112–14.
2. (London and New York: Routledge, 1998): see 'Fact/Value Distinction'.
3. (Harmondsworth: Penguin, 1977). The form of the distinction that Mackie argues for is idiosyncratic, being avowedly subjectivist, but I believe that his arguments can be used to support any form, no matter how apparently object-ivist.
4. *Ethics*: 15.
5. See note 3.
6. See note 2.
7. Cf. the point made by Anscombe in 'Modern Moral Philosophy', in her *Ethics, Religion, and Politics: Philosophical Papers*, Vol. III (Oxford: Blackwell, 1981): 31. Let me here express my debt to Anscombe's writings for so much in my own thought and writing on ethical questions – a debt that cannot be tied down to detailed mention or quotation. Likewise, I owe an immense amount to the writings of Peter Geach, Philippa Foot, and Rosalind Hursthouse. None of them are, of course, responsible for the use or distortion I may have made of their ideas. There is currently, in academic circles, a flurry about 'plagiarism'. I am convinced that this is just a fashion, what the sociologists call a 'moral panic'. Some authors stand so much above their generation that one can no more plagiarise them than one can plagiarise Virgil. But out of conformity with current *mores*, let me here declare that any too-close reflection of any other author in what follows is to be attributed to sloppy memory, sloppy footnoting, or both.
8. J.O. Urmson, 'Saints and Heroes', in A.I. Melden (ed.), *Essays in Moral Philosophy* (Seattle: University of Washington Press, 1958). Alasdair MacIntyre, in *Against the Self-Images of the Age* (London: Duckworth, 1971), makes much the same point.
9. See note 3 for the peculiarities of his theory, which I think are irrelevant here. It is unusual in being avowedly subjectivist. Most authors wish to avoid an imputation of subjectivism. But sometimes their defences seem to mean little more than that according to their theories, value claims have to be objective in form, or 'universalisable'.

10. Plato, *Euthyphro*: 7b1–8d1.
11. Mackie, *Ethics*: 36–8. The argument is there stated as well and as soberly as anywhere else I know of.
12. For an academic account of the result of scientific quizzes and polls, see J.D. Miller, 'The Measurement of Civic Scientific Literacy', *Public Understanding of Science* 7 (1998): 208. More accessibly, the *Economist* magazine regularly publishes results of such polls. Even more accessibly, one can find anecdotal results in the column 'Dumb Britain', in the British satirical magazine *Private Eye*, where quotations are given from quiz shows in which contestants have claimed that mercury is red, that the animal that builds dams is the sheep, and that Hadrian's Wall was built to keep out the Zulus. Compare Geach, *The Virtues* (Cambridge: Cambridge University Press, 1977): 15.
13. *The Virtues*: 15.
14. Ibid: 15–16.
15. Anscombe, 'What is it to Believe Someone?', in C.F. Delaney (ed.), *Rationality and Religious Belief* (Notre Dame: University of Notre Dame Press, 1979). Oddly enough, George Orwell – no philosopher – spotted it long before: 'As I Please', in *Tribune*, 27 December 1946.
16. Geach, *Truth and Hope* (Notre Dame: University of Notre Dame Press, 2001): 47.
17. *Ethics*: 38–42.
18. Ibid: 38.
19. *Truth and Hope*: 38.
20. *Ethics*: 38.
21. Or at least, to be cautious, time does not exist in time, and space does not exist in space.
22. *Ethics*: 39.
23. Geach, 'Good and Evil', in P. Foot (ed.), *Theories of Ethics* (Oxford: Oxford University Press, 1967): 64–73. Foot herself has recently referred to this article as 'sadly neglected', in her *Natural Goodness* (Oxford: Clarendon Press, 2001): 2.
24. *Ethics*: 52.
25. Ibid: 57.
26. Foot, 'Utilitarianism and the Virtues', *Mind* 94 (1985): 196–209.
27. Some perhaps will feel unwilling to agree with me when I say that goodness is not an absolute but a relative notion. They will fear, perhaps, that such an account as this may lead to subjectivism – that is, a position in which goodness is thought to be dependent on someone's subjective state of mind. But all I have claimed is that goodness is a relative notion, and thus dependent on a relation to something else. This relation to something else might be to individuals in an objective way, or to their social contexts or their natures, or to all three in different ways.
28. David Lewis, *On the Plurality of Worlds* (Oxford: Blackwell, 1986): sec. 1.1, esp. at 5, and 1.9, esp. at 92–3.
29. Foot, *Natural Goodness*: 5–65.
30. 'Are Moral Considerations Overriding?', in her *Virtues and Vices* (Oxford: Blackwell, 1978): 186.
31. I have made this point before, in 'Virtues, Motivation, and the End of Life': 113–14.

32. See, for example, 'Morality as a System of Hypothetical Imperatives', *Virtues and Vices*: 157–73.
33. 'Modern Moral Philosophy': 32.
34. One thinks of Anscombe, Foot, Finnis, Geach, Hursthouse, and Williams in Britain. America might show more variation, and the rigid orthodoxies may also be disappearing.
35. Foot, 'Utilitarianism and the Virtues': 196–209.
36. Geach, *The Virtues*: 99–103.
37. I also touched on this point in 'Virtues, Motivation, and the End of Life': 112–13.
38. See also Anscombe, 'Modern Moral Philosophy': 30–2.
39. Geach raises moral objections to some of Socrates's dialectical practices, even in the last weeks of his life, in 'Plato's *Euthyphro*', in his *Logic Matters* (Oxford: Blackwell, 1972): 31–44.
40. On voluntarism in pre-Reformation thought concerning God's law, see the summary in the *Routledge Encyclopedia of Philosophy*, 'Religion and Morality'. On the Catholic/Protestant split after the Reformation, see Council of Trent, Session VI, Decree on Justification, Chapter 11, in H. Denzinger, *The Sources of Catholic Dogma* (St Louis: Herder, 1957): sec. 804 (see Anscombe, 'Modern Moral Philosophy': 31n). Admittedly, there are the counterexamples of Catholic voluntarists such as Descartes and Pascal, and it is not easy to find Protestant voluntarists who cannot be suspected of other extreme views, such as antinomianism. But on the connection between medieval voluntarism and Luther's thought, see A. MacIntyre, *A Short History of Ethics*, 2nd edn (Notre Dame: Notre Dame University Press, 1998): 119–22.
41. See, for example, S. Johnson, 'The Uses of Retirement', *The Rambler*, no. 7, 10 April 1750.
42. Cf. 'Modern Moral Philosophy': 32.
43. 'Lícito' and 'ilícito' are too explicitly theological.
44. *Oxford English Dictionary*, 2nd edn (Oxford: Oxford University Press, 1989), entries *right* (sb) (1) and (2), and *wrong* (sb) (2).
45. *OED*, where the pair is cited under the entry *wrong* (sb) (2), I. 1, and the reference given to Wulfstan, in the early eleventh century (*Homily* xlii, 203), 'wrang to rihte and riht to wrange'.

4
Incommensurability and Basic Goods: A Tension in the New Natural Law Theory

Henry S. Richardson

1 Introduction

In the 'new natural law theory,' the idea of basic goods plays a pivotal role.[1] Because, together, they comprise the elements of 'integral human flourishing,' the basic goods maintain continuity with the Aristotelianism that Aquinas bequeathed to the natural law tradition.[2] Because their status as goods, on this view, is self-evident (*per se nota*), they provide this new natural law theory with a firm foundation for ethics while enabling it to skirt old worries about deriving an 'ought' from an 'is.'[3] Because the basic goods are mutually incommensurable, they leave intelligible room for practical reasoning to operate 'creatively' in shaping an individual's practical concerns.[4] And because even their instances are incommensurable with one another, they allow this view to be 'good-based' in an obvious sense without compromising the Pauline Principle – the precept that evil is not to be done that good may come of it.[5] The basic goods thus position the new natural law theory to provide an attractive and well-founded view that frames morality within a broader conception of human flourishing, leaving appropriate room for individuality while preserving strict moral principles.

This view is conceptually richer and more subtle than the consequentialist and deontological theories that dominated most Anglo-American ethical theory in the twentieth century. If it could succeed in deploying the concept of basic goods in order to fulfill all of the functions I have just described, the view would have a compelling claim to acceptance. The basic goods would serve as a bridge between the theoretical grounding of ethics in a conception of human nature, on the one side, and a richly layered ethical theory that gives centrality to the good while resisting consequentialism, on the other.

In this chapter, I develop one reason for doubt. I will show that these theorists' well-grounded acceptance of value incommensurability undercuts their effort to make the basic goods central. I will argue that the strong form of incommensurability that the new natural law theory invokes to make room for creative practical reasoning and to prevent itself from being colonized by a maximizing form of consequentialism makes trouble for the theory's central claim that there are basic goods. Specifically, I will show that the following two theses of the new natural law theory are mutually inconsistent:

THE SOURCE THESIS (S): *Necessarily, all reasons for action derive entirely from the small, finite set of basic goods.*

THE THOROUGH INCOMMENSURABILITY THESIS (TI): *Every instance of a basic good is evaluatively incommensurable with every other wholly distinct instance.*[6]

In what follows, I explain these theses and indicate why the new natural law theorists are committed to them. I then show how TI makes trouble for S and how their commitment to defending the Pauline Principle leaves the new natural law theorists little room for maneuver in coping with this conceptual tension between TI and S. What should be jettisoned, I suggest, is S, the defining thesis of the new natural law theory.

2   The new natural law theory

The label, 'new natural law theory,' I borrow from a critic of the family of views that I here address.[7] These views share a general mode of presenting Thomistic natural law theory as applied to practical reason and ethics. The principal authors I discuss are Germain Grisez, a pioneer of the new natural law theory; John Finnis, one of its best-known exponents; Mark C. Murphy, one of its most sophisticated defenders; and Alfonso Gómez-Lobo, one of its clearest expositors.[8] There are important philosophical differences among these authors, which I shall mention from time to time. None of these, however, qualifies their attachment to S or TI, nor affects the interpretation of the theses in a way that removes their inconsistency. The most prominent disagreements among these four theorists concern the dimension in which this theory is perceived to be 'new,' namely its disavowal of grounding normative principles or propositions directly in human nature. In order to explain these disagreements, I must first say more about the kinds of proposition that might be thus grounded. I hope that readers already familiar with these authors will forgive my elementary exposition; perhaps it will at least help convince them that my 'new natural law theorist' is not an artificial construction. Although the 'new natural law theory' I describe is, to the best of my belief, one to which all four of the authors just mentioned actually subscribe, my characterization involves some active reconstruction.

Whether old or new, natural law theory in the Thomist tradition is, as Murphy puts it, 'welfarist: it asserts, that is, that the fundamental reasons for action are aspects of agents' well-being.'[9] Thomistic natural law theory is thus good-based in a way that the natural law theory of the Stoics, which had a greater influence on Kant, was not.[10] Note that this welfarism is not necessarily individualistic or impartialist. There is some disagreement among the defenders of the new natural law theory as to whether an agent's fundamental reasons for action essentially refer only to elements of that agent's welfare, and incorporate the good of others only via goods such as friendship, or whether, instead, the fundamental reasons are agent-neutral. Grisez, for instance, insists that the 'integral human fulfillment' limned by the basic goods 'is not individualistic satisfaction of desires; it is the realization of all the human goods in the whole human community.'[11] Murphy, by contrast, holds that the theory's welfarism gives an obvious reason to take the agent-relative characterizations of the reasons provided by the basic goods to be metaphysically or theoretically more fundamental.[12] Nonetheless, he suggests that to each of the fundamental, agent-relative reasons provided by a basic good corresponds an agent-neutral reason that is also *practically* fundamental.[13] Abstracting from these differences, the point remains that the new natural law theory, like its Thomistic ancestors, is welfarist.[14]

The new natural law theory differs from the old with regard to how it is possible to establish that a given set of basic goods constitutes the elements of human welfare or integral human fulfillment. On older views, it was held that this could be established by a theoretical examination of human nature. The normative importance of the basic goods as limning human flourishing would appear, according to this older view, from a theoretical examination of natural teleology in the human case. What principally sets apart the new natural law theory is the contrasting position that this kind of theoretical derivation of the basic goods is unnecessary, if not impossible. On the new view, the good is known principally by practical reason, and that the basic goods are to be sought is not itself derivative from anything; rather, in the case of each basic good, it is self-evident that it is to be sought.[15] The basic goods are like Aristotle's 'starting-points' or 'first principles' (*archai, principia*): they are the premises of demonstrative practical reasoning, whose importance cannot be demonstrated.[16] Because this insistence on the practically non-derivative status of the basic goods is principally what sets the new natural law theory apart from the old, S is the defining commitment of the newer theory.

Again following Aristotle and Aquinas, room is left open for supporting the normative importance of the basic goods 'inductively' (by drawing, non-propositionally, on 'felt inclinations and a knowledge of possibilities') or 'dialectically' (by working back and forth between theoretical and practical knowledge).[17] Still, this possibility supplements, and does not supersede, the new natural law theory's claim that, for example, 'the principle that truth is worth pursuing, knowledge is worth having, is...an underived principle. Neither its intelligibility nor its force rests on any further principle.'[18] Accordingly, the new natural law theory crucially distinguishes demonstrative practical reasoning from non-demonstrative practical reasoning and aligns the notion of 'derivation,' as in the claim that the basic goods are non-derivative reasons, with demonstrative connections.

The demonstrative connections that these theorists have in mind probably ought not to be thought of narrowly as deductive entailments. Rather, in practical reasoning, the modes of demonstrative reasoning, or of derivation, are those typified by the Aristotelian practical syllogism – end–means connections of one kind or another. In a widely accepted way, Murphy distinguishes two kinds of connection of this sort:

> An instrumental reason arises from another instrumental or non-instrumental reason, and as instrumental, it derives all of its normative force from that other reason. A specificatory reason (that is, a reason to promote some state of affairs that is an instance of some state of affairs that one has reason to promote, as when one has a reason to play basketball inasmuch as one has a reason to take exercise) arises from another reason, and as specificatory, it derives all of its normative force from that other reason.[19]

Now, plainly, this oversimplifies; but we see the point. It is an oversimplification, in that additional reasons may support the selection of a given instrumental means or a given specification. For instance, selecting basketball as the preferred way of exercising can be supported on the ground that since one's friends play basketball, one can play it with them. Even when the picture is thus complicated, though, we can still imagine the links traced by practical reason reaching back to one or more basic reasons via a combination of instrumental and specificatory links.[20] These are links of what Timothy Chappell calls 'subsumptive practical rationality,' which he characterizes as 'one kind of practical rationality – the kind that explains, motivates, and justifies actions.' As he puts it, this form of practical rationality 'explains by subsuming one explanation under another until a basic good is reached.'[21] That a basic good is non-derivatively a good means that its being a good is independent of any subsumptive link to any other good.

Strictly speaking, the claim that each of the basic goods is self-evidently a good – or something choiceworthy or to be sought – is a further claim, logically independent of their non-derivative status as practical principles. It is coherent to hold that a given self-evident truth can be demonstrated. The new natural law theorists are all committed, however, to this further claim about the non-derivative status of the basic goods. It helps to differentiate their position sharply from one that holds that basic goods are to be derived from a philosopher's metaphysical grasp of human nature.[22] Conjoined, the claim that the basic goods' normativity is underived and the claim that it is self-evident yield a strong reading of the Thomistic claim that these goods are *per se nota*: they are self-evidently goods, and hold this status *per se*, or non-derivatively. That each of these is self-evidently a good implies that each *can* function as a starting-point for practical argument; that each is non-derivatively a good implies that its *only* role in practical arguments is as a starting-point.

Once they have the list of self-evident goods, or categories of goodness, on hand, the new natural law theorists use it to give an account of human flourishing. Although the lists these authors give vary slightly, this variation will not concern me. None of these authors claims to have discovered the uniquely correct way of categorizing human goods. What is of more interest is their common hope to provide a list that is exhaustive. By providing 'a catalog of the basic goods,' as Murphy puts it, they provide the basis of 'the natural law theorist's account of the fundamental reasons for action, of what makes actions intelligible.'[23] The type of account involved is practical, in that it concerns the intelligibility of human actions. Particular actions may well instantiate more than one basic good; but if the theory is successful, any intelligible purpose will instantiate 'some or all of them.'[24] The basic goods, then, are the 'ingredients' of human flourishing.[25] There is a small, finite number of them – perhaps between five and twenty, and in any case more than one. As I shall sometimes say, for short: there are *several* basic goods.

That the basic goods can thus structure an account of human flourishing gives the new theorists a strong claim to be 'natural law' thinkers. Thus, although this normative account of human flourishing is not *derived* from human nature, human nature must be such that it dovetails with the list. Grisez puts the link in terms of capabilities: 'The human nature which is the standard for morality' – and, I think he means, for practical reasoning in general – 'is not a formal essence and set of invariant relationships, as was suggested by inadequate, scholastic natural law theory. Rather, the standard is the basic possibilities of human individuals as bodily creatures, endowed with intelligence, able to engage in fruitful work and creative play, psychically complex, capable of more or less reasonable action, in need of companionship, capable of love, and open to friendship with God in whose image they are made.'[26] Accordingly, although the list of basic goods provides the *content* of the human good, these new natural law theorists can still reach back for a link to human nature in order to explain the *concept* of the human good.[27] In this way, the basic goods serve as the linch-pin of an ambitious theoretical account of practical reason.

This link to human nature justifies the 'natural' in the label; but what about the 'law'? Such a list of basic human goods could be plugged into a consequentialist view, according to which in every situation the action that ought to be done is the one that yields the best consequences. As we shall see, the new natural law theorists deny that we can ever determine, for any choice involving wholly distinct options, which option yields the best consequences. In addition, they construct their moral theory in a way that resists consequentialism. Instead of plugging their rich conception of the good into a simple, maximizing conception of practical rationality, they see that conception of the good both as specifying an antecedently available principle of practical reasonableness and as giving rise to multiple, distinct principles of practical reasonableness. On this basis, if the theory all fits together, it would be well able to generate the kinds of strict moral principle, such as the Pauline Principle, that we associate with a traditional natural law view. I will briefly describe how this is supposed to work.

The framing principle of practical reason is a central feature of the new natural law theory. Grisez brought it to prominence in his interpretation of Aquinas, and following Aquinas, calls it 'the first principle of practical reason' (FPR).[28] This is the principle that 'good is to be done and pursued and evil is to be avoided.'[29] Because it ranges over all kinds of goods, and because the specification of the concept of evil waits on further, more specific precepts of practical reasonableness, this principle is 'pre-moral.' In line with the theologically grounded teleology of Aquinas's view, pursuit of goods is not symmetrically matched with avoidance of bads. Following Aquinas in this respect, the new natural law theorists content themselves with developing lists of basic goods, and do not put forward lists of basic bads. Aquinas's general position, in the background here, is that badness is a privation of good.[30] Accordingly, the further specification of the first principle of practical reason proceeds in two stages. First, the basic goods are listed, so as to specify the 'good' to which it refers. Second, drawing on the basic goods and especially on the basic good of practical reasonableness, precepts of practical reasonableness are developed so as to specify the 'evil' to which the first principle refers. Fundamental to this account of practical reasonableness is the distinction between promoting goods and refraining from attacking or violating them.[31]

This relationship between the basic goods and the FPR raises an initial question about the concept of a 'basic good.' How is 'beginning' with the FPR compatible with the non-derivative importance of each basic good? One might expect there to be a derivation, along the following lines:

1. Good is to be pursued.
2. Knowledge is a (basic) good.
3. Hence, knowledge is to be pursued.

But while each of the new natural law theorists would recognize (1)–(3) as a sound inference, none of them would recognize it as playing a role in the practical derivation of reasons. Among them, they differ in the prominence accorded to the FPR. In Grisez's and Gómez-Lobo's exposition, the FPR is central.[32] In Finnis's and Murphy's, it is not. This difference, however, is *merely* one of exposition. Grisez, who most emphasizes the FPR, writes that 'the general determinations of the first principle of practical reasoning are [the] basic precepts of natural law [setting out the basic goods]. They take the form: Such and such a basic human good is to be done and/or pursued, protected, and promoted.'[33] Hence, even Grisez, who gives a central place to the FPR, holds that each of the basic goods is embedded in its own, self-evident practical precept, of the form of (3). There is no need to derive these from the FPR. Furthermore, apart from the determinations or specifications of the FPR that come from the basic goods – and, through them, the principles of practical reasonableness – the FPR provides no practical guidance.[34] As Gómez-Lobo puts it, it is a 'formal' principle, true (he argues) by virtue of the meaning of its terms, and correspondingly empty of practical content, taken by itself.[35] For this reason, Finnis, who drops the FPR from his exposition, and at one point even implies that there is no such principle of natural law, does not thereby differ dramatically from Grisez or Gómez-Lobo in his theory of practical reason.[36] That the basic precepts directly associated with each basic good all share the form of the FPR might be important for the theory's links to metaphysics and theology, but is not important practically. The FPR thus does not undercut the 'basic' status of the basic goods; in other words, even though the above inference (1)–(3), and similar derivations, are generally recognized by the new natural law theorists, they are not seen as required for the basic goods to have reason-giving force.

By contrast, the various precepts of practical reasonableness, which draw on the basic goods, do offer important practical guidance. Different authors offer different precepts of practical reasonableness. Quickly scanning Murphy's, one can easily see their range. Some of the precepts would naturally be thought of as prudential ('against inefficiency'), while others seem moral in their content ('against dismissing or devaluing persons within the context of agent-neutral ends' and 'against intentional, instrumental destruction of instances of basic good'). Still others ground virtues ('against flightiness and stubbornness,' 'against idleness').

It will be important to the argument that follows to understand that these principles of practical reasonableness are supposed to derive in some way from the basic goods. Our authors suggest different paths of derivation. In Grisez's presentation, the principles of practical reasonableness (or, in his terminology, of 'morality') derive from what is necessary to enabling and securing 'integral human fulfillment,' which, in turn, is an idea constructed out of the various basic goods, considered agent-neutrally as well as agent-relatively.[37] Murphy, by contrast, defends his principles of practical reasonableness as being implied by facts about the basic goods: they direct one not to act in ways that presuppose the falsity of such facts.[38] Finnis seems to employ, by turns, each of these strategies of justification.[39] Among the most important facts about the basic goods that are invoked in these derivations are those on which we shall shortly focus: their plurality and mutual incommensurability.

We must recognize that there may be some important structuring elements in the theory of practical reasonableness that do not derive from the basic goods. For instance, Chappell has argued that in conjunction with the FPR the plurality and incommensurability of the basic goods entail that the three attitudes towards goods mentioned by the FPR – those of promoting them, respecting them, and refraining from attacking or violating them – cannot be collapsed into the one attitude of promotion.[40] If this is correct then, if it is true that there are plural, incommensurable basic goods, a crucial set of structural distinctions derives from the FPR itself – in particular, the distinction between promoting and not attacking a basic good. Another set of structural distinctions may involve the difference between pursuing (or refraining from attacking) the basic goods in one's own life and pursuing (or refraining from attacking) them impartially. Murphy has suggested that perhaps agent-neutral reasons derive from the basic goods just as agent-relative ones do.[41] Grisez, on the other hand, seems to treat the 'first principle of morality,' which invokes an agent-neutral or impartial conception of 'integral human fulfillment,' as independent of the FPR.

Accordingly, in building the argument that follows, I will presume only a qualified dependence of the principles of practical reasonableness on the basic goods. The idea that the basic goods are the source of value might be taken to suggest that *all* differences in reasons supervene on differences at the level of basic goods. However, because some of the fundamental distinctions of practical reasonableness may, on the new natural law theory, be independent of the basic goods, I will assume that such supervenience holds only when the differences between options are confined to one of the six types generated by the two-fold agent-neutral/agent-relative distinction and the three-fold distinction between promoting, respecting, and not attacking. In fact, my argument will depend upon this supervenience holding only when the differences are confined to the agent-relative promotion type. In particular, I will take it that the following relation is supposed to hold between the reasons generated by the basic goods and the full set of applicable reasons, taking account of the principles of practical reasonableness:

PERSONAL PROMOTION SUPERVENIENCE (PPS): *Where two options differ neither in the basic goods attacked or respected nor in the persons whose goods are promoted or attacked, then if there is no difference in how the two options instantiate the basic goods for any person, then the reasons for and against the two options must be the same.*[42]

In other words, setting aside issues arising from the distinctions between promoting and refraining from attacking and between reasons arising from one's own good and reasons arising from the good of others, the principles of practical reasonableness cannot generate any reasons that discriminate between two options if there is no underlying difference in how those options instantiate the basic goods. This principle will prove important to the argument later on, as it will exclude certain roles for the principles of practical reasonableness. Before turning to that argument, however, we need first to consolidate what we have learned about the concept of a basic good.

3 Basic goods and the meaning of the source thesis (S)

Depending on how one defines the notion of a basic good, more or less of what is controversial about S will rest on the existential claim that there are basic goods. I will parse things as follows: drawing on the last section's general account of the new natural law theory, I will *define* 'basic goods' as 'aspects of individual welfare that constitute fundamental reasons for action.'[43] Here and throughout, I mean by 'a reason' a consideration carrying (what this tradition seems comfortable referring to as) normative force and not merely motivational force. A fundamental reason is one whose normative force does not derive from any other reason.[44] The verb 'constitute' should not cause trouble. I use it simply because I am not sure about the best way to describe the metaphysics of goods in relations to that of reasons, compatibly with the new natural law view. Suppose that the contents of reasons can be instances of goods. If so, then 'that constitute' could be replaced, yielding the following: 'basic goods' are 'aspects of individual welfare whose instances are the contents of fundamental reasons for action.' Those who prefer some other way of pinning down the metaphysical categories of goods and reasons should substitute their own preferred gloss of 'constitute' here. Incautiously, one might simply say that these aspects of individual welfare *are* fundamental reasons for action.

In light of this definition of basic goods, we may factor S into two sub-theses:

THE DERIVATION THESIS (D): *There are several fundamental reasons for action, and necessarily all reasons for action derive entirely from them.*

THE WELFARIST THESIS (W): *Each fundamental reason for action is an aspect of individuals' welfare or well-being.*

In the discussion that follows, I will be concerned with both of these sub-theses; but I should signal here that my argument sets aside welfarism as such.

The only corollary of W on which my argument turns is the following:

GENERALITY (G): *The fundamental reasons are general types that can have multiple instances.*

That the new natural law theorists are committed to G will importantly enter my argument that S and TI are inconsistent. I believe that all of the new natural law theorists I am here discussing are committed to the generality of fundamental reasons. Finnis, for instance, refers to each basic good as 'a general form of good that can be participated in or realized in indefinitely many ways on indefinitely many occasions.'[45] This commitment is not surprising. Indeed, there are reasons to think that all reasons are general.[46] Further, in order to ground an account of integral human flourishing, the basic goods must be general types that can be found in many different humans' lives. Accordingly, we should understand the notion of 'aspects' that appears in W as picking out generally describable or statable aspects of human well-being. When we thus understand the term 'aspects,' G emerges as a corollary of W.

Before turning to the second reason that G is important to the new natural law theorists, I pause to clarify the notion of an 'instance' involved. These general goods that are essential aspects of human well-being can indeed, as G anticipates, have multiple instances. These, instances, in turn, can be either general or particular.[47] An instance of the former, general type is playing basketball, taken as an instance of the basic good of play. An instance of the latter, particular type is my playing basketball last Tuesday at the local playground.[48] Importantly, then, the idea of an instance of a good embraces all potential specifications of that good.

The new natural law theorists' second reason for being committed to G is that it crucially aids in the defense of one of their further claims, namely their claim that every instance of a basic good is, considered as such, good.[49] Perhaps this further claim is a corollary of D, for if an item has positive normative force that stems from its being an instance of a basic good, and if one considers it only 'as such,' setting aside, in thought, any negatives that may flow from it accidentally or instrumentally or that may otherwise inhere in it, then how could it not be good? Be that as it may, however, this further claim comes under pressure from purported counterexamples. Health may be a basic good; but as in the time of the Vietnam War, being healthy may make a young man susceptible to being drafted into a dangerous and unsafe enterprise. Is having feet that are not flat really a good? Well, the answer comes: considered *as* an instance of health, and so in isolation from accidental disadvantages, it is.[50] Is knowledge of the number of blades of grass on a given plot on a given afternoon really worth having? Well, the answer comes: considered *as* an instance of knowledge, and in abstraction from the triviality of the content, it is.[51]

Turning now to D, note first of all that the claim that the basic goods are the source of value is not meant by the new natural law theorists as a mere summary comment about our moral psychology. Rather, this claim is meant to get at the underlying facts about what reasons there are. These theorists can allow that our actual patterns of practical reasoning are quite various, for they can hold that any valid pattern of practical reasoning that we engage in that is not a case of subsumptive reasoning must draw on reasons that supervene upon a set of reasons that *could* be subsumptively arrayed so as to reach the same conclusions. Their implicit claim is that, however we actually reach practical conclusions, the reasons that actually favor or disfavor the various options in fact derive, in a way that could be laid out subsumptively, from fundamental reasons. The differentiations drawn by other modes of practical reasoning would, like some of the principles of practical reasoning already adverted to, *supervene* on differentiations that follow, subsumptively, from the fundamental reasons (the basic goods). A correct subsumptive course of reasoning would lay out the way reasons actually come to attach to options; any other mode of practical reasoning merely indirectly reflects this underlying set of practical truths.

This account of D should explain why it (and so also the full thesis S) states an alleged necessary truth about the source of reasons. The claim is that there is no other source, ultimately, from which reasons for action can derive. As we have just noticed, other patterns of derivation are *conceivable* and seem, indeed, to be followed by reasoners. But if these are really to track the structure of reasons, there must exist a valid, subsumptive derivation tracing things back to the fundamental reasons. What makes this seem a necessary fact is not any conceptual truth; rather, it is put forward as some sort of deep, metaphysical truth. In the context of the new natural law theory, we may assume, this metaphysical necessity could be cashed out, eventually, either theologically or by reference to human nature, or both.

Now that we have some grip on each of these elements of S, we can put D together with G, the one aspect of W on which my argument turns, to state in a consolidated way those aspects of S that make for trouble:

THE QUALIFIED SOURCE THESIS (S*): *There are several fundamental and general types of reason for action, and necessarily all reasons for action derive from one or more of these fundamental and general types of reason for action.*

S* is weaker than S because it drops the latter's welfarism, keeping only the commitment to generality that, as we saw, is implicit in welfarism. In the argument that follows, I will show that S* is inconsistent with TI. Since S* is a weakening of S, it will follow, *a fortiori*, that S is inconsistent with TI. Before giving this argument, I must first explain TI and why the new natural law theorists are committed to it.

4   Thorough incommensurability (TI) and its grounds

The thorough incommensurability thesis is, again, the following:

> THOROUGH INCOMMENSURABILITY (TI): *Every instance of a basic good is evaluatively incommensurable with every other wholly distinct instance.*[52]

What is this notion of evaluative incommensurability? To get at it, let us first assume, with the natural law tradition, that all considerations bearing on choice are reasons and that all reasons are ultimately good-based (or evaluatively based).[53] Within these assumptions, there remain two importantly distinct questions we can ask – whether the options are evaluatively comparable in an overall way, and whether they are evaluatively commensurable. Initially to define these notions in an objective way, we may say that options are objectively incomparable overall if there is no fact of the matter either as to which option is all-things-considered better nor as to whether they are all-things-considered either of equal value or evaluatively on a par.[54] Independent of the question of comparability is the question of whether or not there exists any single scalar property or single dimension of goodness that adequately reflects or represents the contributions made to their overall comparative status (as better and worse, on a par, or incomparable) by the various evaluative respects in which the options differ. If there is such a dimension, then the options are objectively evaluative commensurable; if there is not, they are objectively evaluatively incommensurable.[55] What TI asserts is a kind of evaluative incommensurability.

The new natural law theorists probably have in mind a slightly less objective sense of the term 'incommensurability.' Allowing for the exceptional status of divine reason, we should probably define evaluative commensurability as holding, not when *there exists* a commensurating dimension, but when it is possible for finite agents adequately to represent the reasons for and against choosing one option over the other in terms of a single scalar property or a single dimension of goodness.[56] In asserting that wholly distinct options are evaluatively incommensurable, then, TI asserts that it is not possible for finite agents adequately to represent in terms of a single scalar property or dimension of goodness the contributions of the various respects in which the options evaluatively differ.

One reason for insisting, in the present context, on the distinction between incomparability and incommensurability is that the new natural law theorists simultaneously assert that every choice between wholly distinct options involves value incommensurability and affirm the possibility of sound and reasonable overall evaluative judgment in such choice situations. Furthermore, the practical judgment they defend in no way involves bracketing or setting aside the incommensurable considerations.[57] Rather, it grapples with them head on. And given the general objectivism of the view, they do not rest this scope for reasonable judgment on the creative or constitutive power of merely subjective evaluation. Rather, their position is that practical judgment can proceed in an objectively sound way in making choices between incommensurable options. In short, they deny that commensurability is a prerequisite of rational (or reasonable) choice. On this point, I am in full agreement with them.[58]

Accordingly, TI, which holds that every instance of a basic good is incommensurable with every other, does not imply that rational or reasonable practical choice is impossible. Rather, what it implies is that rational or reasonable practical choice typically cannot proceed by means of arraying all of the relevant reasons along a single dimension and then deciding by maximizing on that dimension. In their attacks on consequentialist ethics, the new natural law theorists are united in holding that whenever the options are wholly distinct we cannot meaningfully commensurate them in this sense.[59]

The new natural law theorists are committed to TI for two kinds of reason. As I have mentioned, they depend on TI to fend off consequentialism. In arguing against consequentialism, they also provide independent reasons for believing in TI. One of these independent reasons, emphasized by Grisez, draws on a Thomistic conception of moral evil.[60] Another, emphasized by Murphy, puts forward more commonsensical considerations about the nature of the choices we face.[61] Although my own argument asserts a conceptual incompatibility between TI and S*, and hence does not depend upon the truth of TI, going over these latter two arguments will serve several purposes. It will further help clarify the meaning of TI. In addition, it will help explain why the new natural law theorists are committed to TI in itself, and not merely as a means of combatting consequentialism.

Heuristically, it will be useful in approaching these arguments to keep in mind the kind of case in which, compatibly with TI, commensurability can be recognized.[62] Consider the choice that a home-buyer faces between two houses, *c* and *d*. Suppose that the home-buyer cares only about price and proximity to work, and that no other dimensions of goodness or badness are relevant to the choice. Suppose that *c* and *d* are equally close to work, on all reasonable interpretations of that notion, and that *c* costs $10,000 more than *d*. On these stipulations, there is only one reason that bears on the choice between *c* and *d*, and it is this price differential. There is no other reason favoring *c* that does not also identically favor *d*. Hence, this kind of case, in which the only difference between the options lies in the degree to which they realize or participate in one dimension of goodness, is paradigmatic of options that, in Murphy's terminology, do not count as 'wholly distinct.' As the reader will recall, TI affirms only that wholly distinct instances of basic goods are commensurable.[63]

Turning now to the new natural law theorists' arguments for incommensurability, their argument from the possibility of moral evil does not establish a result as general as TI. The conclusion it supports is that incommensurability must be present in every case of morally significant choice. In the background of this argument is the distinction made by the natural law view – in both its new and old forms – between the reasons for action generated by the basic goods and the normative requirements expressed by the various specific precepts of practical reasonableness. Moral evil consists in a violation of one of the latter set of normative requirements, not merely in acting against the balance of reasons, as these are established independently of the precepts of practical reasonableness.[64] In this tradition, it is important to see morally evil action as both knowing and rational. In particular, necessary conditions for morally evil action by an agent *a* in a given choice situation include both:

RATIONAL OPTIONS: *a has at least two options that are not contrary to the balance of reasons as* a *perceives them to be*

and

NON-IGNORANCE ABOUT REASONS: *a is not significantly ignorant of any of the reasons bearing on the options.*

To act evilly, one must have had the option to choose well, and to have known it. These two necessary conditions for morally evil action, it is claimed, imply a third, namely that the options not be commensurable.

To see why, consider further what the commensurability of the options would mean. By definition, if two options are evaluatively commensurable, then all of the reasons bearing on the choice between them can adequately be arrayed in terms of a single evaluative dimension. Options that differ in only one evaluative dimension, such as houses c and d under the stipulations above, are commensurable, but not wholly distinct. But the commensurability of two options does not imply that they actually differ only in one evaluative dimension, and so is logically compatible with their being wholly distinct. What the notion of evaluative commensurability does imply, however, is that all these potentially multiple differences can be adequately captured, without loss or residue,[65] in a unidimensional representation of the strength of reasons supporting each option. If this commensurating maneuver is successful, then it will be true to say that the reasons for one option are adequately represented by a score of x on that dimension and the reasons for the other option are adequately represented by a score of y on that dimension. Translating all the relevant reasons into this dimension, then, we get effectively the same situation as in the choice between c and d: there is ultimately only one reason that bears on the choice between these two options, namely that one of them is superior to the degree $(x-y)$ in the units of the commensurating dimension. In any case in which the balance of reasons does not already strongly favor one of the options, the generation (or newly acquired perception) of this summative reason will provide the agent with practically significant new information. To fail to know it would be to fail the non-ignorance condition. To perceive it, however, would be to fail the rational options condition, for it ineluctably indicates that the balance of reasons favors one option over the other. Therefore, if a morally significant choice is a choice in which morally evil action is possible, every morally significant choice is between incommensurable options.

Not every choice is morally significant, however. The new natural law theorists' defense of TI, in its full generality, seems to rest on some less formal observations about the nature of the practically significant choices we face. Following Murphy, one may divide the more general argument in two: the first step pertains to the claim that each basic good is incommensurable with each other basic good; the second to the claim that even instances of a single basic good are mutually incommensurable. In defending the first step, Murphy remarks that

> one can face choices regarding the devotion of one's life to one type of good rather than another: to become a physician (life) or a philosopher (knowledge), to get married (friendship) or to take holy orders (religion). And it does seem clear that when one encounters these choices, one can intelligibly choose one or the other.[66]

Yet there does not seem to be any dimension that can plausibly claim to commensurate the claims of these different, practically competing basic goods, compatibly with the overall objectivism of the view, which is independently argued for.[67] Pleasure and happiness seem the only plausible candidates; but the pleasures that provide objective reasons for action are immanent to activities of achieving or pursuing some basic good or goods, while happiness is itself a distinct basic good that does not supersede the others.[68] More abstractly, the new natural law theorist can also note that since the FPR is formal and the basic goods are self-evidently plural, it is not to be expected that there could be any single, substantive, unifying dimension of goodness.

The second step is to extend the defense of incommensurability to different instances of a given basic good. Instantiations of a single basic good can fail to present 'wholly distinct' options in the same way that instantiations of multiple basic goods can; again, this defense of incommensurability is limited to wholly distinct options. As one sufficient condition, Murphy suggests, 'instantiations *i* and *j* are wholly distinct if *i* and *j* contribute to distinct dimensions of the same category of basic good.'[69] Further explicating this idea, and adding a complementary one, he notes that any of the basic goods

> might have a number of dimensions to it (think of the different kinds of knowledge that there are, and how it might seem senseless to say that one is a greater participation in knowledge than the other), or might have instances that are related only analogically, so that there is no univocal notion that could be used in providing a common measure of greater or lesser instantiation (think of the different ways one might participate in play).[70]

While, as Murphy recognizes, these considerations do not amount to a proof of inter-instance incommensurability, they are nonetheless fairly convincing. Some cases of knowing *can* be ranked as greater or lesser participations in knowledge. For instance, one who learns the times tables through 20 learns more than someone who merely learns the times tables through 12. In precisely this kind of case, however, the two options are not wholly distinct: one includes the other in a straight-forward sense. If we keep in mind that TI is limited to wholly distinct options, it will indeed seem highly plausible that different dimensions of goodness can arise within each basic category and that some of the items within a given category bear only an analogical resemblance to one another – a link weak enough to block a reductively quantitative comparison. For instance, to adapt an example of Finnis's, it does not make sense to say that knowing how much printer's ink was used in printing this copy of this book is *more* of an instance of knowledge, or participates *more* in the good of knowledge, than does knowing the truths that the book conveys.[71] The philosophical and the printing-related, we might say, are different dimensions of knowledge.

Now that we understand the concepts of incommensurability and of wholly distinct options employed by TI and see how the new natural law theorists extend their arguments for incommensurability both to cross-category choices and to choices involving only one (category of) basic good, we can turn to the relation between this incommensurability claim and the assertion that the basic goods are the source of value. Just as my argument will focus on S*, a weak form of S, so, too, my argument will focus on the following weak version of TI:

THE THESIS OF COMMON INTRA-CATEGORIAL INCOMMENSURABILITY (I*): *It is commonly the case that, in choices involving wholly distinct options that differ only in the way in which only one basic good is instantiated, the options are evaluatively incommensurable.*

This thesis leaves aside cases involving the differential instantiation of more than one basic good and claims only that incommensurability commonly holds within a basic good, not that it always does. If I* is logically incompatible with S*, then so too, *a fortiori*, is TI.

5 The incompatibility of the qualified source thesis with intra-categorial incommensurability

We have just seen that the explication of the possibility of intra-categorial incommensurability involves the idea that a given type of basic good can be realized – or participated in – in ways that vary along multiple dimensions and even in ways that bear only an analogical resemblance to one another. In the argument that follows, I will forego any advantage that might stem from pursuing the possibility of instances that are merely analogically related, and concentrate on the multi-dimensionality of the alleged basic goods. (If anything, the kind of 'splitting' strategy I use would go through more easily if the instances were merely analogically related.) My claim is that this multi-dimensionality is incompatible with S*, the qualified source thesis.

S* holds that all normative reasons for action derive from a limited set of fundamental reasons. For the new natural law theorists, given their other commitments, this limited set is the set of basic goods. Because S* abstracts from whether the fundamental reasons are aspects of individual welfare, we are focussing only on their claim that what they call 'basic goods' are the fundamental reasons. A fundamental reason, again, is one whose normative force does not derive from any other reason.

We shall want to find a case in which only one basic good is prominently involved. Because knowledge is generally so useful, it is hard to find cases regarding the good of knowledge that have no significant instrumental links to other goods. Accordingly, we would do well to switch from the good of knowledge to the good of play, which is relatively easy to see as an activity pursued solely for its own sake. Indeed, although play *can* be pursued for many ulterior reasons, it is also thought of as a paradigm case of an activity that has no point beyond itself.[72] Like knowledge, play has multiple dimensions. Among these are the degree to which it engages our imaginative capacities and the degree to which it engages our capacities of recall or memory. Each of these is a dimension of the value of play, in that, other things equal, the more play engages either of them, the better that instance of play is. Two instances of play that vary solely on one of these dimensions, and differ in no other evaluatively relevant respects, would be commensurable, and would fail to represent wholly distinct options. But consider the parlor game, charades, and the card game, Concentration. The former requires lots of imagination, while the latter requires memory above all. Ranking differently on these different dimensions of play, these two games are evaluatively incommensurable.

Now consider the case of One-eyed Jack. Since he does not want to be dull, he will allocate a fixed amount of time each week to play. Up until now, however, his sole form of play has been playing Concentration for an hour every evening. Assume that Jack has no disability that would prevent him from engaging in imaginative play. Now, despite the fact that these forms of play reflect incommensurable values, these options are not incomparable. Indeed, I claim that it would be objectively preferable to the *status quo*, other things equal, for Jack to play charades three evenings a week and Concentration the remaining evenings. Assume that no other basic goods are consequentially at stake and that the two options differ, with respect to basic goods, only in the degree to which they instantiate these two dimensions of the good of play. What can possibly account for the objective preferability of Jack's switching partly over to charades?

The good of play, considered as such, is impotent to explain this fact. As we have seen, as instances of play, these two games are incommensurable.

Neither is more a case of play, or better as an instantiation of play, than is the other. To explain the superior choiceworthiness of Jack's shifting partly to charades, we need to invoke the two dimensions of play that these two games differentially realize: imaginative play and memory-exercising play. Here, it is important to remember the distinction between incommensurability and incomparability. We start with an intuitive comparison of Jack's two options, one of which seems clearly better than the other. In explaining this comparison, compatibly with the incommensurability of these two dimensions of play, we cannot proceed to construct or discover a single dimension on which we show that charades receives a higher score. Nonetheless, the distinction between these two dimensions helps to indicate something that Jack's life has left out.

In so appealing to these dimensions of play, they are functioning as reasons. There is no reason not to take them to be reasons. They are of the same metaphysical type as the allegedly fundamental reasons, the basic goods. Like the basic goods, they are general types – just a little more specific. Further, as far as I can see, the goodness or choiceworthiness of memory-exercising play and imaginative play is just as evident or self-evident as is that of play itself. Indeed, adding this kind of specification can enhance the self-evidence of a good's choiceworthiness: compare knowledge of eternal truths with knowledge as such. Since memory-exercising play and imaginative play, considered as goods, have different practical implications in the case at hand, they must be different goods. It follows that, although each is an instance of the good of play, they cannot *both* be identical to the good of play (being distinct from each other); and by parity of reasoning, if they are goods, they are *each* non-identical with that of play itself.

This, then, is the difficulty. According to D, reasons for action necessarily derive from the basic goods. As I have explained, the notion of derivation involved in this claim entails that it must be possible to set out this derivation in a series of subsumptive links that, taken together, justify and explain the action on which they bear. In Jack's case, however, the reasons for switching partly over to charades cannot be explained by reference to the basic good of play as such. One may say, if one likes, that it is explained, instead, by reference to the basic good of play considered not as such but as a manifold comprising multiple, incommensurable dimensions including memory-exercising play and imaginative play. But since there is no bar to considering these last two as distinct goods, a true and complete derivation of the reasons applicable to Jack's case could flow from them, leaving out all reference to the basic good of play. Since reference to the basic good itself can add nothing to the rational cogency of the derivation, and since the basic good of play as such cannot explain the objective preferability of the switch, it cannot be necessary to deriving the reasons for it.[73] Recognizing incommensurability thus undercuts D, which itself is part of S*.

Defenders of the new natural law theory will likely respond that what is operative in Jack's case is some principle of practical reasonableness, and not directly any basic good. The principle at work could be some principle requiring 'balance'[74] or against wholly 'dismissing aspects of well-being.'[75] But this response is ruled out by the evaluative relationships that must hold if the principles of practical reasonableness are to be consistent with D. As we saw in discussing the principles of practical reasonableness more generally, their advice supervenes on differences that could, in principle, be laid out at the level of the basic goods. Some of the most fundamental, structural distinctions deployed in those principles, such as that between promoting and refraining from attacking, or that between the agent's good and that of others, may not be so capturable. But the new natural law theory does depend, for its consistency, on PPS, which affirms that the supervenience holds when what is at stake is confined to the goods promoted by and for a single agent. Such is Jack's case. The facts in Jack's case being what they are, PPS implies that the principles of practical reasonableness can make no difference to the structure of reasons already described.

The difficulty raised by Jack's case cannot be plausibly met by the hope to provide a more refined list of basic goods. To see why not, consider how the difficulty can keep getting iterated. Suppose we decide that imaginative play and memory-exercising play are two distinct basic goods. Suppose, as before, that Jack's only play consists of a nightly hour of Concentration. Now consider a different option – perhaps not as good as a partial shift to charades, but still an objective improvement over his current situation. He could shift some of his playing time to doing crossword puzzles. This, too, is an instance only of memory-exercising play. But it playfully exercises the capacities of verbal memory, and not merely the capacities of pattern memory. To explain why it would be more choiceworthy for Jack to shift some of his time to cross-word puzzles, we need to recognize the distinctness of these two kinds of reason or good, verbal-memory-exercising play and pattern-memory-exercising play. These being different evaluative dimensions, we must expect that the broader category of memory-exercising play has no power to commensurate them. Accordingly, as in the initial argument, memory-exercising play as such will be displaced from any necessary role in a subsumptive derivation by the two more specific value categories.

Once things get carried this far – and there is no reason to think that the process of discriminating reasons cannot continue – it ceases to be plausible to think that one will rest with a fixed list of fundamental reasons from which the normative force of all other reasons can be derived.[76] If I* holds of a set of basic goods, this argument will apply to at least some of them.

In particular, this same strategy of argument may be applied to block those who would evade my appeal to PPS, two paragraphs back, by asserting that what explains the preferability of Jack's switching is some particular *good* of practical reasonableness – say, *balance*. Like the other basic goods this purported one, too, admits of incommensurable dimensions. One element of balance is the *number* of different activities in one's life. Another, incommensurable element of balance is the degree to which these activities are different – their qualitative *range*. Sticking with Jack, we might compare two options: the Concentration/ charades option, as above, and an option that splits his play time among five different memory-play games. By hypothesis, these options cannot be compared in terms of which yields more balance. Thus, the difficulty raised by the original version of Jack's case returns, here, for the view as outfitted with the additional good of balance.

The good of play may be thought peculiar, somehow; but, again, the only reason I chose it was for ease of exposition. All of the basic goods have incommensurable dimensions. Knowledge varies in depth, breadth, and extent. Friendships vary in intimacy and degree of mutual respectfulness, and so on. The only reason to choose play was to avoid having to be heavy-handed about stipulating that other things are evaluatively equal.

In sum, the intra-categorial incommensurability that I* affirms destroys D's claim that there is a set of fundamental reasons that play a necessary role in the derivation of all reasons for action. Since the argument also assumed the generality of basic goods, what has been shown is that S* and I* are incompatible. It follows, *a fortiori*, that S and TI are incompatible. The new natural law theorists' endorsement of incommensurability as a means of staving off consequentialism and as a way of protecting the possibility of morally significant choice ends up undercutting their central effort to set out basic goods that serve as the sources of normativity.

6 Room for maneuver?

How damaging is this result for the new natural law theory? We have already seen that S* and I* are each deeply rooted in the theory; but perhaps the inconsistency that arises from holding both could be averted by weakening one or the other of these two theoretical commitments.

Starting with S*, we may begin by noting that the foregoing argument has no tendency to show that there are any goods that are not instances of the ones the new natural law theorists identify as basic. Hence, the argument leaves untouched the following thesis:

THE BASIC GOODS ARE NECESSARY CONDITIONS OF GOODNESS (BANG): *There is a set of goods that are basic just in the sense that everything that is a good either is a member of that set or is an instance of at least one of the goods in that set.*

If the new natural law theorists were to retreat to this thesis, however, their view would go out with a whimper. This thesis does assert that one can provide an exhaustive classification of what is good. If a link between the goods and human nature can be established, then BANG would also allow one to allocate to human nature a significant role in the theory of normativity. The theory of normativity that resulted, however, would little resemble the new natural law theory, for it gives up on D, the claim that normativity *derives* from the basic goods.

The other main possibility is to weaken I*. Since the incompatibility between S* and I* arises from the incommensurability of instances of a single basic good, this kind of incommensurability could be denied. For instance, the view might retrench to the following thesis:

INTER-CATEGORIAL INCOMMENSURABILITY (ICI): *Each basic good is evaluatively incommensurable with every other basic good, and each instance of one basic good is evaluatively incommensurable with every other wholly distinct instance of another basic good.*

As long as incommensurability among instances of a given basic good is not asserted, it might be thought, the view can avoid the problems raised by the case of One-eyed Jack.

There are two problems with this incommensurability-restraining response, however. The first is that it flies in the face of the facts. We have seen good reason to conclude that instances of basic goods *are* incommensurable. Or, to put the matter a little more cautiously: Insofar as there is good reason for recognizing the mutual incommensurability of the basic goods that stems from their being distinct dimensions of evaluation, there is equally good reason for recognizing incommensurability within each type of basic good. Distinctness of evaluative dimensions does help explain incommensurability and, as we have seen, there is good reason to recognize distinct evaluative dimensions within various of the basic goods. Perhaps, however, defenders of the new natural law theory could dig in their heels behind ICI and – somehow resisting the argument from iteration – insist that if one discovers incommensurable dimensions within a purported basic good, this only means that one has not yet arrived at a fully adequate list of basic goods.

In taking such a stance, however, the defenders of the new natural law theory would run squarely into the second problem with retreating from I* to ICI, which is that ICI provides an insufficient basis for defending the Pauline Principle. This fact has long been recognized by defenders of consequentialist ethics. In grappling with consequentialism, the new natural law theory starts at a disadvantage because it, too, is a good-based view. Accordingly, it does not begin by having at its disposal the means of resisting the idea of maximization that are available, say, to a status-based view.[77] How, then, to put Samuel Scheffler's question, can it explain 'how . . . it can be rational to forbid the performance of a morally objectionable action that will have the effect of minimizing the total number of comparably objectionable actions that are performed and will have no other morally relevant consequences?'[78] As Scheffler notes, the case for consequentialist maximization at which this rhetorical question gestures avoids claiming that there is any way of summing up the overall goodness of a state of affairs. Instead, it confines itself to the kind of 'dominance' ranking that we saw with the case of houses *c* and *d*, as it limits itself to just one dimension of goodness.

To see why the distinctions between promoting and not attacking basic goods and between agent-relative and agent-neutral ways of considering them will not suffice to answer Scheffler's challenge,[79] consider Richard Brook's case of the Lion's Den:

> You are at the zoo with two children who are making a scene. Becoming angry, you toss them into the lion's den. Horrified, you come to your senses and notice that they can only be saved if you toss a third child (who just toddled along) into the back of the den. The beast would be distracted and you could quickly leap in and save the first two. What should you do? Whatever you do, you have initiated a chain of events that results in a child's death.[80]

This is not a particularly realistic case – although in these days of terrorists using passenger airplanes as missiles, who knows what is realistic? It is a case, however, that sharply pits the Pauline Principle against consequentialist maximization; and it has the virtue of allowing us to bypass the issue of whether agent-neutral and agent-relative reasons are incommensurable with one another, as it confines itself to a single agent's similar attacks on one basic good.[81] Scheffler's question here becomes, 'How can it not be rational for me to minimize the number of people I kill, other things being equal?' The new natural law theory must properly answer this question if it is to reconcile its commitment to the Pauline Principle with its evidently good-based character.

The new natural law theory as outfitted with the strong incommensurability claim, TI, would have a way of achieving this reconciliation. As two distinct instances of badness, the agent's options in this case, as in every case, would be incommensurable. Starting with Grisez, the new natural law theory simply refused to truck with consequentialist maximization, using its assertion of thorough-going incommensurability to explain why maximization never makes sense. If it fell back to ICI, it would no longer have a clear basis for resisting consequentialist maximization in cases involving options that differ in only one dimension of goodness and only one basic mode (promoting, respecting, attacking) of practical orientation to it. Indeed, since the reasons supporting each option are not, in such cases, wholly distinct, it would seem that the new natural law theorists would be obliged to admit that the choices such options offer are not even 'morally significant.' Yet this is hardly what they would want to say about a case such as the Lion's Den.[82]

7 Conclusion

I have shown that the new natural law theorists' assertion that instances of a given basic good are evaluatively incommensurable is incompatible with their central claim that the basic goods are the source of normativity. Furthermore, there seems to be no way to avoid this inconsistency without paying a severe price – either by seriously compromising the sense in which the basic goods are supposed to be 'basic' or else by weakening the view's capacity to support the Pauline Principle. I am in no position to determine the best way forward for a natural law theory. I can, however, say a little about my own preferred response to these difficulties.

My argument that shifting from TI to ICI would undercut the Pauline Principle presupposed that the view remains a good-based one. The new natural law theory, as we have seen, is importantly good-based, in that even the precepts of practical reasonableness, such as that which forbids the intentional, instrumental destruction of instances of a basic good articulate reasons that supervene on facts about the basic goods. Perhaps, though, this latter claim should be given up. Perhaps such a principle of right (if we may call it that) should be recognized as having an intuitive basis of its own, just like the basic goods, such that PPS should be given up. Such a move, which would grant equal primacy to the right as to the good, would be one important step in the direction of the kind of moral theory I myself would favor, which is neither a consequentialism nor a natural law view.[83]

This move by itself, however, ignores the first argument against shifting to ICI, namely that I* better fits the facts. Since I am convinced that incommensurability is indeed widespread and ramifying in the way that the iterative argument suggested, I would prefer to drop D – and so both S* and S – and do without the claim that there is a privileged set of goods that count as the source of normativity. There may be a set of goods that is classificatorily useful and enlightening, à la BANG; but there is no set of goods (or of goods and principles) from which all normativity ultimately must be derivable. In my view, D gives too much importance to subsumptive and other quasi-demonstrative modes of practical reasoning. The contrast that the new natural law theorists use to set up D is overblown. Their claim is that although the basic goods *can* be inductively or dialectically supported, they *cannot* be derived. I tend to think, rather, that all practical justification involves a mixture of holistic, bottom-up support and deductive or quasi-deductive elements. On this picture, although perhaps something can be derived, nothing need be. Given this justificatory holism, there is no necessity of finding underivable, self-evident practical premises.[84]

Current adherents of the new natural law theory may not wish to follow me in dropping D. If the argument of the current chapter is correct, however, it is, in any case, time for a new new theory.

Notes

1. I am very grateful to Ruth Chang, Timothy Chappell, Mark C. Murphy, and the members of Philamore for critical and constructive comments.
2. This link to Aristotle, via Aquinas, is an important theme in all of the authors discussed here. It is mentioned, variously, in Germain G. Grisez, 'The First Principle of Practical Reason: A Commentary on the Summa Theologiae, I–II, Question 94, Article 2', *Natural Law Forum* 10 (1965): 168–201; Germain G. Grisez, *The Way of Lord Jesus*, Vol. 1: *Christian Moral Principles* (Chicago: Franciscan Herald Press, 1983; hereafter *CMP*): 184–5; John Finnis, *Natural Law and Natural Rights*, corrected edn (Oxford: Clarendon Press, 1982 [1980]; hereafter *NLNR*): 103; Mark C. Murphy, *Natural Law and Practical Rationality* (Cambridge, England: Cambridge University Press, 2001; hereafter *NLPR*):

ch. 1; Alfonso Gómez-Lobo, *Morality and the Human Goods: An Introduction to Natural Law Ethics* (Washington, DC: Georgetown University Press, 2002; hereafter *MHG*).

3. These worries are centrally addressed by John Finnis. See John Finnis, 'Natural Law and the "Is"-"Ought" Question: An Invitation to Professor Veatch', *Catholic Lawyers* 26 (1980–81): 266–77; and Finnis, *NLNR*, esp. 36–42.

4. Grisez, *CMP*: 186–7.

5. Ibid: 216–22; Finnis, *NLNR*: 118–25; Murphy, *NLPR*: 204–7.

6. The qualification 'wholly distinct' is suggested by Murphy, *NLPR*: 185. I will return to it.

7. Russell Hittinger, *A Critique of the New Natural Law Theory* (Notre Dame, Indiana: University of Notre Dame Press, 1987).

8. See the works cited in note 2. I have omitted Timothy Chappell from this list: Timothy Chappell, *Understanding Human Goods: A Theory of Ethics* (Edinburgh: Edinburgh University Press, 1998; hereafter *UHG*) defends many of the tenets of the new natural law theory; and that work as well as his later writings, such as Timothy Chappell, 'The Implications of Incommensurability', *Philosophy* 76 (2001): 137–48, take up the argument that the incommensurability of goods undercuts consequentialism. Chappell, however, seems less clearly committed to the source thesis than are the other writers I discuss. In addition, unlike the other writers, who aim to give exhaustive lists of the basic goods, Chappell holds that there is no necessary limit on the number of types of goods.

9. Murphy, *NLPR*: 46.

10. On this point, Murphy cites Gisela Striker, 'Origins of the Concept of Natural Law', *Proceedings of the Boston Area Colloquium in Ancient Philosophy* 2 (1986): 79–94.

11. Grisez, *CMP*: 186.

12. Murphy, *NLPR*: 176.

13. Ibid: 180–1.

14. Murphy's definition of welfarism crucially puts 'agents' in the plural possessive.

15. Or perhaps one should simply say, following Chappell, that it is 'evident' that each of the basic goods are to be sought: Chappell, *UHG*: 36. The point is that their choiceworthiness needs no demonstration.

16. Finnis, *NLNR*: 63.

17. For the possibility of inductive support, see Finnis, *NLNR*: 77; and Finnis, 'Natural Law and the "Is"-"Ought" Question': 268. For the possibility of 'dialectical' support, see Murphy, *NLPR*: 21.

18. Finnis, *NLNR*: 69.

19. Murphy, *NLPR*: 181.

20. In addition, once the precepts of practical reasonableness are on the scene, these add far more subtle ways in which distinctions can, in principle, be traced back to the basic goods.

21. Chappell, *UHG*: 35–6.

22. See Murphy, *NLPR*: 14, citing Finnis, *NLNR*: 34 and Finnis, 'Natural Law and the "Is"-"Ought" Question': 275.

23. Murphy, *NLPR*: 11–12.

24. Finnis, *NLNR*: 92; cf. Murphy, *NLPR*: 101. The qualification about 'intelligible' purposes is suggested by Murphy's sensible insistence that some human actions (intentional in some sense) are unintelligible: Murphy, *NLPR*: 1, 11.

25. Gómez-Lobo, *MHG*: 38; cf. 9.
26. Grisez, *CMP*: 183.
27. Murphy, *NLPR*: 95. Murphy's own effort to link the basic goods to a teleological account of human function, consistently with their non-derivative normativity, is most impressive. See his ch. 1.
28. Grisez, 'The First Principle of Practical Reason'.
29. Ibid.: 168. Aquinas's Latin reads: 'Bonum est faciendum et prosequendum, et malum vitandum'.
30. See Thomas Aquinas, *Summa Theologica*, trans. Fathers of the English Dominican Province, 5 vols (Westminister, MD: Christian Classics, 1981): I, q. 5 a. 3.
31. Grisez, *CMP*: 215; Finnis, *NLNR*: 118; Murphy, *NLPR*: 204; Gómez-Lobo, *MHG*: 46.
32. Grisez, *CMP*: 179; Gómez-Lobo, *MHG*: 2.
33. Grisez, *CMP*: 180.
34. Grisez seems to hold that the FPR does provide practical guidance. He writes that 'the first principle of practical reasoning always controls practical thinking. Yet one can find oneself doing something which cannot attain any intelligible good; then the first principle makes it clear that one's action is pointless and this leads to a cessation of effort' (Grisez, *CMP*: 180). Note, however, that this practical guidance depends on a substantive filling out of the list of intelligible goods. Indeed, the judgment that an act will not lead to *any* intelligible good presupposes an *exhaustive* list of basic goods.
35. Gómez-Lobo, *MHG*: 5.
36. Thus, in his catalog of three kinds of principles of natural law (*NLNR*: 23), Finnis leaves out any mention of the FPR. Rather, he simply describes the basic goods as 'the basic principles of all practical reasoning' (59).
37. Grisez, *CMP*: 185.
38. Murphy, *NLPR*: 160–1.
39. Finnis, *NLNR*: ch. 5. Sometimes, however, Finnis also seems directly to appeal to the intuitive reasonableness of a given principle, making otherwise unexplicated assertions about what is or seems 'unreasonable.' Insofar as he thus relies on considered judgments about the right that are independent of the good, Finnis covertly adopts an ethical method more in line with what I will, in the end, be recommending.
40. Chappell, *UHG*: 74–82.
41. Murphy, *NLPR*: 181.
42. This supervenience may be imagined in layers. If, as the new natural law theorists hold, the principles of practical reasonableness derive from the basic goods, then some of the differences at the level of basic goods will show up *via* principles of practical reasonableness. For instance, it may be that, given a principle of practical coherence, one person's life history may make an option preferable that another person's life history would not. The supervenience point is that, as a metaphysical matter, this difference between these two people's situations can in principle be cashed out in terms of a difference in the basic goods that the choices offer. One way to imagine this is to imagine enriching the description of the options, so as to discriminate between option-A-as-chosen-by-a-person-with-history-type-1 and option-A-as-chosen-by-a-person-with-history-type-2. I am grateful to Timothy Chappell for raising the issue.

43. Murphy, *NLPR*: 6.
44. Ibid: 181. Murphy there distinguishes two ways in which a reason can be fundamental, and seems to indicate that the more important sense is the non-epistemological one I use to explain the notion of a basic good. One might define a weaker sense of fundamentality, according to which a reason is fundamental just in case it has *some* normative force not deriving from any other reason; but since the new natural law theory is interested in tracing all normative force to its 'sources,' it seems more straightforward to go directly to the stronger sense.
45. Finnis, *NLNR*: 61. Grisez, likewise, describes the basic goods as 'general determinations' of the FPR (*CMP*: 180) that are to be 'realized indefinitely – that is, they are always to be realized, and new ways of realizing them can always be found' (182). Murphy describes the basic goods as 'highly general' (*NLPR*: 20). Gómez-Lobo takes it that basic goods can have multiple 'instances' (*MHG*: 9).
46. For instance, Joseph Raz, *Practical Reason and Norms* (Princeton: Princeton University Press, 1990): 19n., holds that all reasons are facts, and that 'facts are not individuals but logical constructs.' Compare T.M. Scanlon, *What We Owe to Each Other* (Cambridge, Mass.: Harvard University Press, 1998): 57. As Jonathan Dancy has pointed out to me, this claim that reasons are not individuals (or particulars) can be accepted by those particularists who are concerned instead to deny that the generalities which are reasons are *always* reasons whenever they are instantiated.
47. I am indebted to Linda Wetzel for discussion of the possibility of general instances. Compare Linda Wetzel, 'What are Occurrences of Expressions?', *Journal of Philosophical Logic* 22 (1993): 215–20.
48. Notice that, to give a fully convincing example of a particular instance of a good, I gave one set in the past. One plausible possibility is that our future-oriented deliberation deals only with generally characterized goods. How should one draw the line between general goods and particular ones? Is my friendship with Mr E a particular good or a general good? It would seem still general, despite its incorporation of a proper name, as I can pursue and enjoy it at different places and times.
49. I put forward one such purported counterexample in Henry S. Richardson, 'Beyond Good and Right: Toward a Constructive Ethical Pragmatism', *Philosophy & Public Affairs* 24 (1995): 124. As far as I can see, Finnis is not fully committal on this point, but instead stresses the defensive maneuvers that would protect the thesis that every instance of a basic good is, as such, good: Finnis, *NLNR*: 62.
50. Gómez-Lobo, *MHG*: 36.
51. Cf. Murphy, *NLPR*: 108. I elide two of Murphy's points. One of his responses to the objection that knowledge of the number of blades of grass on a given plot does not seem valuable simply bites the bullet: 'facts about grass density are those in which people can, intelligibly, take an interest.' His use of the 'as such' response comes in the claim that 'the badness of having . . . false views [about such matters] seems best explicable by knowledge being good as such.' For that latter point to work, however, it seems that he would need also to deploy the 'as such' move more positively, since having false views on a matter can be avoided by having no views about it, which is typically sensible regarding grass density.

52. Note that TI applies pairwise to instances of goods. It follows from this that the commensurability it denies is what has been called 'weak' commensurability. Strong commensurability obtains only if there is some one dimension – such as pleasure or utility, substantively interpreted – in terms of which the reasons for and against every option in every pair of options agents ever face can adequately be represented. Weak commensurability demands only that for each choice there be some dimension in terms of which one can adequately array the reasons, allowing that different dimensions might play this role for different choices. See David Wiggins, *Needs, Values, Truth: Essays in the Philosophy of Value*, Aristotelian Society Series, Vol. 6 (Oxford: Basil Blackwell, 1987): 258–9.

53. There are obvious Kantian grounds for doubting that all reasons are good-based. For doubts about whether all practical considerations are reasons, see John Broome, 'Normative Requirements', in *Normativity*, ed. Jonathan Dancy (Oxford: Blackwell, 2000).

54. On the relation of being on a par, see Ruth Chang, 'The Possibility of Parity', *Ethics* 112 (2002): 659–88. Because of my focus, here, on deliberation and decision, I define 'comparability' more narrowly than does Chang by applying the term only to the case in which items can be ranked all things considered.

55. On the distinction between evaluative incommensurability and incomparability, see Henry S. Richardson, 'Commensurability', in *Encyclopedia of Ethics*, 2nd edn, ed. Lawrence Becker (London: Routledge, 2001): 258–62. I had not realized until researching the present chapter that Grisez has long insisted on the distinction between comparability ('commensuration [that] occurs in choice') and commensurability ('commensuration . . . antecedent to choice'): Grisez, *CMP*: 156. This distinction lies behind my insistence that the commensurating scale be a real property or a dimension of goodness; for if this restriction were not imposed and one could simply pick or construct a dimension, of course it would always be possible to construct it so as to reflect the comparative status of two options as antecedently determined by choice.

56. One way to put the exceptional status of God – as, perhaps, on a view such as Leibniz's – might be to say that God's infinite understanding allows him adequately to array all reasons along the single dimension of goodness as such. We generally lack that capacity.

57. Hence, they do not proceed in the spirit of Isaac Levi, *Hard Choices: Decision Making Under Unresolved Conflict* (Cambridge: Cambridge University Press, 1986).

58. See Henry S. Richardson, *Practical Reasoning about Final Ends* (Cambridge, England: Cambridge University Press, 1994): ch. 6.

59. Grisez, *CMP*: 152; Finnis, *NLNR*: 112–15; Murphy, *NLPR*: 182–7; Gómez-Lobo, *MHG*: 39–40. See also Chappell, *UHG*: ch. 3.

60. Grisez, *CMP*: 152–3. His argument there restates that of an earlier journal piece.

61. Murphy, *NLPR*: 182–6. Murphy develops his argument as a generalization of Grisez's, employing a conception of 'practically significant choice' in lieu of Grisez's 'morally significant choice.' In this form, I do not believe the argument works. The necessary conditions for intelligible practical choice do not entail, as the necessary conditions for intelligible moral choice do, in this tradition, that the agent is free of significant normative ignorance. Hence, the conditions

of intelligible practical choice do not allow one to suppose that the agent has recognized that the commensurated reasons may be dispensed with in favor of the simpler, commensurating set.

62. Cf. John Finnis, Joseph Boyle, and Germain G. Grisez, *Nuclear Deterrence, Morality, and Realism* (Oxford: Oxford University Press, 1987): 258; and Murphy, *NLPR*: 268, n. 14.

63. Murphy, *NLPR*: 185.

64. On this distinction, see also Candace Vogler, *Reasonably Vicious* (Cambridge, Mass.: Harvard University Press, 2002), esp. 66–71. Vogler is, in some sense, working within the Thomistic tradition. A rigorous distinction between normative requirements and the considerations that contribute to the balance of reasons, developed independently of this tradition, is found in Broome, 'Normative Requirements'.

65. To see what I mean by 'residue,' here, consider the kind of case that Slote invokes in explaining the idea of satisficing. Thus, consider a house-seller, and suppose that it first appears that the only relevant consideration is the price. Then suppose, however, that once the bids start going over $1 million, the seller starts saying things to himself like 'if I sell it for that much, I'll have difficulty avoiding the taxes that come with a failure to reinvest my capital gains in my new primary residence.' As soon as he has said that, he has made clear that price is not, after all, the only consideration that matters. Hence, in this case, the dimension of price could not capture all of the reasons, without residue. For a general argument that the idea of satisficing only incompletely captures the importance of evaluative multi-dimensionality, see Henry S. Richardson, 'Satisficing: Not Good Enough', in *Satisficing*, ed. Michael Byron (New York: Cambridge University Press, 2004).

66. Murphy, *NLPR*: 184.

67. For arguments against subjectivist accounts of goodness, see Murphy, *NLPR*: ch. 2.

68. Murphy, *NLPR*: 100, 134.

69. Ibid: 185.

70. Ibid: 187.

71. Finnis, *NLNR*: 62. Finnis there appears to suggest that, after all, these two instances might be commensurable, as he suggests that, 'except for some exceptional purpose, it is worth more' to know the conveyed truths. But this talk of normal purposes violates his own ban, enunciated on the preceding page, on speaking of the purposes for which knowledge is sought. In assessing an instance of a basic good as such, we ought to set aside all ulterior purposes.

72. Finnis, *NLNR*: 87.

73. It is important to remember, here, that the notion of derivation at work in D is demonstrative, at least in the sense that characterizes subsumptive practical reasoning.

74. Cf. Finnis, *NLNR*: 110.

75. Cf. Murphy, *NLPR*: 198–201.

76. Notice that this discrimination between two types of memory also suffices to answer the defender of the new natural law theory who asserts that what is going on in the original Jack case is that the good of play is intersecting with two other basic goods: aesthetic experience in the case of imaginative play

(a bit of a stretch, but let it go) and knowledge in the case of memory-exercising play (it's so great to *know* where that pair of threes is).
77. See, for example, F.M. Kamm, 'Non-Consequentialism, the Person as an End-in-Itself, and the Significance of Status', *Philosophy and Public Affairs* 21 (1993): 354–89.
78. Samuel Scheffler, 'Agent-Centred Restrictions, Rationality, and the Virtues', in *Consequentialism and its Critics*, ed. Samuel Scheffler (Oxford: Oxford University Press, 1988): 249–50.
79. It may well be that, as argued in Timothy Chappell, 'The Implications of Incommensurability', *Philosophy* 76 (2001): 137–48, the distinctions between promoting, respecting, and not attacking basic goods suffice to defeat a maximizing consequentialism. Even if so, Scheffler's challenge lives on, as in the case about to be described, to threaten the ability of a good-based view such as the new natural law theory to maintain the Pauline Principle.
80. Richard Brook, 'Agency and Morality', *Journal of Philosophy* 88 (1991): 197. I discuss this case in Richardson, 'Beyond Good and Right': 118.
81. Murphy interestingly argues that each basic good generates both agent-neutral and agent-relative reasons that are incommensurable with each other: Murphy, *NLPR*: 181, 186.
82. This is obviously only a cursory and preliminary examination of the theoretical options available for coping with such difficulties. Perhaps, for instance, one should introduce temporally indexed distinctions into the basic modes of practical orientation so as to distinguish between (a) now successfully attacking a basic good and (b) now acting so that I will have successfully attacked a basic good. Perhaps, by contrast, the notion of an 'attack' on a basic good should be shorn of success conditions, such that the attack on the life of the two children is complete even before it is settled that the lion will eat them. See the useful discussion in Whitley Kaufman, 'The Lion's Den, Othello, and the Limits of Consequentialism', *Southern Journal of Philosophy* 37 (1999): 539–57.
83. See Richardson, 'Beyond Good and Right'.
84. Here, I follow Rawls's rejection of a 'Cartesian' conception of practical justification: John Rawls, *A Theory of Justice*, revised edn (Cambridge, Mass.: Harvard University Press, 1999 [1971]): 506.

5
The Polymorphy of Practical Reason

Timothy Chappell

1 Natural law theory in outline

Natural law theory (NLT) offers an approach to normative ethics that is simple, distinctive, and persuasive. It posits a variety of different sorts of basic goods, things which are good in themselves rather than merely instrumentally good. These goods are the basis both of motivation and of justification: most if not all of our practical reasons arise from them, and to justify an action is to explain something about its relation to the goods. Our practical reasons are, irreducibly, polymorphous; and the source of that polymorphy is the variety of the goods.

So NLT defines the right in terms of a logically prior good. NLT cannot follow the majority of deontologists (e.g. Ross 1930; Rawls 1971; Thomson 1990; McNaughton and Rawling 1992) in rejecting the 'teleo-logical' approach to ethics, or in taking (for instance) rights, rules, or *'prima facie* duties' to be analytically basic to ethics. On the other hand, NLT takes the goods to be so fundamentally diverse that there is no prospect, in NLT, of developing anything like the consequentialists' characteristic maximising approach to normative questions. For NLT, the various goods constitute fundamentally different standards or dimensions of normative assessment.

As a result, NLT recognises no single currency of value whereby the various goods can be numerically calibrated against each other. This in turn means that practical reason's assessments of what to do cannot be based upon any such calibration. Instead, the main work of practical reason is done by asking, about any proposed action, what sort of attitude that action expresses to each of the goods involved.

NLT does not require the agent to take a maximising attitude to any of the goods that confront him. It cannot require this, for two reasons.

The first is that the notion of maximising is not well defined in NLT. The second is that, even if it were well defined, maximising one good G1 would nearly always involve failing to maximise some other good G2. So any action that satisfied a maximising requirement of practical rationality in respect of one good would *ipso facto* fail to satisfy that same requirement of rationality in respect of another good. Now it is no better to breach this requirement of rationality in respect of one good than in respect of any other. So the combination of a plurality of goods with a maximising requirement for practical rationality will make it impossible to draw a distinction between the practically rational and the practically irrational. That is, it will destroy our normative theory altogether.

Instead, NLT requires the agent to take either of two different attitudes to the goods that confront him. The first of these attitudes is pursuit. Since NLT bases both motivation and justification upon the variety of the goods, it naturally licenses – and mandates – the agent to pursue any of the goods, and gives him a *ceteris paribus* freedom as to which of them exactly he is to pursue. According to NLT, this freedom is the theoretical basis of the important moral phenomenon of supererogation.

The second attitude is respect. NLT tells the agent to regard each of the goods as a good – as something valuable, something that it would be intelligible to respond to, something potentially worthy of pursuit – even when he is not actually pursuing it. But not just any action is consistent with such an attitude. To respect a good is to rule out certain possible actions and policies, because those actions or policies would involve a failure to respect the good in question – as we may also say, a violation of that good. According to NLT, this ruling-out is the theoretical basis of the important moral phenomenon of constraints.

Confronted with a plurality of goods, practical rationality permits an agent to pursue some goods in that plurality and not pursue others, provided that the agent does not pursue his preferred goods no matter what the cost to other goods is. For any good that the agent does not pursue, there are limits to the permissible trade-offs that the agent may make with that good in order to gain a good that the agent is pursuing. To respect or honour a good is to refuse to trade it off, use it as a means, treat it as incidental to what one is really after, in just any way at all. It is to refuse to treat that good as if it were not only not a good that is focal to one's agency, but not a good at all – something of zero value. In other words, it is to refuse to violate that good. (With these remarks cf. Chappell 2003: 170–1.)

Such, in outline, is the programme of (NLT) as I understand it. The theory is increasingly well understood, and ethicists are growing in their appreciation of its potential as a major and serious alternative to the three-way opposition that is most usually set up in normative ethical theory – roughly, Kant *versus* Mill *versus* virtue. For all that, NLT is still not as well understood or appreciated as it deserves to be. In this chapter I offer a variety of important clarifications of NLT's programme, aimed at the points where they seem to be most needed.

My clarifications come under five headings, which I shall review one by one: (1) Maximisation; (2) The ontology of the goods; (3) A contrast between reasons; (4) Incommensurability; and (5) Violation.

2   Maximisation

Doubts about the possibility or plausibility of a maximising response to a plurality of goods may begin when we consider incommensurability (cf. section 5). They may also – and for obviously related reasons – arise when we consider the kind of life that someone would have if they seriously tried to maximise all the goods at once. As I have pointed out before (Chappell 1998: 14–15, 2003: 163–5), the people whom we normally call good people do not even try to do as well as they can by every available good. And if they did, the consequences would be almost unimaginable. If everyone accepted a requirement of practical rationality to maximise all the goods at once, then no one could live the distinctive lifestyle of a professional violinist, or a lumberjack, or indeed a philosopher. All good lives would be essentially similar, differing only where differentiation aided 'the division of ethical labour'. There would be nothing like the polymorphous diversity of good lives that we actually see. All of which is evidence either that we are systematically mistaken in our views about what lives are good; or else that there is something wrong either with the consequentialist doctrine of maximisation, or with the consequentialist doctrine of commensurability, or with both doctrines. I take it I have listed these alternatives in order of increasing likelihood.

A third source of serious doubts about the very possibility of maximising (for which cf. Chappell 2001a) has nothing to do with incommensurability. For an agent to maximise is for her to take the best available option. But anyone who is a voluntary agent at all always has infinitely many options. Options are possibilities, and possibilities form a mathematically dense array: between every two similar possibilities P and P*, there is a third possibility P**, which (on some plausible similarity metric) is more similar to P than P* is, and more similar to P* than P is.

Thus even when someone's range of options is severely restricted, there are still infinitely many ways in which she can choose to act if she can choose to act at all. (So, for instance, a paralysed man who can only move one finger, and that too to a minimal extent, does not have exactly two options – to move it or not. Since actions are not reducible to physical movements, there are indefinitely many things that the paralysed man might be [in the middle of] doing by moving his finger, for example spending a month tapping out a Morse translation of *The Iliad* to an amanuensis.)

Since every option range is of infinite size, no agent can ever know, or even have a justified belief,[1] that she is taking the best available option. This means that the instruction to maximise cannot be used as her decision procedure by a person who is acting. Nor can it be used as a criterion of rightness by someone who wants to assess what that agent does. But if the instruction to maximise cannot be used in either way, then it seems that it cannot be used in ethics at all. The exhortation to maximise is pointless, empty rhetoric.

This sounds like a good reason to give up the idea that a practically rational response to a plurality of goods must be maximising – that no response will be practically rational unless it takes the best option available. For in fact no practically rational response to a plurality of goods ever could be maximising.

Other reasons for doubts about maximisation can be given, too. Consider a delightful little story from Pollock (1983). An infinitely long-lived connoisseur, with an infinite capacity for utility, has a bottle of Everbetter wine. Everbetter is a wine with the curious property that, however many days you leave it to mature, it will always be even better if you leave it just one day more. Now the connoisseur is a maximiser: he thinks the secret of practical rationality is encapsulated in the instruction, 'Take the best available option.' But any day that the connoisseur picks as the day to drink the wine has an unfortunate property: it is a less good day to drink the wine on than tomorrow. So he will never get to drink it unless he abandons his maximising account of practical rationality.

Sorensen (1994) rejects this argument against maximising rationality. According to him, the connoisseur does get to drink the wine, 'on a day that is as real as the day he began his task [of reaching the end of the infinite series of days]: it is observed that the connoisseur cannot complete the process in any number of days. But that observation is only worrisome if one restricts "any number" to finite numbers.' Sorensen's proposal seems to be that the connoisseur can drink the Everbetter on a transfinitely numbered day. But can the connoisseur ever reach a transfinitely numbered day? The paradoxes in supposing transfinite numbers are real – that is, realised in anything – are massive; and we are supposed to be dealing with practicable, realisable, cases. If Sorensen's point is that there is no difference between the goodness of the wine on day aleph and on day aleph + 1, the proper retort is that there is no difference between day aleph and day aleph + 1, either; so Sorensen has not provided a real description of a possible case.

A different tack for the maximiser against Pollock's argument is this: 'What the connoisseur should compare is not the utility of drinking the wine on day N with the utility of drinking the wine on day N + 1. It is the utility of drinking the wine on no day with the utility of drinking the wine on some day.' The trouble with this is that there is no one thing that is 'the utility of drinking the wine on some day'. Since the wine is always improving, the utility of drinking the wine is different, and greater, with every new day. So long as the connoisseur remains a maximiser, he retains his reason perpetually to postpone Wine-Drinking Day. If the connoisseur picks today as Wine-Drinking Day, he not only has to bear in mind the utility gained by getting to drink the wine at all. He also has to bear in mind the utility lost by not drinking the wine on a later day when it will be better.

Intuitively, of course, it is perfectly obvious what the connoisseur ought to do. He should just write off this lost extra utility and pick as Wine-Drinking Day any day when the wine is good, or good enough. But to do this is to settle for an option that is patently not the best option available. Alternatively, it is to prefer what is obviously the worse of a pair of options to what is obviously the better of that pair. In other words, it is to give up being a maximiser.

For these reasons at least, then, a maximising theory of practical rationality is unavailable. This conclusion helps to support NLT by ruling out one of the most popular alternatives to it.

It is worth pausing, incidentally, to note just how popular this alternative is. Maximising assumptions are everywhere, not just among, say, Bayesians or rational choice theorists, but more generally in moral philosophy and philosophy of action. To give one glaring example: since Davidson (1980), and even before, it has been absolutely routine for theorists of practical reason to assume that rational action occurs when the agent acts on his *best* judgement, or (equivalently?) on his judgement of what is *best*. So far as I can see, these are maximising ways of talking. If the arguments just given are correct, they are seriously misleading.

3 The ontology of the goods

But which are the goods? And what is it for anything to be a good? It is a commonplace – and I have little to add to this commonplace here – to present lists that answer the first question by giving examples: 'Accomplishment, the components of human existence [i.e. life and health, liberty, autonomy, "what makes life human"], understanding, enjoyment, deep personal relations' (Griffin 1986: 67); 'Life, knowledge, play, aesthetic experience, sociability, practical reasonableness, religion' (Finnis 1980: 80–9); 'Happiness, knowledge, purposeful activity, autonomy, solidarity, respect, and beauty' (Railton 1984: 109–10).

It is equally commonplace to deduce an answer to the second question by generalisation on the basis of these lists. The most popular conclusion among natural law theorists is something along Aristotle's, Aquinas's, and Finnis's lines: the goods are 'aspects of human flourishing', or 'fulfilments of human capacities'.

This answer to the second question seems mistaken to me, because of its anthropocentrism – an anthropocentrism that I consider to be one of Aristotle's less inspired innovations relative to Plato. Intuitively, there are counterexamples to the idea that the goods are all aspects of human flourishing. The well-being of the Amazonian ecosystem, or of my pet dolphin, is a good, and even an aspect of flourishing; but not of *human* flourishing. The truth, again, is a good, but it would still be a good even if it was directly opposed to human flourishing: as Nietzsche remarks somewhere, 'there is no necessary connection between the truth and the well-being of mankind'. Come to that, Aquinas's God is not an aspect of human flourishing (or at least he is not only that), though clearly Aquinas counts him as a good, indeed as the supreme good.

Moreover, if the goods were all defined as aspects of human flourishing, that would simply raise the question why human flourishing was such a good thing. Why not a moral focus on cockroach flourishing, or on Martian *eudaimonia*? The anthropocentric account of what it is to be a good seems to get the order of explanation back to front. Knowledge and friendship (for instance) are not goods because they are aspects of human flourishing. Rather they are aspects of human flourishing because they are goods, and because human flourishing (unlike cockroach flourishing) is a sufficiently sophisticated form of flourishing to include them.

If you see things this way round – the Platonist way round – then the question why human flourishing is such a good thing need not be left unanswered and unanswerable, as it seems to be on the anthropocentric approach. Beyond mere dogmatic assertion, there will be a reason that we can give as to why human flourishing is a good thing, in a way that cockroach or canine flourishing simply is not. The reason will be that human flourishing involves such great goods as knowledge and friendship, and cockroach and canine flourishing do not.

This line of thought helps to point us in the direction of a better account of what it is for anything to be a good. The idea will be that the goods are not, or not essentially, aspects of human flourishing. What they are essentially is this: they are the ideal standards that apply in the different normative dimensions. Things can be worse or better in ever so many different ways; and the variety of goods corresponds to that variety. Each good stands as an ideal limit, a 'horizon of perfection', for the development of the kind of improvement that it governs.

This idea suggests an explanation of how the goods ground practical reasons. Reasons arise when we see potentials for good: that is, when we see the difference between how things are and how things could be in the light of one of these ideal limits. Compare Anscombe (1957)'s well-known metaphor of 'direction of fit' in her characterisation of desire. Her – rather Sartrean? – idea was that while beliefs correspond to ways the world is, desires correspond to ways the world *is not*, but could or should be. I am suggesting that this sort of disparity is precisely a disparity between the actuality and the norm. You could also call it a gap between an *is* and an *ought*.

This conception of the goods also shows why J.L. Mackie is absolutely right to compare the moral objectivist's good to the Platonist's Forms:

> Plato's Forms give a dramatic picture of what objective values would have to be... [As with a Form], an objective good would be sought by anyone who was acquainted with it, not because of any contingent fact that this person, or every person, is so constituted that he desires this end, but just because the end has to-be-pursuedness somehow built into it. (Mackie 1977: 40)

In a sense, the variety of goods just is a variety of Platonic Forms: a variety of types or dimensions of intrinsic to-be-pursuedness. Mackie, of course, thinks that this is a problem for the moral objectivist, because he thinks that the whole idea of intrinsic to-be-pursuedness is hopelessly mysterious from a naturalistic point of view. No doubt it is; but that is so much the worse for naturalism, not so much the worse for intrinsic to-be-pursuedness. For naturalism itself presupposes intrinsic to-be-pursuedness. Naturalism, after all, is supposed to be *true*; and truth is a prime example of an end that we are not merely constituted to desire, but which (in Mackie's words) 'has to-be-pursuedness somehow built into it'.[2] So anyone who wants to use naturalism as a basis for raising Mackiean 'queerness' as a problem for the variety of goods that the pluralist proposes had better be prepared to raise queerness as a problem for the enterprise of naturalism itself.

4 Reasons

Practical reason is irreducibly polymorphous. Part of what it means to believe that is to believe in a variety of goods. But in fact there is more to the polymorphy of practical reason than the variety of the goods. For we may distinguish two sorts of practical reasons, which I shall call teleological and non-teleological.

Agents' teleological reasons are set by the basic goods. What these goods are is determined by the nature of objective moral reality; how we respond to them – whether we take these ends as our ends, or as central objectives in the constitution of our lives – is determined by our free choice.

Non-teleological reasons are the reasons that agents still have, no matter what goods there are (and hence no matter what teleological reasons there are). They too are determined by objective moral facts, though again the way we respond to them is a matter of choice for us.

Here is an example of the contrast between teleological and non-teleological reasons. Friendship is a *telos*, which entails that I have a practical reason to pursue friendship; and this reason is a teleological one. But I also have practical reason to pursue any end, including the good of friendship, efficiently. This reason does not derive from any good in particular. Since any good at all would need to be pursued efficiently, I would have this reason no matter what the goods were, and no matter which goods I recognised. Hence, this practical reason is non-teleological.

Some other examples of non-teleological practical reasons are second-order reasons, or reasons of still higher orders. For instance, I have a second-order practical reason to discover what the goods give me reason to do, and reason to do it once discovered. I also have a third-order practical reason to discover that I have reason to discover what the goods give me reason to do; and again I have a third-order practical reason to think that I have reason to do it once discovered. And so on. It does not appear that these higher-order reasons could derive from any of the basic goods themselves. Hence, these practical reasons too are non-teleological.

A third sort of non-teleological practical reason plays a key role in Kant's ethical theory, because it is a crucial working part in his argument for the categorical imperative. This is the reason that I have, no matter what my ends, to protect my own agency so that I can achieve whatever my ends are. Since 'no matter what my ends' is part of the definition of this sort of practical reason, it follows that we will have this sort of reason on any particular account of our ends, or of the goods. Here then will be a third sort of non-teleological practical reason.

The question of how non-teleological practical reasons interact, or should interact, with teleological ones is an interesting and complex one. I shall not be exploring it here. My concern is simply to point out that, although NLT is recognisably a teleological theory, still NLT is not committed to saying that all reasons are teleological reasons. This helps us to see a number of things. For example, it clarifies how NLT relates, or might fruitfully be related to, another very plausible ethical theory – Kantianism.

5 Incommensurability

Polymorphous goods give us polymorphous practical reasons. They give us reasons that simply cannot be combined by that murky consequentialist operation known as weighing goods (or reasons); nor by some more mathematically sophisticated form of combination, such as the construction of parallelograms of forces representing strengths of preference, vector-sums taking reasons as inputs, or indifference curves representing our attitudes to various mixes of outcome. Many social-choice theorists and welfare economists have tried to find an algorithm to give a formal mapping of the ins and outs of practical reason's responses to the variety of goods. The main fascination of such formal work, it seems to me, lies in its perennial and inevitable failure. Another interesting question is why anyone should ever have expected it to succeed; another again is what would count as success in this sort of work, and why that sort of success would be worth having.

So NLT is deeply committed to the incommensurability of the goods. But it is important to note what this commitment to incommensurability does and does not mean. It does not mean, for instance, that NLT is committed (like Taurek 1977) to saying that 'the numbers do not count'. If we treat the various goods as dimensions of normativity, as suggested in section 3 above, then we will see that NLT rationally favours (*ceteris paribus*) an action that does well in more of these dimensions to an action that does well in fewer of them – just as it is rational, other things being equal, to prefer an apple, an orange, and a banana to an apple and an orange (because the latter choice gives you everything the former choice gives you, and something else as well). It is too early, at this stage, to say exactly what the rationality of this preference implies for problematic rescue cases such as those considered by Taurek (though I hope to have shed more light on this sort of question by the end of the chapter). But at any rate we can say with some assurance that the rationality of that preference does not imply commensurability. Obviously no one who prefers more kinds of fruit to fewer is rationally obliged to think that apples, oranges, and bananas all represent the same sort of value. Likewise, NLT's preference for doing well in more dimensions rather than fewer in no way implies that NLT takes the goods to be reducible to a single good, or measurable against each other in any way at all.

On the other hand, NLT neither needs, nor is particularly helped by, incommensurability in the strict sense often used by the formal theorists. In this sense two goods G1 and G2 are incommensurable if and only if there is no fact of the matter as to whether G1 is of more value than G2, G2 is of more value than G1, or G1 and G2 are equal in value. In general, NLT does not at all subscribe to this sort of view: there is nothing in NLT to stop us saying that one good is more important than another. (For example: Noughts and Crosses, as a game, is a good, because it is an instance of the good of play. But it is patently a less important good than life, or truth, or knowledge.) Nor, similarly, is NLT debarred from saying that two goods are equally important. (So, for example, your life is no less important a good than mine.)

The kinds of commensurability that NLT really needs to resist are two. One is strict numerical comparability, of the kind that is involved in consequentialist arithmetic. NLT can allow that different goods are equal in importance, or that they differ in importance; what it cannot allow is the fantasy that there is a cardinal-numerical way of modelling the different grades of importance. (Or, come to that, a complete ordinal ranking of the goods and their instances. Some value-relations really are indeterminate, though others are not. It is a fact that Noughts and Crosses and Snap are both less important goods than the good of life. But, it seems to me, there's no fact of the matter whether Noughts and Crosses is more, less, or equal in importance compared with Snap.)

The other kind of commensurability that NLT should resist is additivity. Roughly but vividly, this is the idea that, for example, twenty lives taken together make, not twenty different goods each of which is as important as a single life, but a single good which is twenty times as important (weighs twenty times as much) as the good of the single life. For NLT to resist additivity is for it to deny that the rescuer choosing between rescuing twenty people and rescuing a single person has one reason to rescue the twenty, and one reason to rescue the one, and that his reason to rescue the twenty is twenty times as strong as his reason to rescue the one. This way of talking is tempting, no doubt, and much damage has resulted from giving in to the temptation. But the truth – which NLT can capture – is that the rescuer has twenty reasons to rescue the twenty where he has only one reason to rescue the one. (Compare the point made above about choosing between an apple, an orange, and a banana on the one hand, and an apple and an orange on the other.) His reasons to rescue the twenty still win out. But they do not win out by outweighing his reason to rescue the one, so much as by out-arguing it. Reasons are not additive, and they do not come in weights; the way in which they compete with each other is rational, not mechanical. It has the structure of an argument or a narrative – not the structure of a weighing operation.

The crucial importance of NLT's attitude to different kinds of commensurability and incommensurability is nowhere more evident than when we turn to my fifth clarification, which concerns the notion of violation.

6 Violation and respect

How do you tell a consequentialist from a natural law theorist? By looking at what they do to the goods they are *not* pursuing.

You could accept a good deal of the framework of NLT and still be a (moderate, liberal) consequentialist. Of course, many consequentialists in fact deny such theses of NLT as the claim that there is a plurality of goods, and that rational agents often have freedom of choice as to which of the goods in that plurality they are going to pursue on any particular occasion. But at least *prima facie*, there is no obvious reason why a consequentialist has to reject these theses. The main thesis of NLT that a consequentialist *must* reject is the thesis that when you are not pursuing a good, then you must respect or honour that good, and must not violate or dishonour it.

So it is that this thesis – which for brevity I will call 'Respect', or 'the Respect thesis' – becomes the key issue in the dispute between NLT and the consequentialists. Accordingly, my aim in the rest of this chapter is to vindicate NLT against consequentialism by defending the Respect thesis. In the process, I hope to shed some light on the crucial but rather mysterious terms 'honour', 'respect', and 'violate'. Maybe I can even shed light on the still more mysterious phraseology that Germain Grisez, John Finnis, and other natural law theorists sometimes use to spell out 'honour', 'respect', and 'violate', as for instance when they tell us that any agent must not 'impede, damage or destroy' any unpursued good (Grisez 1983: 216–17), or that any agent must not 'act directly against' any unpursued good (Finnis 1980: 123), and must instead 'remain open' to that good (Grisez 1993: 635).

Why then must a consequentialist reject Respect? Here are three reasons. First, as already pointed out, Respect is clearly a standard foundation for the standard variety of historically recognised absolute moral prohibitions; and the consequentialist has no place in his theory for these absolutes. (Unless he is a rule consequentialist; and even then, the role that he gives these absolutes is an instrumental one, quite different from their constitutive role in the absolutist tradition that the consequentialist instinctively opposes.)

Second, the consequentialist will reject Respect because he will think that Respect succumbs to a 'vacuously true or substantively false' dilemma. As he sees it, 'respecting a good that you are not pursuing' can only mean factoring into the moral sum the cost of not pursuing that good, and of whatever you do to that good instead of pursuing it. But under consequentialism, this moral cost is factored in *anyway*. The moral sum in question is the one that leads you to pursue some other good. And all costs to other goods are automatically factored into that sum. That's what consequentialist moral calculation is like – it is comprehensive.

So to the consequentialist, 'respecting a good' can only mean 'not pursuing it, whilst pursuing some other good with the consequentialist's usual synoptic caution about resultant costs'. For this reason, the consequentialist will conclude that there are only two alternatives. Either there is no content to the idea of respect for goods that is not already captured by the idea of pursuit of goods. In this case the Respect thesis turns out true, but already fully accounted for elsewhere in the consequentialist's theory. Or else there is more to the idea of respect – a content that is not captured by the notion of pursuit. In that case, the consequentialist will want to know what more there is to respect, and is unlikely to be satisfied by the likeliest answers.

For consequentialists are proud of the clean-cut simplicity of their theory:

> Non-consequentialists all commit themselves to the view that certain values should be honoured...But they all agree...that certain other values should be promoted...Thus where consequentialists introduce a single axiom on how values justify choices, non-consequentialists must introduce two.
>
> But not only is non-consequentialism less simple for losing the numbers game. It is also less simple for playing the game in an *ad hoc* way. Non-consequentialists all identify certain values as suitable for honouring rather than promoting. But they do not generally explain what it is about the values identified which means that justification comes from their being honoured rather than promoted...Not only do [non-consequentialists] have a duality then where consequentialists have a unity: they also have an unexplained duality. (Pettit 1991: 238)

This is the third reason why consequentialists will reject the Respect thesis. They see it as an unnecessary and unhelpful complication of practical rationality to say, as non-consequentialists do, that there are two ways of responding to values – pursuit and respect. (As my quotation shows, Pettit's own terms are 'promotion' and 'honouring'; the terminology can be varied *ad libertatem*, though we shall need in section 7 to enter a *caveat* about what Pettit means by his terms.) All the work that needs to be done, according to the consequentialists, is done by the notion of pursuit and its negation. Insofar as it does not simply reduce to the notion of pursuit and its negation, the notion of respect is therefore surplus to theoretical requirements.

What is most striking about this consequentialist critique of NLT's Respect thesis is the way it takes for granted the notion of a *moral sum*. Consequentialists routinely talk of factoring into a single sum a variety of moral costs and moral gains, and producing a single practical verdict as the output of that sum. Provided this makes sense, the consequentialist will be right to say that there is no separate content to the notion of respecting goods. Hence he will also be right to say that everything we need to do in ethics and the theory of practical reason can be done by way of the single notion of pursuing goods. In which case the Respect thesis will have been proved false. We will also have the results that moral absolutes cannot be grounded by appealing to Respect (recall the consequentialist's first reason for opposing Respect), and that the consequentialist's tidy way of responding to values is preferable to the non-consequentialist's untidy way (recall the consequentialist's third reason).

So all of these issues depend on the intelligibility of talk of moral sums. I have argued in section 5 that such talk is *not* intelligible, because of the kind of plurality that is true of the goods. The central point to make in defence of the Respect thesis is that the goods are incommensurable. That is why we need the Respect thesis – as the exchange with the consequentialist that I have just reviewed makes clear. It is because the goods are incommensurable that there is more to respecting goods than not pursuing them. This is why it is not untidiness but theoretical necessity that leads NLT to posit two attitudes to the goods, respect and pursuit, not merely one, promotion. And that in turn explains why NLT has a good theoretical basis for the constraints that it proposes.

7 An ambiguity about honouring goods

This is enough to explain the place and purpose of the notion of violation within NLT. It is also enough, incidentally, to show how different NLT's notion of 'respect' or 'honour' for goods is from some other notions of respect/honour that have been influential recently.

In particular – and this is a point that I perhaps did not stress enough in Chappell (2001b) – NLT's conception of honouring is completely different from the conception that seems to be the main target in Pettit (1991). Pettit's target is a conception of honouring that pretty well identifies the honouring/promoting distinction with the agent-relative/agent-neutral distinction. As the point is put in McNaughton and Rawling (1992: 837):

[Pettit's] distinction between honouring and promoting a value translates naturally into our distinction between agent-relative and agent-neutral rules. Take the example of honesty, or the slightly more complex one of loyalty to friends. [Where S stands in for 'ceteris paribus, should ensure that', and x, y and z are variables ranging over agents, we can state two pairs of rules relating to these two values, as follows:]

AR $\quad \forall x \, (xS \, [x \text{ is honest}])$ (1)

AN $\quad \forall x \, (xS \, [(\forall y \, (y \text{ is honest}))])$ (2)

AR $\quad \forall x \, (xS \, [\forall y \, (y \text{ is } x\text{'s friend} \rightarrow x \text{ is loyal to } y)])$ (3)

AN $\quad \forall x \, (xS \, [\forall y \forall z \, (z \text{ is } y\text{'s friend} \rightarrow y \text{ is loyal to } z)])$ (4)

McNaughton and Rawling's Rule (1) tells each agent to ensure that he himself is honest. So Rule (1) is agent-relative – it is a rule telling us to honour the good of honesty. Rule (2), by contrast, tells each agent to ensure that agents in general are honest. So Rule (2) is agent-neutral – it is a rule telling us to promote the good of honesty. Again, Rule (3) tells each agent to ensure that he himself is loyal to anyone who is his friend. So Rule (3) is agent-relative – it is a rule telling us to honour the good of loyalty. Rule (4), by contrast, tells each agent to ensure that agents in general are loyal to those who are their friends. So Rule (4) is agent-neutral – it is a rule telling us to promote the good of loyalty.

This description makes it crystal clear that the McNaughton/Rawling/ Pettit distinction between promoting and honouring goods is nothing like NLT's distinction between pursuing and honouring (or respecting) goods. NLT's distinction certainly cannot be identified with the agent-relative/agent-neutral distinction; for the attitudes to goods that NLT calls 'pursuing' and 'respecting' are *both* agent-relative attitudes. For me to pursue a good is to ensure that *I* go after it; for me to honour a good is for me to ensure that *I* do not violate it. In this sense, for NLT all the ethics that matters is agent-relative.

This means that NLT has a simple answer to Philip Pettit's charge that non-consequentialism switches in an *ad hoc* way between two alternative responses, responding in an agent-relative way to some goods (by honouring them) and in an agent-neutral way to others (by promoting them). The answer is that NLT is not guilty of this ad-hockery, because NLT says that *all* responses to the goods should be agent-relative ones. True, NLT recognises a certain amount of 'play', a certain scope for the ungoverned and unpredictable judgement-call, between respecting and pursuing goods. But this is not ad-hockery: it is the agent's freedom.

This is one reason why pursuing goods is sharply distinct from promoting them. Promotion is, in any case, a maximising attitude, and falls within the ambit of the criticisms of maximisation that I offered in section 2. But that is not the only thing wrong with promotion. A second and equally disabling problem for the concept of promotion comes out clearly when we consider what McNaughton and Rawling call 'agent-neutral' rules. NLT rejects the very idea of such rules as a striking absurdity – and, we may add, a characteristically consequentialist absurdity. How could it possibly be a moral rule worth my trying to act on, let alone a rule that I could possibly allow to override the agent-relative rules, that I should 'ensure, other things being equal, that agents in general are honest'? Why do not I wish for the moon while I am at it? It is barely possible to take such formulations as rules for the individual agent, rather than as mere vapid aspirations. If they tell us anything concrete at all, they seem to tell us mainly to be pathologically addicted to minding other people's business.

8 The content of the notion of violation

In section 6 my main objective was to explain the theoretical point of the notions of violation and respect of goods. In section 7 I distinguished NLT's notion of respecting or honouring goods from the conception, visible in the work of McNaughton, Rawling, and Pettit, that closely aligns the honouring/promoting distinction with the agent-relative/agent-neutral distinction.

Now the place of the concept of violation in NLT is one thing – the extension of that concept is quite another. According to NLT, exactly what counts as a violation of any good, and why? This, of course, is a huge and difficult question in itself, and I cannot hope to answer it comprehensively here. All the same, in this section I shall round off the chapter by offering some brief remarks about how NLT might answer it.

First remark: one paradigmatic way of violating a good is often to destroy it or its instances, or to attempt to destroy it. So, for example, intentionally and directly killing people is wrong because killing people is destroying them,[3] and people are individual goods. (More about 'intentionally and directly' under my fifth remark.)

Second remark: different goods are violated in different ways. For some goods it seems implausible, or overstretched, to talk of actions violating them at all. How do you act so as to violate the good of Noughts and Crosses, or haute cuisine? And why would it matter much if you did? In these cases the idea of actions of violation seems absurd. What seems less absurd is the idea that there might be attitudes or dispositions that violate such goods (cf. Chappell 1998: 85–6). A general churlishness, puritanism or boorishness, for example, might be an absolutely wrong way to be as a person, even if no particular action expressing that vice is itself absolutely wrong.

Third remark: there may be (instances of) less important goods such that, in an emergency, their violation is justified if it will save (an instance of) a more important good. My first remark makes it plausible to think that destroying the *Mona Lisa* is a violation of the wonderful aesthetic good that that picture represents. So what should you do when the crazed art-hater tells you to rip it up, or he will rip your daughter up with his twelve-inch knife? Probably, you should rip it up.

Destroying the *Mona Lisa* is a terrible and irreversible act of artistic sacrilege. On the other hand, if you do not do it then your daughter will die; and arguably, the *Mona Lisa* is a less important good than the good instantiated by the individual human life of your daughter.

Whether or not that is the right answer in this particular case, it does help to make clear a general pattern of permissive argument that may be evoked by 'the *Mona Lisa* problem', as I call it. The idea is that because some goods are more important than others, sufficiently dreadful circumstances can justify – not merely *what would otherwise be* violation of the less important good but – *actual* violation of the less important good. That, I think, is importantly right – provided we do not try to extend the point to cases where equally important goods are at stake – as, for instance, in choices between human lives.

This point about emergency circumstances brings me to my

Fourth remark: what counts as a violation of any good is contextually determined – to a degree. It is tempting and natural to think that context ought to make a difference to what counts as a violation. In some ways this is true. I have just explored one way it is true under my third remark; I shall explore another under my fifth. It is not true, however, that what counts as a violation is *solely* contextually determined. There are general facts about our behaviour that provide general, and not merely particular, answers to the question, 'What is this agent doing?' And, I believe, it is in each case this general answer that is the starting point for moral assessment.

More about that under my

Fifth remark: the action/omission distinction (AOD) and the principle of double effect (PDE) are both crucial in defining exactly what counts as a violation, and why. The whole idea of NLT is that there is a difference between failing to promote (or better, pursue) a good and violating it – a difference that consequentialism is characteristically unable to accommodate. AOD and PDE play a crucial role in explaining how this can be so, because they are central to NLT's explanation of how it is that an agent can fail to aim at a given good, can even indeed exact a high cost from that good, without in any way being 'opposed' to it or setting himself up to 'attack' it.

In NLT, the agent has a certain freedom as to how he treats any of the goods that he is not aiming at in a given action. But only up to a point: there are limits to what he can do to those non-pursued goods, limits set by the concept of violation. This makes it an interesting question for NLT exactly where these limits are. And the answer to that is going to depend on how clear it is that our actions are directed against those goods, where the way to decide whether an action is more or less, or not at all, 'directed against' some good will be to examine how the conditions of actionhood apply to this action.

But – as I have argued elsewhere (Chappell 2002) – AOD and PDE are precisely philosophical theses about the conditions of actionhood. For AOD claims that actions incur a higher degree of actionhood (and hence of responsibility) than omissions do, while PDE claims that actions incur a higher degree of actionhood (and hence of responsibility) under those descriptions under which they were intended than under non-intended descriptions. So the question how the conditions of actionhood and responsibility apply to a given human performance involves – not exclusively, but centrally – the question whether or not that performance falls within the scope of PDE, or AOD, or both. Hence, the question whether a given performance is or is not a violation will often need to be referred for adjudication to PDE and AOD.

We can see some examples of how this sort of adjudication may go if we turn to my sixth and final remark in this last section:

Sixth remark: PDE and some problem cases.[4] Consider the following:

1. *Injection*: The doctor injects a lethal dose of painkiller into the terminally ill patient, saying that he foresees but does not intend the patient's death.
2. *Cargo*: To prevent shipwreck, the ship's captain throws the cargo overboard in the storm, saying that he foresees but does not intend the loss of the cargo.
3. *Virgin*: To avoid rape, a devout virgin jumps out of a fifth-storey window, saying that she foresees but does not intend her own death.
4. *Hysterectomy*: A doctor removes the cancerous womb of a pregnant woman, saying that he foresees but does not intend the unborn infant's death.
5. *Bridge*: A general orders the blowing up of a bridge to prevent an enemy army's advance, saying that he foresees but does not intend the deaths of the civilians on the bridge.
6. *Tactical Bomber*: The air force commander orders the bombing of an armaments factory which is next to a primary school, saying that he foresees but does not intend the deaths of the children at that school.
7. *Craniotomy*: Attending a difficult and dangerous confinement, the doctor crushes the skull of the infant to prevent the mother from dying along with her infant. The surgeon says that he foresees but does not intend the infant's death.

Proponents of PDE claim to see differences between these stories as to what counts in each case as a means or an end on the one side, and an unintended side-effect on the other. A critic might rejoin that there is no important distinction of that sort to be drawn in these cases (assuming, which many critics deny, that a distinction can be drawn at all). All seven agents profess to be distinguishing what they intend from what they foresee; and all seven agents, according to PDE's critics, might as well be allowed this claim. If there are moral differences between the seven cases – as of course there surely are – they do not rest on PDE. And this, the critics say, shows the theoretical inefficacy of that venerable distinction.

This criticism can be answered. Showing how will help to support my claim that we need PDE to make sense of the details of what counts as a violation of any good. The right answer to the criticism begins by stating, briefly, an account of intention. What is it to intend X and not Z by doing Y?

The answer to this is complicated, because there are *two* distinctions that are relevant here. First, as noted elsewhere in this book by Mark C. Murphy (and by me in Chappell 2002), there is a distinction between the action-description under which you do the act, and any other description that may be true of it. Secondly, however, there is a distinction between whatever is *normally causally separable* from the act that you do, and whatever is not so separable.

Going with the first distinction, you can say that you intend X and not Z by doing Y simply because the action-description under which you act intentionally is 'to do X by doing Y', and is not 'to do Z by doing Y' (or 'to do X and Z by doing Y' – or any formulation that includes doing Z). Going with the second distinction, however, you will intend *both* X and Z by doing Y just so long as X and Z are both normally causally inseparable from Y.[5]

Both distinctions have advantages and disadvantages. The first distinction has the advantage of intuitiveness when we are introspecting. If I set my mind to switching the light on, then it just does not seem right to say that I intend *both* to switch the light on *and* to increase present electricity consumption, even though I know perfectly well that that increase is normally causally inseparable from my switching the light on. After all, *many* things will be normally causally inseparable from my switching the light on; but I surely cannot have them *all* in mind when I go ahead and switch on the light. So, the idea is, I cannot be intending them all. And to say that I *do* intend them all – even if, so to speak, I do not mean to – has an air of paradox about it.

On the other hand, there are cases where almost exactly that paradoxical thing is what we find ourselves wanting to say; and the second distinction gives us a way of saying it. Suppose that I, being of sound mind, put a bullet through your head. I protest that my mind is set only on putting a bullet through your head to test the trigger mechanism on my handgun, even though I know perfectly well that your death is normally causally inseparable from my putting a bullet through your head. In this case, surely, we have a strong inclination to say that I kill you intentionally by putting a bullet through your head – *even if* it is true that the action-description under which I act is that of testing the gun by putting a bullet through your head, and not that of testing the gun by killing you.

The first distinction provides us with a close and introspective criterion of what it is to intend something; the second gives us a less proximate and external criterion. Which should we use? I think there is something to be said for using both. For it is undeniable that the first criterion captures more accurately the difference in direction of fit between intention and foresight; but it is also undeniable that the second criterion disallows certain claims about what someone intends that we are likely to think *ought* to be disallowed. For example, in my bullet-through-the-head case, we do not just want to say that the death of the victim is something that the killer is merely negligent for not foreseeing. Rather, we want to say that the killer's intention is – at least in one sense – an intention to kill.

More broadly, the fact that these two distinctions can both be made about intention suggests that there are subtleties here that *ought* to be recognised in a decent theory of responsibility. Perhaps what we should suggest is that there are two levels of actionhood which should be distinguished here – and hence two levels of responsibility (see Chappell 2002). There will be cases where a plausible appeal to PDE involves saying that one is acting under one description but not another even though the two descriptions are normally causally inseparable; there will also be cases where a plausible appeal to PDE only invokes normal causal separability. At the level of the first distinction, we may say that X is intended in the strongest sense when X is part of the agent's plan of action. At the level of the second distinction, we may say that X is intended in a weaker sense when it is normally causally inseparable from all or part of the agent's plan of action.

It is a simple matter of introspection to test whether X is intended in this first sense. ('A simple matter' – or at least, a *relatively* simple matter. Which is not to say that there cannot be deception, including self-deception, about what one intends.) As for the test for the second sense of intention, I want to suggest that it can be stated something like this:

> A intends X and not Z by doing Y iff Y is not normally causally separable from X, whereas Y is normally causally separable from Z.

So where X, Y and Z are three action-types, and doing X is not normally causally separable from doing Y, but doing Z is: if you intentionally do Y (either as an end or as a means), then you also intentionally do X (either as an end or as a means); but you do not (necessarily) intentionally do Z.

Are these the right criteria? We might test them by applying them to the seven problem cases described above. When we do this, obviously the first criterion will, in each case, give the result that PDE applies. This result is guaranteed simply by the fact that, for example, 'injecting painkiller' and 'giving a lethal injection' are different descriptions, and can therefore, by the first test, *automatically* be the objects of different intentions. But as noted, the trouble with the first test is that it seems to make *too many* action-descriptions distinct from each other. So how does the second criterion fare? Well, it seems, at least, to do some of the work that needs doing:

1. *Injection*: Injecting painkiller is normally causally separable from giving a lethal injection. So when you intentionally inject the painkiller, it does not have to be that you intentionally give a lethal injection by that very act. There is therefore scope in this case for the application of PDE.

   (*Caveat*: *Scope*, I said: I did not say straight out that PDE *justifies* the doctor's action. Whether it will or not depends on other factors in the context, such as the proportionality of the intended act to the known but not-intended side-effect. The same *caveat* will apply to all of these seven cases.)
2. *Cargo*: Throwing the cargo overboard is not normally causally separable from losing the cargo. So when you intentionally jettison the cargo, it does have to be that you intentionally lose the cargo. Hence there is no scope for PDE in this case: if the captain is justified in jettisoning the cargo (as he presumably is), it is not PDE that justifies him.
3. *Virgin*: Jumping out of a fifth-storey window is not normally causally separable from killing yourself. Hence there is no scope for PDE here; if the virgin's action is justified, it is not justified by PDE.

4. *Hysterectomy*: Removing a cancerous womb is normally causally separable from abortion. So there is scope for PDE here.
5. *Bridge*: Blowing up a bridge to prevent an enemy army's advance is normally causally separable from blowing up civilians. So there is scope for PDE here too.
   Likewise,
6. *Tactical Bomber*: Bombing an armaments factory is normally causally separable from bombing a primary school. Again, there is scope for PDE here.
   And, finally,
7. *Craniotomy*: Crushing an infant's skull is not normally causally separable from killing the infant. Hence there is no scope for PDE here; if such an action is justified, it is not justified by PDE.[6]

In these verdicts the notion of 'normal causal separability' is crucial: it is this that sets the reasonable limits on what anyone can legitimately claim to be intending, or not intending, in anything that they do. But of course the criterion is a difficult one to apply. In particular, why – you might ask – should the criterion be the general one of *normal* causal separability? Why not the particular criterion of causal separability *in this case*?

The answer lies in the point I made in my fourth remark above. We morally assess actions as falling into fairly broad types. These types are, at least, the bedrock of our moral assessments: it is only on the foundation of that bedrock that the complexities and exceptions can get built in. It is not even possible to begin moral assessment by looking at the particular case, without seeing first what kind of case it is in general – unless perhaps you have a complete calculus of consequences to hand, which no one has.

As Crisp (2001) points out in a deft critique of particularism, an all-out holism of reasons simply makes moral assessment impossible, because it makes the subject-matter of moral assessment unintelligibly homogeneous. The only way to draw moral verdicts out of such homogeneity, so far as I can see, is the act-consequentialist way. But I do not need to argue here that that is not an acceptable way out for the particularist, or indeed for anyone else.

Another question about the second distinction's verdicts on the problem cases is this: 'Why these action descriptions (e.g. "blowing up civilians") and not others (e.g. "blowing up civilians on a bridge that the enemy will shortly use")? Doesn't everything hang on which action descriptions you pick?'

The answer is yes; but I have no answer to offer to the extremely difficult question of how to give a canonical regimentation of such descriptions. In fact, I suspect that there is no such regimentation, beyond what intuition can tell us. (If so, this has the uncomfortable but unsurprising consequence that there must be cases which are indeterminate for PDE. The consequence is, of course, not lethal: indeterminacy somewhere is not the same as determinacy nowhere.)

However, insofar as I have an answer here, it is the same point again: analysis of action has to start with broad types. As I have shown, though, it does not have to end with them. In the framework that NLT provides, the analysis of action can become very particular indeed: we can find ways of justifying very fine-grained verdicts about what counts as a violation of any good, and what does not. In this context, what may well happen sometimes is that we find ourselves falling back from the 'external' way of drawing the PDE distinction to the 'internal' way. In so falling back, we may be acknowledging a higher level of responsibility; but perhaps such a fall-back is inevitable in some cases.

Of course, it is just this fine-grainedness of judgement – and just this propensity for finding fall-back positions – that has itself often excited the critics' impatience with the proponents of NLT and with arguments that they have put forward about particular cases. And sometimes justifiably (see the Grisez quotation in note 6); but overall the verdict is surely unfair. The fact that NLT has so much to tell us, not only about the theoretical place of the notion of violations of the good but also about the content of that notion, is no handicap to the theory. Rather, it is another evidence of its richness – a richness that I hope this chapter has demonstrated in at least five different respects.

Notes

1. What would justify such a belief? Not an appeal to experience ('This type of action was the best option in the past'). Even if an action of this type worked *well* in the past, my argument shows that the agent cannot know (or justifiably believe) that it was the *best* option in the past. Nor an appeal to computation costs ('This option is very probably the best that I am going to find without searching for a better one for an unfeasibly long time; *therefore* it is the best'). As before, there is no reason to think that the agent knows the probabilities involved (or has justified belief about them), precisely because the agent *could not* have such knowledge (or belief) without *already* having access to at least some information about which options really do maximise.
2. For more on this, see Finnis (1977).
3. Not all believers in life after death need to deny the claim that 'killing people is destroying them'. The Christian doctrine of the Resurrection, for example,

can be understood as the doctrine that God miraculously *reverses* the destruction of people that is involved in their deaths.
4. Thanks to Antony Duff, Gerard J. Hughes and David S. Oderberg for discussion of these cases.
5. Note that my distinction between two senses of intentional action is quite different from that made by Kamm (2000), who distinguishes 'doing something in order to bring about an effect' from 'doing something because we will bring about an effect'. In any case, I am sceptical about the moral significance of Kamm's distinction.
6. *Pace* the grisly procrusteanism of Grisez (1993: 502): 'the baby's death need not be included in the proposal adopted in choosing to do a craniotomy. The proposal can be simply to alter the child's physical dimensions....'

References

Anscombe, G.E.M. (1957) *Intention*, Cambridge, MA: Harvard UP.
Chappell, T.D.J. (1998) *Understanding Human Goods*, Edinburgh: Edinburgh UP.
Chappell, T.D.J. (2001a) 'Option Ranges', *Journal of Applied Philosophy* 18: 107–18.
Chappell, T.D.J. (2001b) 'A Way Out of Pettit's Dilemma', *Philosophical Quarterly* 51: 95–9.
Chappell, T.D.J. (2002) 'Two Distinctions that Do Make a Difference: The Action/Omission Distinction and the Principle of Double Effect', *Philosophy* 77: 211–34.
Chappell, T.D.J. (2003) 'Practical Rationality for Pluralists about the Good', *Ethical Theory and Moral Practice* 6: 161–77.
Crisp, R. (2001) 'Particularising Particularism', in B. Hooker and M.O. Little (eds), *Moral Particularism*, Oxford: OUP, 23–47.
Davidson, D. (1980) 'How is Weakness of the Will Possible?', in his *Essays on Actions and Events*, Oxford: Clarendon Press, 21–42.
Finnis, J.M. (1977) 'Scepticism, Self-Refutation, and the Good of Truth', in P.M.S. Hacker and J. Raz (eds), *Law, Morality, and Society*, Oxford: Clarendon Press.
Finnis, J. (1980) *Natural Law and Natural Rights*, Oxford: OUP.
Griffin, J. (1986) *Well Being*, Oxford: OUP.
Grisez, G. (1983) *Christian Moral Principles*, Quincy, Illinois: Franciscan Press.
Grisez, G. (1993) *Living a Christian Life*, Quincy, Illinois: Franciscan Press.
Kamm, F. (2000) 'The Doctrine of Triple Effect and Why a Rational Agent Need Not Intend the Means to His End', *Aristotelian Society Supp.* 74: 21–39.
Mackie, J.L. (1977) *Ethics: Inventing Right and Wrong*, Harmondsworth: Penguin.
McNaughton, D. and Rawling, P. (1992) 'Honouring and Promoting Values', *Ethics* 102: 835–43.
Pettit, P. (1991) 'Consequentialism', in Peter Singer (ed.), *A Companion to Ethics*, Oxford: Blackwell, 230–40.
Pollock, J. (1983) 'How Do You Maximise Expectation Value?', *Noûs* 17: 409–21.
Railton, P. (1984) 'Alienation, Consequentialism, and the Demands of Morality', *Philosophy and Public Affairs* 13: 134–71; reprinted in S. Scheffler (ed.), *Consequentialism and its Critics*, Oxford: OUP, 1988, 93–133.
Rawls, J. (1971) *A Theory of Justice*, Oxford: OUP.
Ross, D. (1930) *The Right and the Good*, Oxford: OUP.

Sorensen, R. (1994) 'Infinite Decision Theory', in Jeffrey Jordan (ed.), *Gambling on God: Essays on Pascal's Wager*, Savage, Maryland: Rowman & Littlefield, 139–59.

Taurek, J.M. (1977) 'Should the Numbers Count?', *Philosophy and Public Affairs* 6: 293–316; reprinted in J.M. Fischer and M. Ravizza (eds), *Ethics*, New York: Harcourt, 1992, 214–27.

Thomson, J.J. (1990) *The Realm of Rights*, Cambridge, MA: Harvard UP.

6
The Structure and Content of the Good

David S. Oderberg

1 Introduction

One of the virtues of natural law theory (NLT) is that it takes ontology seriously. Rather than beginning with an abstract conception of duty, or of motivation, or of value, or of character, it takes the objective and concrete nature of things, of human beings in particular, as the explanatory starting point of ethical enquiry. In this is precisely the flaw that its opponents claim to detect, inasmuch as NLT is charged with making implausible assumptions about human nature – its existence, let alone its features – or about the fundamentally teleological character of action, or about the existence of cosmic order.

As with any ethical theory confronting objections to its foundational doctrines, NLT can face such charges head-on or else in an indirect fashion. Indirectly, it can show how the working out of the theory from that foundational basis yields results that are coherent in themselves and also with our deepest moral convictions (to the extent that these can still be identified in our current, conceptually fragmented society), as well as offering resolutions of core problems common to all ethical investigation and avoiding others that specifically attend rival theories. Meeting such requirements will constitute indirect proof that the ontology on which NLT is based is a plausible one. Typically, NL theorists use a combination of direct and indirect argument, but there is inevitable bias in favour of one method or other.

On the whole, the new generation of NL theorists that has arisen in the wake of John Finnis and Germain Grisez seems more inclined to an indirect method of argument for the plausibility of the NL ontology. In particular, they have generally approached it from the motivational side, as it were: by understanding the intelligibility of acting for the sake of some end, for instance, the theorist argues for that end as an intrinsic, and therefore basic, good. Arguments that proceed directly from a consideration of essence or function, on the other hand, tend to take a back seat.[1] This *agent-centred* approach, as I call it, is an essential component of the case for NLT. There is also, however, what I call a *world-centred* approach, and this tends to be the hallmark of the historic NL tradition, in particular the thought of scholastic philosophers, notably St Thomas Aquinas. For these thinkers – the generalization is risky, but on the whole accurate – objective features of the world are the starting point for arguments to the necessary structure of human motivation and of the obligations, rights, virtues, and other moral phenomena on which that motivation depends.

One of the central ways in which the historic world-centred approach must differ from a contemporary approach of the same kind is that it is no longer dialectically possible to take as self-evident many of the elements of ontology that were self-evident to theorists of a past age. The existence of human nature is perhaps the most obvious example. Hence a comprehensive, contemporary restatement and defence of NLT requires its adherents not to shirk from their metaphysical responsibilities, making use too of the full range of data available from anthropology, biology, psychology, and other relevant sciences. My aim in this chapter, however, is far more limited. Taking a broadly world-centred approach, I want to examine some of the current disputed questions in NLT, and these fall into two distinct but overlapping categories: questions as to the *content* of the natural law, in particular the identity of the basic goods; and questions as to the *structure* of the natural law, in particular those concerning whether there is a hierarchy of basic goods, whether there is a supreme (or, as Mark C. Murphy calls it, superordinate) good, and the nature of the relationship between the basic and the non-basic goods.

The field of enquiry that has been opened up by contemporary NLT is rich and sure to yield robust fruit. NL theorists can be proud of having put back on the map a theory that, for analytical philosophers, was only a few decades ago barely worth consideration. The following discussion, then, is proposed as a limited contribution to that burgeoning and fertile debate.

2   Questions of content

All NL theorists begin with a conception of the basic goods as the foundation of morality. It is both surprising and satisfying (given the state of contemporary ethical theory) to observe the extent to which they agree on just what those basic goods are. Here are some examples:

- John Finnis: Life; knowledge; play; aesthetic experience; friendship; religion; practical reasonableness.[2]
- Alfonso Gómez-Lobo: Life; the family; friendship; work and play; the experience of beauty; knowledge; integrity.[3]
- Timothy Chappell: Life; truth, and the knowledge of the truth; friendship; aesthetic value; physical and mental health and harmony; pleasure and the avoidance of pain; reason, rationality, and reasonableness; the natural world; people; fairness; achievements; the contemplation of God (if God exists).[4]
- Mark C. Murphy: Life; knowledge; aesthetic experience; excellence in play and work; excellence in agency; inner peace; friendship and community; religion; happiness.[5]
- In my book *Moral Theory* I gave: Life; knowledge; friendship; work and play; the appreciation of beauty; religious belief and practice.[6]

All of the above theorists, myself included, agree that life, knowledge, friendship, and aesthetic experience are on the list. This is encouraging, but there is also quite a bit of disagreement. It is unrealistic to expect all NL theorists to agree on all of the basic goods, but it is desirable that as much agreement be reached as possible. As a foray in that direction, I want to focus first on what seem to me to be several important areas in which theorists differ, both those cited and others.

2.1 Pleasure and the avoidance of pain

Natural law theorists tend not to place pleasure and/or the avoidance of pain on the list of basic goods. Although this is correct, they also do not often explore just why pleasure should be absent. (Henceforth I use the term 'pleasure' as shorthand for 'pleasure and/or the avoidance of pain.') Moreover, Timothy Chappell does put pleasure on his list of basic goods.[7] He claims that an action can be fully intelligible solely in virtue of its being performed for the sake of experiencing pleasure (his example is that of smelling the coffee in a delicatessen) or avoiding pain (his example being that of taking an aspirin to get rid of a headache).

To see why this view is mistaken we must look at the way pleasure and pain have to be integrated into moral ontology. The first thing to note is that Chappell concedes that if pleasure is to be a basic good, it can only be either the pure physical sensation or else psychic or mental delight ('a mood or an emotion'[8]), since the other possible senses of 'pleasure' are too vague or heterogeneous. We can agree on the latter point but also go further. For there is no *faculty* of pleasure as such, by which I mean no *active power* of enjoyment (or aversion) as such, as opposed to enjoyment of this or that thing or activity; and this applies also to bodily or psychic feelings. The point can be brought out by contrast with the good of knowledge. There is a faculty of knowledge as such because there is a single genus of object to which knowledge is directed, namely truth. The NL theorist affirms that truth as such is good, which is why knowledge is good. (Sometimes the NL theorist refers to the pursuit and acquisition of truth, or of understanding, instead of knowledge, but there is no harm in this.) There is no sense to be made of a *bad* truth, as opposed to an unpleasant, awkward, trivial truth, and the like. The same applies to goods such as life and friendship, or beauty.

When it comes to pleasure, the matter is different. There is no such thing as pursuit of pleasure *as such* – not even the hedonist strictly pursues pleasure as such, but pleasure in *certain kinds of activity*, in his case mainly the carnal pleasures. The very fact that we have to divide pleasures into bodily and mental shows that there is no human ability or active power directed at pleasure in itself, but rather that pleasure is divided up among and accompanies the use of other powers, such as reason, sense, will, appetite, emotion, and so on. So it is true to say that 'pleasure is but the accompaniment of the normal exercise of abilities which exist for the accomplishment of some other purpose.'[9]

We cannot, though, postulate *activity* as the genus of object to which pleasure is directed in the way that we can postulate truth as that to which knowledge or understanding is directed. For 'activity' is itself too heterogeneous to count as an object that we can call, like truth or friends or beauty, *good in itself*. A way of putting the same point is to note that in response to the thought that activity is good in itself the natural question to ask is, 'What kind of activity?' We can call this the 'it depends' response, and observe that it does not apply to truth or friends, for example. It is mistaken to respond to the thought that friends or truth are good in themselves by saying, 'it depends': for truth and friends are precisely the sorts of thing that it is good in itself to possess. There is no such thing as a bad truth or a bad friend in the specific sense meant here, which is consistent with the possibility of friends who do bad things or truths whose possession has bad consequences. The NL theorist accepts that the pursuit or acquisition of basic goods can have bad effects (hence the centrality of the intended/ foreseen distinction), and that goods can be pursued by bad means (hence the need for the Principle of Double Effect, which encompasses the previous distinction).

The point about pleasure, rather, is that it can accompany a bad activity, and this in the sense that it can be bad because of its very *content*. Hence it will not do to object to Chappell's position by saying that one can take pleasure in being a heroin addict or a bank robber – for these involve violations of other goods such that their proscription is consistent with taking pleasure to be a basic good. Again, there is bad knowledge in the sense that it can be put to a bad use (learning how to build a bomb so as to carry out a terrorist act) or acquired in a bad way (scientific experiments on non-consenting patients). But the learning of how to build a bomb, or the scientific results derived from an evil experiment, are not *in themselves* bad – they are just more truths whose pursuit, if proscribed, is proscribed for reasons other than that of the contents of the truths themselves. On the other hand, taking pleasure in the sight of an animal's being tortured is bad *because of its very content*, because of the nature of the activity in which pleasure is taken. Hence pleasure cannot be a good in itself.[10]

To return, then, to Chappell's examples, what do we say about smelling coffee or taking an aspirin? We must doubt their intelligibility in the terms he proposes. In other words, we must go beyond the thought that these are activities whose intelligibility is given by their being pursued for the sake of pleasure and the avoidance of pain in themselves, and look to the activities to which the pleasure and relief are accompaniments. More generally, we must appreciate that whereas, say, physical health or the possession of friends are constituents of the proper functioning of the human being, and being terminal points of teleological explanation are *ultimate* constituents thereof, we simply cannot say that pleasure *per se* is a constituent of proper functioning (let alone an ultimate one), or that conversely pain *per se* is a constituent of *mal*functioning. The pleasure of sensing the enticing aroma of freshly brewed coffee is only intelligible as an accompaniment of an activity that itself participates in some good, whether it be rest and relaxation of the mind (part of life), acquiring some new phenomenal knowledge (consider wine-tasting), perhaps even appreciating beauty (though whether smells or tastes can be beautiful, as opposed to sights and sounds, is a difficult question). Again, taking aspirin to relieve a headache is only intelligible as an accompaniment to the activity of pursuing a state of physical and mental integrity (part of health, which is part of life). Without a further explanation in terms of wanting to eliminate the headache as a malfunction, or better as an obstruction to normal physical and mental functioning, simply taking the aspirin to relieve the pain is an incomplete account of the action.[11] The same goes for smelling the coffee: the pleasure derived from it may uplift, or relax, or stimulate – but whatever its role in the activity, it must be as an accompaniment to the normal exercise of abilities that exist for some other purpose, and indeed as an *enhancement* of them. It is precisely for this reason that we do *not* reach for a painkiller every time we feel a pain, and regard people who do as disordered; *mutatis mutandis* for a person who makes anything more than an occasional pastime out of seeking out enjoyable scents, unless he do so for some other purpose (such as wine-tasting, which like any hobby is a kind of play).[12]

2.2 Inner peace; happiness; achievements

An important candidate claimed by Murphy for the list of basic goods is that which he calls 'inner peace,'[13] defined as 'the state of having no desires that one believes to be unsatisfied.'[14] Lest inner peace be thought of as a privation and so metaphysically unsuited to rank alongside the positive reality of the other goods, Murphy makes clear that it is a 'state of equilibrium, and this equilibrium can without distortion be characterized as a positive reality.'[15]

Murphy sees the inclusion of inner peace as advantageous to NLT *qua* objectivist account of well-being because it implicates desire in the right way, unlike subjectivist theories. Since a desire for x generates only a reason either to secure x or to rid oneself of the desire for x, subjectivist desire-fulfilment theories, which posit the simple reason to secure x as flowing from the desire for x, cannot be correct. Inner peace, on the other hand, can be pursued in just the right way, since securing x or ridding oneself of the desire for x will put the agent in the state of having no unsatisfied desires (of which he is aware).

Unfortunately, however, the postulation of inner peace as a basic good is subject to major objections. The first relates to Murphy's own attempt to sidestep the criticism, alluded to by Derek Parfit,[16] that if having satisfied desires were an aspect of well-being, one would have reason to produce desires merely for the sake of having them satisfied. The easier they were to satisfy, the easier it would be to achieve well-being in that respect, hence one might, all things being equal, have reason to produce as many low-level, uncomplicated, easily-satisfiable desires as possible; which is absurd. By switching to the idea of having no unsatisfied desires, Murphy responds, one denies the existence of a reason to produce desires just for the sake of satisfying them: 'One has a reason to ensure that one lacks unsatisfied desires, but one has no reason to strive to have satisfied desires.'[17]

This response misses the point that 'S has no unsatisfied desires' is logically equivalent to 'S has all desires satisfied or S has no desires.' This is a double blow, because not only on Murphy's definition of inner peace *does* one have a reason to produce desires that are easily satisfied – that is one way of achieving the state of having no unsatisfied desires – but one *also* has a reason not to have any desires at all, that is, to reach a state of pure *anorexia* (in the etymological sense),[18] since that is *also* a way of having no unsatisfied desires. Yet if these are the exclusive, alternative ways of achieving inner peace, something is wrong with positing inner peace as a basic good.[19]

Secondly, Murphy asserts that desires are, at least implicitly, time-indexed. I do not simply want to write a novel, I want to write one before I die. Fred does not simply want dinner, he wants it at 6.30 p.m. Hence it is no objection to inner peace as a basic good that having, as agents typically do, many outstanding, unsatisfied desires at a given time contributes to their lack of inner peace: it is only when a desire is not satisfied at or by the time at which the agent wants it to be satisfied that his inner peace is disturbed.[20] Again, though, this leads to a bizarre result, namely that if I desire to φ at time t, and t passes, it is logically impossible for that desire *ever* to be satisfied, and so to the extent that the lack of satisfaction detracts from my inner peace, my inner peace is forever compromised. I could, of course – and agents usually do – *renew* my desires ('I want to start my novel *next* year'), but on Murphy's view that would be a *distinct* desire, whose satisfaction could never make up for the previous, unsatisfied time-indexed desire.[21] Now it is a fact that agents have, at any given time, many time-indexed desires, and that as time passes an increasing number of them go unsatisfied. Moreover, the effect is cumulative – the older you get, the more the backlog of unsatisfied time-indexed desires builds up. By the end of a person's life, then, he is almost certain to be so weighed down by unsatisfied time-indexed desires that, if Murphy is right, he could hardly be said to have achieved inner peace. This is a sad fate for us, and one made even worse by the thought that, logically speaking, there is *nothing* any of us can do to get our inner peace back. No ethicist, let alone an NL theorist, can accept this result with equanimity. If, however, we go back to *non*-time-indexed beliefs as our standard of whether inner peace is achieved – for example, my desire *simpliciter* to write a novel – then the original objection that Murphy sought to avoid returns, namely that one can have many unsatisfied desires and still have what anyone can reasonably call inner peace.

Maybe, then, we should hang onto inner peace as a basic good but say that it is something else, something unconnected with the lack of satisfaction of desire *per se*? Here my third objection to Murphy comes into play, namely the lack of a theoretical basis, as he concedes,[22] for postulating a basic good of inner peace. He accepts that '[w]e might, then, deny that inner peace is an aspect of flourishing; rather, achieving inner peace is typically, though not always, a means to participating in other goods.'[23] This concession is part of the truth, but not the whole story. The first question one must ask in determining whether a concept denotes something that can plausibly be called a basic good is: Does there exist a faculty or capacity in human beings such that proper use of that faculty or capacity fulfils human nature in a way that does not require further explanation in terms of some more general faculty or capacity? This can be called the *foundation question* of NLT, and answering it showed above that pleasure cannot be called a basic good. It applies equally to anything one might call inner peace; indeed, applying the foundation question to inner peace immediately strikes one as curious in a way that applying it to pleasure does not. For what could this putative faculty for inner peace consist in? Inner peace, whatever it is, looks like something far too broad and heterogeneous to be a basic good.

Indeed, the more we analyze the term 'inner peace,' the more we see that it denotes a complex of states and properties that are attributed to human agents in different ways. Specifically, whatever else inner peace might be, it includes a complex of *virtues* that are among other things instrumental to the participation in basic goods. When we think of a person who has inner peace, we think of someone who has (*inter alia*) temperance, prudence, modesty, and discretion: these kinds of virtue all, in one way or another, exhibit a certain harmony and proportion in the activities of the agent. The agent who has them pursues the good in general, and individual goods in particular, in a way that reflects a well thought-out (even if only implicitly), well-structured and harmonious plan of life. And this is consistent with the agent's giving overriding emphasis to one or several goods at a certain cost to others. Understood as a complex of virtues, then, inner peace is simply not the sort of thing, categorially, that can be a basic good, or indeed a good at all in its own right. It is this metaphysical miscategorization, moreover, that is (as we shall see) at the heart of other errors in the postulation of basic goods.

Inner peace can also be thought of as a higher-level *structural* property of the pursuit of the good in general, more precisely a property of the agent once that agent's pursuit of the good comes to its natural end. Leaving aside for the moment questions of a future life (again, inner peace can also be thought of as a state of beatitude), we can say that inner peace in this respect is a terminal property of the agent in his pursuit of the good – what the agent might (but need not) achieve, or better the moral position the agent might (but need not) reach, when pursuit of the good is no longer possible. This will not be the acquisition of a distinct good, but the acquisition of a state of soul made possible by the way in which, and extent to which, the first-order basic goods have been pursued throughout a lifetime.

Looked at in this latter way, inner peace is similar to another basic good Murphy proposes, namely happiness.[24] This he defines as 'the successful achievement of a reasonable life plan,' although for Murphy the structure of a life plan is not given prior to the agent's actual commitments. (This is allegedly contra Aristotle and Aquinas, though he does not make clear where these thinkers deny that an agent's commitments shape structure. He appears to link it to their affirmation of a hierarchy of goods, which Murphy denies and which I will address later, but for the moment it is hard to see how the existence of a hierarchy, whilst regulating permissible structures, excludes a contribution by the agent to the specific structure of his own life plan given his particular circumstances.)

If happiness as Murphy understands it is just what I have called inner peace in the second sense, then it is clear that happiness cannot be a basic good either. Certainly from a pre-theoretical viewpoint, it appears strange to claim that agents aim at life, friendship, knowledge, aesthetic appreciation, and happiness, as though happiness were categorially at the same level as the other goods. This categorial confusion is implicit in Murphy's remark that 'while the structure of happiness is up to the agent, the material that the agent has to work with is not: it is the nine basic goods.'[25] But the requirement that the nine basic goods are the material the agent has to work with must involve more than the simple fact of the agent's having to pursue those nine goods as basic and no others. It must also involve facts about the structure and content of those goods (they cannot be pursued in any old way). So we are led to the curiosity that the structure of happiness (being one of the nine goods) is both up to and not up to the agent. Or if some aspects of structure are and some are not up to the agent, no clue is given as to how the differentiation is made. And since Murphy appears to be saying the nine basic goods are the matter of happiness, and happiness is one of the nine goods, then happiness is in some way the matter of itself.

Yet this is more than a benign truism, since whilst it makes sense to say that one structures happiness for oneself by pursuing knowledge in a certain way, it is far less clear what it means to say that one structures happiness for oneself by pursuing happiness in a certain way.

We can escape this categorial confusion by adopting the traditional Aristotelian–Thomistic position on happiness: we should identify happiness with *the good*, and we should identify the good as that property which stands in the determinable–determinate relation to the first-order goods such as life, knowledge, and friendship, which agents are bound to pursue if they are to fulfil their rational natures.[26] Happiness is not just another basic good – it is what people necessarily pursue *in virtue of* pursuing the basic goods themselves. As such, happiness has a structure – that structure, partly determined by the agent's commitments, partly determined by the basic goods themselves and their complex interrelationships, which orders the agent's actions. Its content, however, is given exhaustively by the way in which the basic goods are pursued.

We can now see, by similar reasoning, why Chappell's postulation of *achievements* as a basic good embodies an ontological mistake. For Chappell, achievements involve the doing of 'things that are worthwhile, or impressive, or in other ways admirable.'[27] But there is no human faculty of achievement: skill and difficulty may be involved in some way in something's counting as an achievement,[28] but difficulty and skill are no more than properties of actions and of modes of performing actions that are executed in the employment of real faculties such as reason, physical capacity, sensation, or will. Achievement *per se* is but a structural property of a life plan aimed at the good via a pursuit of the basic goods, and individual achievements are always instances of pursuit of one or more goods. Achievement (whether singular or plural) is not another species of good: it is *what you get when you pursue the good.*

Putting aside the ontological confusion, we can make essentially the same point by saying that postulating achievement as a basic good is explanatorily redundant for the reason that any instance of the putative good will, insofar as its contribution to the good life is concerned, be wholly explained in terms of other, genuine basic goods. Suppose one climbed Mt Everest, a typical achievement. In what way would the act contribute to the good life? It would be an example of the pursuit of life and/or knowledge and/or play and/or aesthetic experience. What else is there left to account for – that as well as being these things it is *also* an achievement? But we have specified the nature of the achievement already by describing it as an instance of the pursuit of one or more of the other – real – goods. There is nothing left to explain.

The general lesson from the above discussion is that one must not confuse structural or higher-order properties of the pursuit of the good, or of the life plan in which that consists, with the basic goods themselves. Getting clear on the ontological levels and categories involved is indispensable, among other things, for answering structural questions such as whether there is a hierarchy among the goods and whether there is a superordinate good. I will now examine an ontological error of a rather different kind.

2.3 Integrity; reason and rationality; practical reasonableness; excellence in agency; fairness

The transition to this new point from the previous subsection can be made via a discussion of *integrity* as explained by Gómez-Lobo.[29] This is on his list of basic goods, and he defines it as 'the inner harmony of a human being who does not let her thoughts, attitudes, desires, emotions, utterances, and actions go asunder but brings them into fundamental consistency.'[30] Gómez-Lobo goes on to contrast integrity with hypocrisy and self-deception. It is, he says, 'the result of bringing the good of practical knowledge to bear on our choices.'[31]

The thought that integrity should be on our list seems plausible, but it is mistaken. Note at once that integrity looks very similar to inner peace in the first sense given earlier, and the argument against inner peace in that sense being a basic good was that it is a complex of virtues, and so categorially unsuited to being called a basic good. It is now time to expand this idea of ontological miscategorization. The problem is not one of integrity's being complex: some, perhaps all, of the basic goods are irreducibly complex. (I will say a little more about this later, as I have elsewhere,[32] but a full exploration must be left for another occasion.) The problem is rather that one must not confuse *goods* and *virtues*. A virtue is best defined as a good habit, and a moral virtue as a good moral habit. More precisely, a moral virtue is a good habit of the will whose immediate object is a type of means for the attainment of the good.[33] Since one attains the good *per se* by pursuing (and, one hopes, attaining) one or more basic goods (and these latter by pursuing the non-basic or sub-goods which are constituents of the basic goods, about which more later), a moral virtue is a good habit of the will whose immediate object is a type of means for the attainment of one or more individual goods. So the metaphysical relationship of virtues to goods is instrumental; but nothing substantive hangs on whether one calls the virtue a means in itself, or whether one speaks solely of the virtue's object as being a means. For example, one can rightly say that honesty is a means of pursuing the good of knowledge (or friendship, or some other basic good). Or one can say that honesty aims at actions such as truth-telling, and that these are means of pursuing the good of knowledge. Or simply that honesty has knowledge as its object, and that pursuing knowledge is a means of pursuing the good, although in the latter case it is perhaps better to speak of a constitutive role for pursuing knowledge, since knowledge is a constituent of the good – speaking of means here does not shed any more light, and risks confusion. In any case, the metaphysical relationship of virtue to good clearly excludes virtues from being goods themselves, let alone basic goods. 'Integrity' is patently the name of a virtue (itself constituted by other virtues), and so it makes no more sense to say that human beings pursue integrity than it does to say that they pursue honesty or loyalty. Or if we do allow such talk, we cannot say that what we mean by a person's pursuing honesty is the same as what we mean by a person's pursuing knowledge or friendship. To put the matter simply, virtues are *what agents have* when they pursue the goods. Proper analysis of the notion of pursuit of a good shows that virtues are the *only* way in which agents can pursue the good, and so are characteristics that agents *must* have if they are to pursue it. But even if we allow talk of 'accidental' pursuit of the good (or attainment of the good), we must still affirm that the virtues are the best, that is, singularly most suited, way of pursuing the good, and so are characteristics that agents at the very least *ought* to have.

As for integrity itself, there is plenty of room for discussion as to what it is, that is, what virtues constitute it. When discussing inner peace in the first sense mentioned above I referred to prudence, temperance, modesty, and discretion – and these chime well with Gómez-Lobo's reference to 'inner harmony' and to not letting 'thoughts, attitudes, desires, emotions, utterances, and actions go asunder.'[34] But it is arguable that integrity as typically understood has more to do with consistency, fidelity to principles, honesty, courage, and the like. However we ultimately characterize integrity, we can now see why it makes no sense to speak of pursuing integrity as a basic good.

Chappell includes 'reason, rationality, and reasonableness' as a basic good (or group of closely linked goods).[35] In the same place he even includes 'practical hope,' which he defines as 'the rejection of fatalism,' though it is not clear how it relates to reason, rationality, and reasonableness, except perhaps as an example thereof. Finnis, as is well known, includes practical reasonableness on his list, which he defines as 'the basic good of being able to bring one's own intelligence to bear effectively (in practical reasoning that issues in action) on the problems of choosing one's actions and lifestyle and shaping one's own character.'[36] For Murphy, excellence in agency has two aspects: 'practical reasonableness, in which one's practical judgments and choices are in accordance with what is reasonable, and integrity of judgment and action, in which one's actions are in accordance with one's all-things-considered practical judgments.'[37]

Whatever the differences in detail between these putative goods, the very nomenclature used indicates that they are really virtues: *excellence* or *reasonableness*, even *rationality*, by which latter is meant the habitual exercise of reason, not its mere presence. But why should some NL theorists single out these virtues rather than others as basic goods? Why not propose the immediate intelligibility of an agent's pursuing *loyalty* or *courage* as a fundamental good, an ultimate reason for action? After all, we can understand a person's saying that he was loyal to his friend in a crisis because 'that's just what loyalty is all about,' or that a soldier ran headlong into the front line of the enemy 'because it was the courageous thing to do.' The obvious retort is that courage promotes life (usually the life of another), and that loyalty promotes friendship – hence we do not postulate the virtues of loyalty and courage *themselves* as basic goods. Yet this is precisely the point. Excellence in agency, integrity, reasonableness, rationality – they all promote, are means to, and exemplify the good of knowledge. But they also promote, are means to, and exemplify the good of friendship, and of religion, and all the other basic goods. But it is *because* they are bound up with the pursuit of every single good – their *pervasiveness* in the moral life, as one might describe it – that there is an inclination among some theorists to place them on the list of basic goods. It does not follow from their pervasiveness, however, that they are themselves ultimate objects of pursuit.

On the other hand, a virtue such as fairness – proposed by Chappell[38] – is not pervasive, and does not therefore even have *prima facie* attractiveness as a possible basic good. Chappell defines it thus (he also calls it 'justice'): 'Treating humans as having dignity means treating all humans as having dignity. And that means treating them as all having the same dignity.' Now whether or not that is the best way of defining fairness – at the very least it captures a core part of the virtue – it is clearly not pervasive in anything like the way reasonableness is. It is hard to see, for instance, how fairness is essentially involved in the pursuit of aesthetic appreciation.[39] Fairness has no more superficial title to being on the list any more that courage or loyalty. But more importantly, since all of them are virtues, none of them are, as explained, even ontologically fitted to being on the list.

2.4   A cornucopia of basic goods?

Before moving on to questions of structure, I want to conclude this section with some additional remarks about content relevant to the question of how large the NL theorist should expect the list of basic goods to be. I will leave the related but general question of whether the list is finite or infinite until the next section, since this does not bear directly on the question of content and is closely connected with mereological and related issues of structure. Assuming for the moment, however, that the list is finite, how large ought we to expect it to be?

As a general methodological rule, I contend that the NL theorist ought to be wary of promiscuity in compiling his list of basic goods. Two more specific rules help to show why this should be so. First, the fundamental question that guides the compilation is, as stated earlier, whether there is an active power or faculty the proper operation of which fulfils human nature. It is not the question of what there is that is ultimately valuable, or of what things there are that deserve ultimate respect. That is why, for instance, it is somewhat misleading (if forgivably so) to call truth a basic good. There can be no doubt that truth is one of the things in this world that are of ultimate value. But when specifying what it is that is ultimately good for human beings to do or to have, this being the basic question of NLT, the theorist is looking not just for some value, or some valuable object, but some valuable *activity* or *behaviour* that fulfils the nature of the person. Hence we should say that *knowledge* or *understanding* is a basic good, not truth *simpliciter*, even though the value of knowledge or understanding derives essentially from the value of truth. The first rule, then, is to abide by the fundamental question by not looking for things that are ultimately valuable yet not at the same time kinds of activity or behaviour proper to human faculties.

Another rule for avoiding promiscuity is that the NL theorist should look for the most *general* goods, since these will also be *basic*. A specific good is, by nature, going to be subsumed by a more general good: it will stand to it in the relationship of species to genus. But the species–genus relation for goods is at the same time an explanatory relation: if we want to know why a specific good, say comradeship in arms, is a good at all, we must explain this by its being a specific kind of friendship. Again, to know why, say, having visually appealing architecture is a good, we must refer it to the genus of aesthetic appreciation. Hence it will be the ultimate genera of good that explain why any goods they subsume are goods at all, since any explanation of one good in terms of subsumption by a more general but non-ultimate good will not be the whole story. For instance, it is not enough to explain why building visually appealing houses is good in terms of the good of appealing architecture, since we still need to know why having appealing architecture is a good. (Needless to say, since the species–genus relation is transitive we usually explain the goodness of any specific good by immediate reference to the ultimate genus without bothering to enumerate the various subsumption relations. Nevertheless, such an enumeration can also be highly illuminating.)

Observing species–genus relations is one way of applying the second rule. Another is to look for part–whole relations. The reason why, say, physical integrity is a good is that it is a part of the good of health, which is part of the basic good of life. It would be metaphysically confused to say that physical integrity is a *species* of life, but correct to say that having two legs is a species of physical integrity and thereby a species of life (not by transitivity, but by being a species of something that actually *constitutes* life, namely physical integrity; more will be said about mereological relations in the next section). Similarly, mental effort is a part of work/play, even if the effort be only small; playing chess is a species of mental effort, and so thereby a species of play by being a species of one of work/play's constituents.

Armed with these rules – abiding by the fundamental question, as well as looking for the most general goods by attending to species–genus relationships and part–whole relationships – and also recalling the general discussion about correct ontological categorization, we can briefly deal with some of the other goods that have been proposed as basic but do not really belong on the list. First is the good of family, proposed by Gómez-Lobo.[40] Now we should agree with Gómez-Lobo about the intrinsic value of the family and family relationships, but recognizing this intrinsic value does not entail recognizing family as a distinct basic good. For family is a species of friendship, and it is friendship that is the basic good. One need only recall the Genesis account of the formation of the first family to see that it is friendship that explains the value of family, even though special values also attend to family *per se*, in particular the perpetuation of the human race.[41] Hence we should locate family within the basic good of friendship, not primarily for reasons of ontological parsimony but for the explanatory light the latter sheds on the former: it is the explanation that guides the ontological categorization.

Applying our methodological rules, we can see why it appears strange to have on one's list of basic goods, alongside life, knowledge, friendship, and work/play, such things as Chappell proposes: physical and mental health and harmony; the existence of individual human beings; and the natural world. Take the first and second alleged basic goods. Physical and mental health and harmony are constituent parts of the basic good of life, and so should not be listed separately. To say this is not to ignore the fact that human biological life *per se* is also part of the good, only that as well as biological life, proper biological functioning is part of the same general capacity of human beings (as of other animals) – the basic good is not just one of living, but of living in a physically and mentally healthy way. This is why we say that when a person is severely incapacitated – even reduced to a comatose state – their pursuit of the good of life is radically diminished even though they have not ceased to pursue it altogether. But now it should be clear that positing the existence of individual human beings as a basic good distinct *both* from health *and* from life is explanatorily otiose – for what is left to the content of the good of life if health is separated out into another good and human existence into yet another? It is only by integrating life and health (both physical and mental) that we can have a correct metaphysical understanding of the ways in which health supports life and of the overall proper functioning of the human being. Moreover, as we shall see, this integration is necessary to understanding the structure of principles and rules governing ethical evaluation in respect of life as of other complex basic goods. For what we want from NLT is not just a satisfying metaphysical account of human nature: we want it to underwrite the system of morality.

Note in this connection that Chappell also toys with the idea of 'respect for human beings' as an additional basic good,[42] though it does not make it onto his official list. It is well that it does not do so, because now, instead of confusing virtues with goods, the confusion is between goods on the one hand, and rights and duties on the other. Rights and duties flow from the good.[43] It is because there are goods that agents have rights and duties – to pursue those goods, to non-interference in their pursuit, to defend other agents in their pursuit, and so on (all of these general rights and duties being subject to a network of principles by which they are ordered and qualified). Respect for human beings is precisely one of the duties that flow from the good of life. It is not itself a good, and does not belong alongside the good that makes it intelligible.

Finally, what about the natural world as a basic good? Here it is unsurprising, especially in our environmentally conscious times, that there should be disagreement. The fundamental divide (and not just between NL theorists but between ethicists of all stripes) is over whether the natural world, if a good, is only an instrumental good or whether it has its own intrinsic value. This is not the place to enter into a detailed discussion of this important question, but some observations are in order.

First, if the natural world is indeed of intrinsic and so ultimate value, this is not something that can merely be asserted – it is by no means obvious, and must be argued for.[44] Further, for what it is worth (and as Aristotle taught, it is worth something), it has simply not been the settled and traditional opinion of mankind (in most cultures, with perhaps the animistic or pantheistic ones as exceptions) that the natural world has intrinsic value. The general opinion has been that the natural world is made for man, and that human beings may, within due limits, exploit its living and non-living resources.[45] This creates a certain presumption against its being of intrinsic value.

Secondly, from the particular perspective of NLT, it seems strange to posit the natural world as a basic good because it is hard to see what faculty of human nature is perfected by concern for it as such. More precisely, leaving aside the natural world's obvious instrumental value – which no one disputes – it is difficult to locate a basic goodness in the natural world that is *distinct* from other goods that do fulfil human nature and whose pursuit is exemplified by concern for the natural world. I am thinking in particular of the goods of life, knowledge, play, aesthetic experience, and religion. Even the animists and pantheists referred to earlier saw intrinsic value in the natural world precisely because for them it embodied divinity. What basic good is exemplified by concern and respect for the environment that is distinct from an appreciation of its beauty, or of the wonders it reveals, or from pursuit of its life- and health-giving properties, or from regard for the natural world as in some way, for persons of religious persuasion, embodying, exemplifying or reminding us of the goodness of the God who created it and of the consequent need for respect of His creation?

But suppose one were to agree that there is no conceptual space left over for a specific good of the natural world distinct from the other basic goods pursued (necessarily, I would argue) by our concern and respect for it. Will it not still be the case that the natural world has basic value in virtue of those other goods? The answer is that it will have basic value in the same way as reading a book has basic value or going for a jog – concern for the natural environment will be no more nor less than an instantiation of the pursuit of other goods, and subject to the same sorts of ethical consideration that are brought to bear on those other goods. Treatment of the natural world will depend upon the way concern for it is good for us: as a way of pursuing other basic goods, yet with its own particular characteristics, there is room in NLT for a characteristically *environmental* philosophy that is at the same time fully integrated within the broader theory.

The overall conclusion to be drawn from the above analysis is that the list of basic goods should still be considered relatively short. In particular, the one proposed by Finnis and Grisez *et al.*, minus practical reasonableness and treating work and play as aspects of a single good, still looks the most plausible.

3   Questions of structure

3.1   An infinity of basic goods?

Is the list of basic goods finite or infinite? According to Chappell, it is the latter. He subscribes to what he calls the 'Dynamic Thesis,' according to which the list of basic goods 'couldn't be completed.' He says, 'It's not merely possible for humans to discover (or create) new instances of basic goods. They can even discover new types of basic goods. Art is an example.' His metaphysical justification for this claim is as follows: 'The list of basic goods available to humans is in fact impossible to close while humans are still developing as a species – as I take it they are.' He speaks even of 'radical possibilities for new articulations of what it means to live a good human life.'[46]

Now although the finiteness question is usually not taken up, at least explicitly, by NL theorists, the tenor of their collective approach to the basic goods suggests that on the whole they subscribe to finiteness. I believe they are right to do so.[47] But first we should note two ways in which we can speak correctly of infinity in respect of the basic goods. First, they are infinite in the *exemplificatory* sense. This means simply that there is no limit to the number of instances of a basic good: suppose humanity were to exist forever, and every human carried out a finite number of activities in pursuit of the good, then the number of instances of such pursuit would be infinite – not *actually*, of course, but *potentially*. If there is an infinite number of truths, and so a potentially infinite number of objects of knowledge, then there is a potentially infinite number of individual pursuits of this good, and so on. This is evidently not the sense of infinity intended by Chappell.

Secondly, the basic goods are, or at least might be, infinite in the *mereological* sense. The good of life, for instance, has constituent parts: mental health, which consists of rationality, good sensory functioning, and so on, and these consist of further elements; physical health, which consists of good digestion, good circulation, a healthy immune system, and so on, and these too consist of further elements; also biological persistence *per se*, which overlaps considerably with health but which also includes such elements as a relatively safe way of living and a relatively safe environment, but perhaps also certain cellular and sub-cellular processes that are dedicated to preserving the very existence of the organism. And for all we know, the constituents and sub-constituents of life, at some level, may be infinite. Whether they are infinite is beyond the scope of this discussion, and there is no room to consider whether the same is true of other uncontroversially basic goods; but the general idea is clear enough. Again, though, this is not the sense of infinity intended by Chappell.

With respect to the sense he intends, we may ask quite simply: What reason is there to believe it? It is not enough to speak vaguely of 'radically open horizons' and of 'humans still developing as a species.' The presumption and evidence are clearly in favour of there being no such open-endedness or possibility of radical development. If we are to take current estimates as correct (I accept that it is debatable, but any uncertainty merely strengthens the case for agnosticism about origins, not the case for the discovery of art), examples of Oldowan art go back at least 2.5 million years.[48] Beyond that, there is little agreement about how far back the so-called 'hominid' line is supposed to go, but if 2.5 million-year-old art has been found, there is no reason to think even older specimens will not one day be discovered. Art, of course, has evolved over time – but the essence of art, the skilled creation of images and objects for the delight of the senses (though perhaps for other purposes as well), appears to be as old as humanity itself.

Moreover, for Chappell to speak of justice or fairness as having been discovered is highly misleading. As he explains, 'There was, *presumably* [my emphasis], a time when there were humans, but no such thing as (*consciously adopted* [my emphasis]) justice between them.'[49] To gloss the presumption with 'consciously adopted' muddies the waters: one might take the thought to be that there was a time – a kind of state of nature – in which humans did not practise justice or fairness. But this would be quite compatible with the idea that humans, when they did not practise justice, nevertheless knew what it was and that it was desirable if for whatever reason unattainable in their state. One assumes, however, that Chappell means something more radical, namely that there was a time at which humans did not even know what justice or fairness *were* – they simply had no conception of such goods, but at some later stage 'consciously adopted' them as goods. If true (I am not sure it is even intelligible), it entails that they had no conception of, for example, murder, or rape, or other violations of bodily integrity; but then this means there was a time when humans acted purely like animals, since all the other goods would also have to have been beyond their mental horizon. Could they have had a concept of life or of friendship without one of justice? To take Chappell's thought to its logical conclusion is to assert that there was a time at which humans simply were not rational but *mere* brutes – something not even Hobbes recognized. To say that humans were once not rational is to deny that they were once humans, which is nonsense. (They might, let us suppose for the sake of argument, have had biological *ancestors* that were like this – but they would not have been *humans*.) Yet are we to suppose that humans were once rational enough to solve intricate problems of hunting, building, and social co-operation, but not rational enough to grasp any basic goods? How are we to conceive of such a state?

Suppose, on the other hand, that humans did discover justice or fairness. How does this license the inference that there is a potential infinity of basic goods? Even assuming that humans somehow discovered, one by one, all of the basic goods on any currently proposed list, how does this justify the thought that the list is infinite? Is it an induction? If so, the induction looks pretty weak, but the more important response is that such a story is consistent with the alternative explanation that humans came, over some suitably long period of time, to a full consciousness of all of the finite number of basic goods. If this alternative explanation is plausible, it cancels the one that favours an infinite list.

At the theoretical level, though, we have strong reason to prefer the explanation that involves a finite list. For what we are looking for when we seek to enumerate the basic goods is a list of the most general distinguishable features of human activity that constitute human flourishing. What reason is there to expect the list to be anything other than finite? Human beings have finite minds and finite bodies, and a finite number of capacities both physical and mental. There is no evidence that, even if we did once 'develop' as a species, we are still doing so. The objection to the idea of yet-undiscovered basic goods can be put as a dilemma: either the human faculty or capacity which the undiscovered good fulfils already exists, or it does not. If it does, what could it be? What is that crucial, wholly general faculty or capacity that has escaped philosophical, biological, and anthropological attention? If it does not yet exist, what is the argument for claiming that one day it will? Crucially, what is the argument for claiming that this process can in principle go on indefinitely? And what is the further argument for claiming that if it did, a single species would persist through those discoveries and that it would be *human*? Until these questions are answered by more than mere hand-waving, we have no reason to think that the list of basic goods is anything other than (a) finite and (b) known to us.

3.2 A superordinate good?

A question that has vexed NL theorists is whether one of the basic goods can in any way be ranked as more important than the others. As a matter of fact – and the fact is unsurprising – the only serious candidate for a 'superordinate' good, as Murphy aptly terms it, is religion, which is held by virtually all NL theorists (Gómez-Lobo being a notable exception) to be a basic good. Needless to say, if a coherent form of Nietzschean NL theory could be made out, it would be aesthetic experience that would be posited as the superordinate good. Theoretical considerations relevant to the question, then, are not wedded to the choice of religion as the highest good, but it is this one I will analyze as the most typical and plausible example, bringing in extra observations specifically connected with it.

As Murphy points out,[50] two general kinds of worry beset opponents of the idea of a superordinate good such as Finnis and Robert George. One concerns incommensurability, and the other is the practical problem of how a superordinate good would affect decision-making with respect to all of the basic goods. As to the first worry – Murphy observes correctly that Finnis, George, and those who follow their basic interpretation of NLT cannot use incommensurability against the thought that there is a superordinate good since they themselves contend that one can coherently impose a hierarchy upon the goods in one's own life plan, and if so one might place a single good at the top of the hierarchy. But if this can be done by an agent, there is nothing conceptually repugnant in the idea that such a hierarchy is objective and prior to choice.

More importantly, however, Murphy argues that whilst Finnis and George are clear about what incommensurability rules out, they are less clear as to what it does *not* rule out. Certainly, to the extent that commensurability entails maximization, commensurability must be rejected. Specifically, if it entails that one can quantify basic goods (according to some measure or other) and thereby judge one good to be 'better' than another by being greater in quantity, commensurability must be ruled out. There might, however, be other relationships of comparability between goods that it is not reasonable to rule out. Murphy suggests the 'for the sake of' relation, according to which, while all the basic goods are intrinsically good, some of them are naturally (prior to all choice) for the sake of others.[51] His position, though, is that whilst some readings of the 'for the sake of' relation are more plausible than others, and although a case might, with fleshing out, be made for happiness as a superordinate good (which I earlier rejected as a basic good at all), there is no route through practical or theoretical reason to religion as a superordinate good.

On this point Murphy is, I submit, mistaken, and we can see this by examining his readings of 'for the sake of.' If one wanted to claim, say, that knowledge was for the sake of religion, it would be too strong to take this to mean that one should never fail to treat knowledge as a means to religion: 'it would seem not to do justice to the nature of knowledge as intrinsically good if, by its very nature, it can never be reasonably pursued except as an instrument.' Earlier, however, he formulates the reading as follows: 'if a certain good is by nature for the sake of another, then . . . in one's plan of action, one should never fail to treat the former as a means to the latter.'[52] The emergence of the word 'except' reminds one of the error of interpretation made by newcomers to Kant, as to whether one is allowed to treat another person as a means. It would not be too strong, rather it would be incoherent for the NL theorist to assert that a *basic* good can never reasonably be pursued except as an instrument, since it is definitive of basic goods that this is precisely not true of them. But what about the proposition that one should never fail to treat, say, knowledge as a means to religion? This is compatible with pursuing knowledge for its own sake in the following way.

First, it should be evident that there are some things that are more important to know than others. It is more important to know that God exists than to know the equations of quantum theory or whether there is water on Mars. Faced with my imminent death, and the chance of coming to know of God's existence or of the truth about water on Mars, it is clear which I should choose. The advocate of the superordinacy of religion extends this point to all the other basic goods. Faced with the choice of dying friendless and dying without knowledge of the existence of God, I should choose the former; the same applies to dying a painful death, or without having had any beauty in my life, or dying after a life or unrelieved drudgery, and so on. All of this is compatible with also pursuing the truth about water on Mars, making a new friend, listening to Bach, and the like, for their own sakes, with no further explanation needed to make such activities intelligible. This point extends beyond religious knowledge to religious practice: it is better to die friendless than to die without having performed certain fundamental acts of worship and adoration of God. Hence the controlling good in these cases is not knowledge but religion, whose practice overlaps at least some of the other goods, in particular knowledge and art. Pursuing knowledge is clearly a means to acquiring religious truth – the latter is not a mere instance of knowledge. Learning to think logically, coming to know the natural world, and so on, are means to acquiring religious truth. By contrast, there are no examples of activities in pursuit of the other goods such that it is better to perform those than to perform certain fundamental acts of religion. Thus there is an asymmetry between the good of religion and the other basic goods. Yet one can pursue the latter for their own sake whilst also recognizing the way in which they are necessary means to obtaining truths of religion of which there are none more important.

Secondly, the advocate of superordinacy should not simply claim there are kinds of religious pursuit that are more important than kinds of pursuit of any other good, but that *within each basic good* there are kinds of pursuit that have a religious content making them more important than other kinds of pursuit within the same good. For instance, if I am a painter (i.e. my work is that of a housepainter, not an artist) and I have a choice between painting a barn and painting a church then, all things being equal, I should paint the church. The qualification is essential, because otherwise NLT really would fall prey to George's otherwise specious worries about how one is supposed rationally to stop the superordinate good from overriding every other activity in one's life.[53] A superordinate good is not an exclusive good – it is, as it were, *primus inter pares*. The other goods have an essential claim on the agent's life, but the superordinacy of religion ensures an asymmetry between the claims. So, to continue the example, if my family is starving and painting the church will not even bring me enough money for a loaf of bread whereas painting the barn will, clearly I must paint the barn. Faced, however, with conflicting duties concerning religion on the one hand and some other good on the other, then if I am capable of doing either and am not in some other way excused from the religious duty, then the higher good must prevail.

Within each good there are specifically religious pursuits that are nobler than any other kind of pursuit. For instance, it is better to make friends with people who also care for religion than with those who do not. (In case it needs emphasizing, I do not expect every NL theorist, let alone many other moral theorists, to accept these claims. For them the argument, if it amounts to anything, amounts to a demonstration that there is nothing incoherent or repugnant to the basic tenets of NLT in having a superordinate good, for instance that of religion.) It is better to come to appreciate the beauty of religious art than the beauty of still life. It is better to practise a profession that is pleasing to God than one that is not. And so on. None of which precludes one from enjoying still life, or from jogging to the shops rather than to church (again, all things being equal), or from having an atheist as a friend – and all of these for their own sakes. Speaking metaphysically, the thought is that the good of religion overlaps all of the other goods with parts that are better or nobler than any other part of each good, whereas no other good overlaps all of the other goods including religion with parts that are so characterized. Less technically, the noblest pursuit of each good is the pursuit that has a religious character, whereas this is not true *mutatis mutandis* for any other good. The friend of superordinacy can hold to all of this while keeping George's anxiety about domination by the superordinate good well to one side.

On the above understanding, then, one must never fail to treat the other basic goods as means to the religious good inasmuch as one must never fail to see how the other goods are ordered towards the religious goods by each containing the noblest expression – the religious expression – of the good in question. Might it not be objected, nevertheless, that this is compatible with failing to treat the other goods as means to the religious good on particular occasions? How does a satisfying game of Monopoly contribute to the good of religion? Here the friend of superordinacy needs to invoke the distinction between explicit and implicit means. Surely we would be right to look curiously at a person who treated each game of Monopoly as a paean to the Divinity, every completed office memorandum as an act of homage to the Lord of all creation. George would not be the first in the queue to diagnose such a person as suffering from what one might call, with due respect to that much maligned character from *The Simpsons*, the 'Ned Flanders complex.' (On the other hand, we are not so quick to poke fun at someone who sees the hand of God in every sunset, or Jesus in every child.) A person who consciously or explicitly adverted to the good of religion in everything she did would rightly be regarded as ethically unbalanced.

On the other hand, it is not clear that the NL theorist should be equally critical of the person who *implicitly* sees every activity, every pursuit, every project, *sub specie aeternitatis*. And by 'implicit' I mean that the person, if questioned, is ready to respond that whatever she does, she does with an eye to how her deed either promotes, respects or in some other way accords with the good of religion; also, that if she interrogates herself, she recognizes how that motive partially guides her actions. Such a person ought not merely to strike the NL theorist as balanced, but also as commendable. Yet should we equally commend the person who implicitly sees every action *sub specie cognitionis*? Or *sub specie amicitiae*? The very thought strikes us as bizarre, though it might not seem strange to a Nietzschean (art) or a Moorean (art and friendship) – which latter cases only reinforce the coherence of the idea of a superordinate good, even if one might disagree over what that good is.

To see all one's activities, even the most trivial, *sub specie aeternitatis* is to be ready, on reflection, to ask oneself the question: 'How does what I am now doing contribute to, or at least not obstruct, the gaining of my final end?' In a balanced and thoughtful life, it is as easy to answer that question in respect of a game of Monopoly as it is in respect of attendance at a religious service. It is not merely a question of how to handle a conflict of goods should one decide to deliberate upon it, as Murphy suggests in passing.[54] To have the question at the back of one's mind – and, should occasion demand, at the forefront – is to allow one's life to be regulated by the superordinate good of religion, yet without treating any basic good as a mere means to its pursuit. Yet Murphy, for one, is not disposed to adopt this picture of how one's life should be regulated. He states: 'It is unclear, then, whether the mere fact that agents tend to pursue other goods for the sake of religion far more than they pursue the good of religion for the sake of other goods should lead us to affirm that the other goods are for the sake of religion or just to recognize that the religious good is not as efficient an instrumental means to promoting other goods.'[55] Yet it is not clear what kind of agent he has in mind. Is he contemplating an agent who fully affirms the good of religion, and its highest nobility, yet who sees the other goods as merely 'more apt to be used as instrumental means than the religious good is'?[56] But then in what sense *does* such an agent regard the religious good as really the noblest good? It is an implausible picture to paint of an agent who sees the religious good as both supremely important and as being at something like an instrumental loose end – sitting at the terminus of a chain of practical reasoning simply because it is not of much help at procuring other goods.

Nor does Murphy see any theoretical reasons for positing religion as a superordinate good;[57] but if my analysis is correct, theoretical grounds are abundant, not just for thinking that religion as a superordinate good is a coherent option for the NL theorist, but for considering this to be eminently plausible in the light of religion's function within an overall life plan.

3.3   Hierarchy, structure, principles, and morality

As I remarked earlier, the point of seeking a proper metaphysic of the good is to provide the necessary theoretical underpinning for NLT as a system of morality. This system must include ethical principles, duties, rights, virtues, counsels, an account of moral decision procedure, a method for solving dilemmas and hard cases, for resolving conflicts, and for deciding upon cases of conscience. It is the transition from the good to the ethical that is, I submit, the point of enquiry that has so far lagged behind others in the contemporary revival of NLT. Perhaps 'transition' is not quite the right word: maybe it is better to speak of a *fusion* between metaphysics and ethics. Consequentialists are wont to think that they have achieved a more successful fusion, but the fact is that their working out of a consequentialist ontology has been woefully inadequate, and hence been a point of weakness that non-consequentialists have persistently and successfully attacked. Not that Kantian or other forms of deontological ethics, or virtue ethics, for that matter, have a better record when it comes to elaborating their own moral ontologies.

Whatever the state of the opposition, NL theorists must press ahead with achieving a coherent and satisfying fusion of metaphysics and morality.[58] In the remaining part of this discussion, I want to set out some of the main ideas of what I take to be the way in which such a fusion is to be achieved, looking in particular at the way structural considerations in moral ontology bear upon practical decision-making.

One of the principal ideas behind the fusion of metaphysics and ethics is that the structure of the basic goods guides the structure of the ethical concepts that together constitute a cohesive and consistent moral system. We have already seen the way in which this works for a superordinate good, which I suggested to be the good of religion. How does it apply more generally? Within the limited space available, I want to give examples that indicate how the enquiry should go, while recognizing that one of NLT's exciting challenges for the future is to bring the same considerations to bear upon the whole range of ethical concepts and problems. The ultimate aim is to have a natural law theory that is fundamentally action-guiding. If the best version of NLT cannot yield concrete moral guidance, it is worth nothing. Hence the goal that must always be on the theorist's horizon is practical – advice, solution, decision, and action.

At the most general level, the consensus among NL theorists is that none of the basic goods is more important than the others. This is true, but it must be spelled out carefully, and in a way that is consistent with the idea of a superordinate good. The metaphysical reason for the idea of equal importance is that each basic good engages the rational nature of the human being in such a way that no kind of engagement according to one good is more necessary to human flourishing than any other. The human being flourishes only if all parts of his rational nature are engaged – no single part of that nature is such that the human flourishes if *only* that part is engaged. Now a superordinate good, as I argued, is one that regulates a person's life, at least implicitly, in everything he does. This does *not* imply, however, that a life of flourishing is one in which *only* the superordinate good (let us continue with religion as the example) is pursued and other goods wholly neglected. Indeed, it is hard to make sense of such a life – even the most austere of religious penitents, hermits, and ascetics do not wholly neglect any of the other goods. To say, moreover, that it is better to die knowing of the existence of God but without a friend in the world than to die full of friendship but with no such knowledge is not to assert that knowledge of the existence of God must be sought at the cost of actively and deliberately undermining the good of friendship either in oneself or others.

As some NL theorists have emphasized,[59] there is more than one attitude one may have toward a good. One might, in adopting an austere, penitential life, not seek to promote the good of friendship by making a point of being sociable and forming close relationships; but one is never permitted to undermine friendship either by intentionally harming the relationships of others or acting badly toward one's own friends. Adopting an eremitic life, for instance (the example is extreme and nowadays rare, but extreme examples sometimes make the point better than moderate ones), requires that one cut oneself off from one's family and friends (at least to some extent); but this does not license acts of injustice and cruelty to one's kith and kin, for example. In a life plan, it is not only possible but necessary that the agent structure his pursuit of the basic goods in a way that accords with his individual circumstances, aptitudes, and interests. This necessity for a subjective ranking does not, however, contradict the objective equality of the basic goods (and the superordinacy of the highest good), which the agent is always bound at the very least to respect even if he does not do much to promote certain goods.

Moreover, we can even say that by prioritising certain goods in his life plan, the agent naturally seeks a kind of *compensation* in the pursuit of the subjectively ranked higher goods, and also of the objective superordinate good, for the fulfilment that is lost by ranking other goods lower. Hence, for instance, those who devote their lives to religion in a way that exceeds what is objectively required by its natural superordinacy (consider again the ascetic, or the mystic, or the person who takes vows of religion) tend to speak of a *solace* or *consolation* in their highest pursuit which makes up for the loss of, say, friends, family, or material prosperity. But the same could be said of other life plans, such as that of the person devoted to art or science above all else (apart from the superordinate good).

Much has been said by NL theorists about the equality of the basic goods, and much more remains to be said. What I want to do in the rest of this chapter is to examine the structure of the goods in general, not just the goods *qua* basic, and to see how relations between them – both within a basic good and across basic goods – form the basis of an ethical system. The first thing to note is that incommensurability does not rule out comparative judgements of importance between goods, both in general and within specific contexts of decision-making. It does, as already mentioned, rule out maximization, and hence it excludes a purely quantitative approach to judgments of relative importance. It does not, as argued earlier, preclude the existence of a superordinate good. But it also does not rule out a whole host of qualitative judgments and rational preferences that together form a coherent and attractive system of natural law morality.

To give a simple example, the reason it is morally permissible, in some cases obligatory, to amputate a limb to save a life is that the continued existence of a person's life is more important than the continued existence of one of his parts. This proves immediately that one can and must make judgments of relative importance within goods, in this case the good of life – which has both continued existence and bodily integrity as constituent parts. The principle that guides this sort of judgment is sometimes called the Principle of Totality, namely the principle that one may sacrifice a part to save the whole. To take a more difficult but not, I would argue, controversial example, it is permissible for a starving man to take a loaf of bread from another person who is not himself starving, without that person's consent. Does this mean theft is sometimes allowed? No: what it means is that in a case of danger to life the right to property is extinguished by the right to life, even though both continued existence and property are parts of the general, basic good of life. A number of principles are involved here, all of which point in the same direction. Right moral order requires (i) that things be subordinated to persons; (ii) that merely useful goods be subordinated to necessary goods (the bread is useful for the person who has enough food, but necessary for the person who is starving); (iii) that less urgent needs be subordinated to more urgent needs. Urgency and necessity are not to be given a purely relativistic interpretation, however, even though the judgment in each case must be relative to circumstance. So, for instance, if you have £100 and are about to spend it on your overgrown garden but I need the money to spend on Christmas presents for my children who would be devastated if they had no gifts, my need is not objectively urgent nor is it greater than yours. To take the money from you would in that case be theft.

On the other hand, there are goods that are also part of life and comparable to life itself. What this means is that just as one has the right to defend one's life to the point of killing an unjust aggressor, so the right of self-defence extends to certain other goods whose possession befits a normal and decent life for a human being. These include: major bodily parts and mental faculties; sanity; liberty; sexual integrity; even material goods of great value to a person, such as their house, life savings, inheritance, and means of sustenance. One may, for instance, use lethal force against a rapist, but not against someone trying to steal your purse. Although I have now brought in the concept of a right, I do not propose to elaborate its derivation from the good.[60] For present purposes I will take it as granted by NL theorists that there are rights and that these can be argued for from a consideration of the good. But the point of bringing in rights is that what rights there are, how we can judge whether we have a right to something in a given situation, and how to resolve apparent conflicts of rights, must be regulated by an account of, among other things, comparability judgments about goods.

Such judgments are not just made about parts of the same good, but also about parts of different goods. For example, if I have agreed to meet my friend for a game of tennis but my child needs me to help her study for a crucial exam, then the less urgent good of the game (which falls within both friendship and play) must give way to the more urgent good of helping my child (which falls within family). But what if I have promised my friend I would meet him for the game? The case must still be decided using judgments of relative importance, but there are also special rules of promising which govern the matter. So if my friend had relied on my promise and incurred great expense by spending a lot of money on a new racquet and taking the day off work, perhaps even risking a serious rebuke from his boss for being absent, and so on, it may be that I am placed under a serious obligation to keep my promise and seek to make alternative arrangements for my child (if possible). On the other hand, a simple promise with no consideration, no legal context, and no intention to confer a strict right on the promisee (such that breaking the promise would be unjust), can be plausibly said only to bind by the virtue of fidelity, which virtue relates to the goods of knowledge (faithfulness to the truth) and friendship (the reinforcement of natural expectations between people). Breaking such a promise might be wrong, but not seriously so; nevertheless, the promise ceases to bind altogether if the promisor would not have made the promise had he known of the intervening circumstances. Assuming I would never have made the promise to meet my friend had I known of my child's need for help, I am excused altogether. But the intervening circumstances that conventionally excuse promisors are implicitly understood by all parties to promises to extend from the less to the more important. It will not do for me to break my promise to meet my friend on the ground that I remembered how much I dislike getting up early in the morning and would never have made the promise had I realized how early a start I would have had to make. The minor inconvenience to me (good of life) gives way to the goods of friendship and knowledge (fidelity, consistency with my word).

It can be seen straight away how complex real cases can become, and how quickly. My purpose here is not even to begin to engage in detailed practical reasoning of the kind used in genuine cases, but to give a sketch of how such reasoning must go in virtue of being guided by considerations as to the relative importance of goods. Consider some more principles relating to right moral order: (i) social and civic goods are subordinate to necessary personal and family goods; (ii) free, conventional societies are subordinate to natural societies. Now, within each basic good there are parts that have an essentially private character and those that have a public character. Friendship contains both the private good of family and the public good of community. Knowledge contains both the private good of knowledge pursued for one's own benefit (such as learning a foreign language) and knowledge pursued for the sake of public benefit (such as knowledge of how to run a government). Art contains both the private good of an aesthetically satisfying personal environment and the public good of a satisfying communal environment (public architecture, for example). How, then, are we to balance the private and the public? On the one hand, the subordination of non-necessary personal goods to civic goods (which I take to be implicit in (i)) means that one must pay fair taxes for the benefit of society. On the other, it means that social goods potentially derived from financial contributions that impede what is necessary for an individual or family to support themselves in a decent way will be subordinate to that necessity and hence unfair if imposed. (Debate about fair taxation is a field in itself – all I am doing is setting out very general principles.) The reason socialism, for instance, is an unjust system is that it subordinates necessary personal and family goods to social goods, which is a reversal of the natural order of things: individuals and families do not exist for the benefit of society – society exists to enable individuals and families to realize their own goods.

Principle (ii), just mentioned, takes the idea even further. States and other forms of political organization are conventional arrangements; families, associations of friends, and of others with like interests or pursuits, even local communities, are natural societies that spontaneously arise as a function of human inclination. The subordination of the former to the latter rules out *ab initio* any form of totalitarianism, tyranny, absolutist government, enforced egalitarianism, or Hegelian state worship. The same idea is embodied in the famous Principle of Subsidiarity, which in one of its formulations says: 'The state has the right and duty to direct, aid, and supplement the activities or persons, families, and other social groups in doing what is necessary or at least truly useful for the common good; but it is forbidden to usurp the functions of private persons and groups, and it may not destroy or impair any natural rights of association or of action by such persons and groups.'[61] If it were not possible to make comparative judgments between private and public goods within a basic good, or across basic goods, such principles would not even be coherent, let alone eminently plausible. Indeed, it is the principles themselves that embody the kinds of comparative judgment that are, and must be, made for NLT to be action-guiding.

It must be acknowledged, of course, that principles such as those I have enunciated probably will not strike all NL theorists as plausible; some may think that they import conceptions of society or of morality in general that are extraneous to pure NLT. To convince theorists that they are not only plausible but persuasive can be a tricky task, since their advocates in the historic NL tradition have usually taken them largely to be embodiments of common sense, and when it comes to commonsense propositions the most one can do positively is to commend them to the common sense one hopes is possessed by others. In a more indirect and also negative way, though, the advocate of such principles can lay down a challenge. The NL theorist is, as I have argued, obliged to develop a theory that is applicable to moral decision-making. To achieve this, I contend, it is methodologically inescapable that the theorist build up a set of principles that (to put the point loosely) enables goods to be translated into action. But if the theorist is a genuine *natural law* theorist, she must acknowledge that basic and non-basic goods do not free float in the metaphysical void – they must subsist within a *natural order of things*. The very idea of a natural law theorist who does not believe in a natural order of things is absurd. But it is through the enunciation of principles that the theorist reveals the natural order he takes to exist. The principles *encapsulate* that order. So it is incumbent upon every natural law theorist to articulate the principles that reveal the natural order he takes to exist, and in which the goods subsist. It can only be, then, for common sense, reflection on facts and logic, and intuition, to tell which system is the one around which NL theorists should group themselves.

3.4   Collision of Rights

The same considerations apply to the question of the collision of rights. I say 'collision' because it must be another methodological principle of NLT that objective morality is coherent and consistent. It can contain no genuine conflicts or contradictions because otherwise action would be impossible. Hence the overriding duty of the NL theorist is to elaborate a system of morality that resolves apparent conflicts and brings rights, duties, virtues, and counsels into an harmonious arrangement. Yet apparent conflicts of rights abound. How is the theorist to resolve them? Again, it cannot be done without resort to basic and derived principles.[62]

The fundamental principle is that in an apparent conflict of rights the actually existing right is determined by an examination of the relative factors in each claim. Underlying those factors are a set of principles relating rights to the goods they protect. So, for example, natural rights take precedence over positive rights. The civil law should (and often does) recognize a natural claim to inheritance by someone who is not mentioned in a civilly valid will. But suppose the natural claim is doubtful – the closeness of the claimant's relationship to the testator is a matter of dispute. According to the principle that clearer titles prevail over more doubtful ones, it appears the claimant does not have as strong a claim as the legally valid inheritors. Now suppose the claimant is at risk of destitution if his claim is not recognized, but the legal inheritors are at no such risk. According to the principle that the greater urgency prevails, the claimant should be recognized.

How should such a case be resolved? Clearly more information is required, and principles must be balanced. This is the sort of activity at which the common law is exemplary, and it would be well that NL theorists study the common law (including equity) to see how concrete cases are decided. Bearing in mind, nevertheless, that we must not expect mathematical or quasi-mathematical precision in our balancing of principles, our aim must be to find a principle (or principles) applied to concrete facts, that as clearly as possible outweighs the others that are relevant. In simple cases it is easy: for example, it is beyond doubt that a parent may park her car in a no-parking zone if it is the quickest way to get her seriously ill child to hospital; natural right prevails over positive right, and so the right of the state to expect obedience to the parking regulation is extinguished (*not* permissibly violated). Again, the nobler the subject of a right, the greater that right's prevalence over less noble subjects: this is why children must obey their parents, not the other way around. (Note the technical use of 'noble': it does not mean morally superior in an intrinsic sense, rather that in the ranking of social priority respecting rights and duties, people who happen to be parents are naturally in authority over people who happen to be their children.)

Another principle is that inalienable rights prevail over alienable ones. Suppose I am seriously ill and in possession of some vital medicine for which, it turns out, the chemist undercharged me and I cannot make up the difference. The chemist has a property right to the return of the medicine, but I have a right to save my own life. Since the latter is inalienable but the former alienable (the chemist can waive his right to the medicine), I am entitled to hang onto it. This explains our sense that it would not merely be uncharitable for the chemist to insist on the return of his property, but also *unfair*. Alienability does, however, present some major conceptual difficulties. For instance, is it ever permissible to sell oneself into slavery, for example, if it is necessary for physical survival? If we apply the principle that the more necessary good prevails over the less necessary, life prevails over liberty and one may so act. If true, this would mean that the supposed inalienability of the right to liberty was false. The idea of inalienability is that the basic goods are so central to human dignity that they cannot be voluntarily abandoned altogether: I can give up my right to own a particular object, but not my right as a human being to own property; I can deliberately surrender a limb but not my life; I cannot voluntarily submit myself to a life of deception and error; and so on. Needless to say, the point concerns a deliberate alienation, not a foreseen effect of the pursuit of some proportionate goal – one may engage in hunger strike even to death as a form of protest, one may risk liberty in fighting for one's country, and so on.

But inalienability seems to block any deliberate giving away of basic rights. This might lead some to say that one may not sell oneself into slavery for any reason, any more than one may enslave another even to save his life. I am not sure that this is right, since, as I have argued elsewhere, there are two alternative interpretations of selling oneself into slavery that are consistent with its not involving the alienation of a basic right.[63] One is that there would be no abandonment of the right to liberty, only a consent to submit to the authority of someone else in perpetuity; should one end up being freed or ransomed, one would be able to resume exercise of one's right to liberty, which shows that the right could never have been abandoned in the first place – otherwise how could it be got back? The other, about which I am more doubtful, is that the abandonment of liberty would be temporary, not permanent, and hence not a true alienation. But just as alienation cannot be partial, so it is hard to see how it can be temporary either, since the same question applies: if the right really leaves the possessor, how can it be regained?

Another principle for resolving collisions – one that some NL theorists will no doubt dispute – is that the closer relationship prevails over the more distant one, this being founded on the natural order of one's concerns. Hence, all things being equal – as with all principles this largely means *as long as there are no principles that override in the circumstances* – the rights of close family prevail over the rights of remote family, of both over friends, of all of these over strangers, of fellow countrymen over those from other countries. This is precisely why a person's obligation to feed his family prevails over his obligation to feed his friends or his fellow countrymen, or for that matter the starving of the world. And it is why he should be more concerned for the state of his own country than for the state of another – which is not to say that he should have *no* concern for the latter. Thus a person's duties radiate outwards through more to less proximate claimants for his moral attention, it being impossible for him to do everything for everyone. The claim that ethical partiality is central to NLT will not, as noted, be shared by every NL theorist. But it is founded on common-sense ideas about agency and possibility, and explains core intuitions we have about why we have obligations to certain people over others. It is for NL theorists who do not share this conviction to come up with a moral ordering lacking partiality and yet coherent with basic insights into the natural law.

The above discussion gives a sketch of how NL theory, based on the good, is to be action-guiding. In the competition between principles, no mechanical decision procedure can be applied. Each case has to be considered in the concreteness of its own circumstances, and competing principles have to be weighed and assessed with prudence. Aristotle was right that there is an irreducible core of practical wisdom at the heart of moral judgment. Nevertheless, it should be clear that there is enormous scope for a new generation of natural law ethicists to build on the historic tradition by making explicit what was taken for granted in ages when ethical agreement was the norm, not the exception, by refining and developing principles for dealing with apparent conflict and difficult cases, and by demonstrating the superiority of NL thinking in applying theory to practice. The day of applied natural law theory, stretching beyond the usual concerns of bioethics, cannot be far away.

4 Conclusion

Two principal ideas have animated the above discussion. First, the natural law theorist must bring metaphysics to the centre of argument concerning both the structure and content of the good. The contemporary focus on practical reasoning has tended to dominate recent debate, and it is by no means to be ignored. But it can only achieve so much. Natural law theory comes ready packaged, as it were, with a deep and rich metaphysical tradition that integrates it into other fundamental areas of thought. In this it is, I contend, far superior to any other theory currently at the forefront of moral philosophy. Only by respecting and developing metaphysics – the metaphysics of human nature being perhaps the prime example – can natural law theory have a sound footing.

Secondly, natural law theory is nothing if it is not a theory about how people should live – what choices they should make, how they should organize their lives, and how they are to decide when faced with concrete moral problems, from the most trivial to the most urgent. Because of the understandable emphasis on bioethics in recent decades, NLT in its applied mode has tended to become rather narrow and obsessed by a small circle of interconnected problems of life and death. It must, because of the demands of the current situation, continue working away at these questions. It should at the same time, however, broaden its applied base by tackling the sorts of everyday moral problem that confront most people most of the time.

This can only be done, I have argued, by constructing – rather, building on the already existent – system of principles that fuses the metaphysic of the good with the epistemology of moral decision-making. Included in that system are principles and subsidiary theories that do not engage the theory of the good in a direct and immediate way, but instead act as indispensable supplements to the analysis of rights, duties, virtues, and counsels that make up the material of ethical choice. These include: a theory of conscience; a theory of co-operation;[64] the Principle of Double Effect, on which much interesting and important work has been and remains to be done; the Acts/Omissions Distinction, which, like double effect, has been cast aside by the majority of ethicists only to be revived and reinforced by NL theorists; a theory of ethical decision-making in the face of doubt, incomplete information, and probabilities (here a revival of debate about probabilism and its rivals is to be encouraged); and a theory reintegrating the virtues into NLT, as against the futile if instructive recent attempts to develop 'virtue theory' as an ethic in its own right.

In NLT much remains to be done. Solid foundational work has already been achieved, but the overall programme must move in new directions, indeed into uncharted waters. The more agreement there is among natural law theorists on core matters such as the content of the good, the better; for without such agreement, consensus on the practical side will prove very hard to achieve. Whatever the future for NLT, it is well on the way to taking its place alongside the other theories that are the standard fare of contemporary philosophical instruction and controversy.

Notes

1. Chapter 3 of Mark C. Murphy's, *Natural Law and Practical Rationality* (hereafter *NLPR*) (Cambridge: CUP, 2001), is a good example of this tendency.
2. Finnis, *Natural Law and Natural Rights* (hereafter *NLNR*) (Oxford: Clarendon Press, 1980): ch. IV.
3. Gómez-Lobo, *Morality and the Human Goods* (hereafter MHG) (Washington, DC: Georgetown U.P., 2002): ch. 2.
4. Timothy Chappell, *Understanding Human Goods* (Edinburgh: Edinburgh U.P., 1998): ch. 2.
5. *NLPR*: ch. 3.
6. D.S. Oderberg, *Moral Theory: A Non-Consequentialist Approach* (Oxford: Blackwell, 2000): ch. 2.
7. *UHG*: 38.
8. Ibid: 8.
9. A. Fagothey, *Right and Reason* (St Louis: C.V. Mosby, 1963; 3rd edn): 183.

10. See further Aristotle's discussion in the *Nicomachean Ethics* 1174a9: 'It seems clear, then [since there are things we should not pursue no matter how pleasurable, and things we should pursue even though they bring no pleasure], that pleasure is not the good nor is every pleasure choice-worthy [hairetē], and that some are choice-worthy in themselves, differing from the others in kind or sources' (my translation). Aristotle's analysis is endorsed by Aquinas in the *Commentary on the Ethics*, Book X, Lecture 4 (trans. C.I. Litzinger, O.P.) (Notre Dame: Dumb Ox Books, 1993): 600–1.

11. Not that the aspirin-taker has to be able to articulate the full explanation!

12. Murphy, who also rejects pleasure as a basic good (*NLPR*: 96–100), comes at the same thoughts via a consideration of the alleged reason-giving force of pleasure and pain. My discussion coheres neatly with his own analysis, by which pleasure and pain only provide reasons for action through desires to pursue the pleasure or avoid the pain. Murphy argues persuasively (pp. 71–6) – if not necessarily beyond all doubt – that a desire for x only gives rise to a reason to pursue x *or to lose the desire for x*. Applied to pain and pleasure, these can then be denied to be fundamental reasons for action since they do not give reasons to avoid/pursue them as such, only to avoid/pursue them or to eliminate the desire to avoid/pursue them.

13. *NLPR*: 118–26.

14. Ibid: 123.

15. Ibid: 125.

16. D. Parfit, *Reasons and Persons* (Oxford: OUP, 1984): 497.

17. *NLPR*: 119.

18. The point is independent of any question about whether 'S has a reason to φ or ψ' is equivalent to 'S has a reason to φ or S has a reason to ψ,' which equivalence Murphy plausibly denies (*NLPR*: 72). The point could be made just as easily in terms of S's having a reason to have all desires satisfied or to have no desires at all.

19. Perhaps the extinction of all desire is the aim of some extreme forms of religious doctrine, but no NL theorist will sign up to it, nor ought they.

20. *NLPR*: 122.

21. Murphy might respond that the later, satisfied time-indexed desire *cancels* the prior, unsatisfied time-indexed desire, and so restores inner peace. But *if* this makes sense it can only be because there is a non-indexed desire *simpliciter* whose satisfaction does the work of restoring inner peace (acting as the common content of the two indexed desires and so enabling cancellation). But if this is so, we will be back with non-indexed desires as the ones that make the real contribution to inner peace, and the initial objection rears its head again, which Murphy had countered by introducing indexed desires in the first place.

22. *NLPR*: 125–6.

23. Ibid: 125.

24. Ibid: 133–5.

25. Ibid: 134.

26. I say more about this determinable–determinate relation in 'On an Alleged Fallacy in Aristotle', *Philosophical Papers* 27 (1998): 107–18.

27. *UHG*: 41.

28. Ibid: 42.
29. *Morality and the Human Goods*: 23–4.
30. Ibid: 23.
31. Ibid.
32. 'On an Alleged Fallacy in Aristotle'.
33. I take this definition from B. Wuellner, S.J., *Dictionary of Scholastic Philosophy* (Milwaukee: Bruce Pub. Co., 1956): 132, but have replaced his reference to the attainment of the last end of man with my reference to the attainment of the good. The reason is not that there is anything fundamentally different between the two formulations – attainment of the good just is attainment of the last end – but that I want to keep the discussion explicit about the good understood as a complex of basic goods.
34. *MHG*: 23.
35. *UHG*: 39.
36. *NLNR*: 88.
37. Ibid: 114–18, at 114.
38. *UHG*: 41.
39. Which does not, of course, mean that one may be *un*fair in the course of pursuing this good!
40. *MHG*: 13–14.
41. For those who take the account in Genesis to be other than historical, or who eschew religious accounts altogether (I do not count myself among their number), it still reveals important ideas about friendship and family that make universal sense, whatever one's (lack of) religious persuasion.
42. *UHG*: 41.
43. See further *Moral Theory*: 53ff.
44. Chappell asserts that it is a basic good, offering no further argument, indeed giving the matter one sentence; *UHG*: 40.
45. I mean 'exploit' in a non-pejorative sense.
46. All quotations from *UHG*: 44.
47. I have already endorsed finiteness (with brief argument in favour) in 'On an Alleged Fallacy in Aristotle': 117, where I say that 'just as all human action would be "empty and vain" (to use Aristotle's words) if practical reasoning did not come to an end, so it would be empty and vain, or more precisely impossible, if there were an infinite number of basic goods which an individual had to pursue in order to pursue the good as such.' See also *Moral Theory*: 41.
48. See the informative and well-illustrated website http://www.originsnet.org/home.html.
49. *UHG*: 44.
50. *NLPR*: 190–8.
51. Ibid: 193.
52. Ibid: 193 for both quotations.
53. See, for example, the passage from George quoted by Murphy at NLPR: 191.
54. Ibid: 195.
55. Ibid: 196–7.
56. Ibid: 196.
57. Ibid: 197.
58. In Chapter 2 of *Moral Theory*, I sketch the main lines of the fusion, but do not pretend to anything like the comprehensiveness and detail that are required.

59. Such as Chappell, *UHG*: ch. 3.
60. See *Moral Theory*: ch. 2.
61. B. Wuellner, S.J., *Summary of Scholastic Principles* (Chicago: Loyola UP, 1956), principle 508C, p. 101.
62. I discuss collision of rights at length in *Moral Theory*: 76–85.
63. See my 'Voluntary Euthanasia and Justice', in D.S. Oderberg and J.A. Laing (eds), *Human Lives: Critical Essays on Consequentialist Bioethics* (London: Macmillan, 1997): 22–40 at 236. See also 226, where duress is mentioned as another possible factor militating against free abandonment.
64. On which see my 'The Ethics of Co-operation in Wrongdoing', in A. O'Hear (ed.), *Modern Moral Philosophy* (Cambridge: CUP, 2004).

7
Harming and Wronging: The Importance of Normative Context

Suzanne Uniacke

1 Introduction

The principal purpose of this chapter is to draw explicit attention to the importance of normative context for two central elements of much contemporary non-consequentialist thinking about morally permissible and impermissible conduct. These two elements are moral *constraints* and moral *rights* as they are invoked across a wide range of issues in practical ethics. At the outset, I clarify the type of moral constraint and right that I have in mind and set out the particular relationship between them that makes normative context important to both. In the course of the chapter, I develop an explanation of what I mean by 'normative context' and of its importance to a widely accepted moral constraint and corresponding right.

2 Moral constraints and moral rights

A central feature of the contemporary non-consequentialist moral thinking under discussion is that it invokes constraints against particular types of acts because of their inherent features, that is, *in virtue of the types of acts they are* – as acts, for example, of intentional harming or of lying. It also holds that *as persons* we possess moral rights to act in particular ways and to be treated in particular ways. These constraints and rights constitute moral considerations that are independent of an appropriate commitment to a principle or duty of benevolence. On this view, concern for the beneficial outcomes of particular actions is relevant to moral judgement and decision *within* what the relevant moral constraints and rights allow. So, for example, it would be impermissible to cause one person's death as a means of providing life-saving organ transplants for several other people. This would treat a person merely as a means of promoting the welfare of others; it would contravene a constraint against intentional harming (in this case homicide); it would violate a person's right to life.

Moral constraints are negative in that they enjoin *against* certain types of act. Typically, such constraints are held to prohibit conduct that aims to harm, coerce, or deceive people. The particular moral constraint that is central to my discussion is usually construed as a prohibition against harming others or, more precisely, against aiming to harm them. Sometimes the harm concerned is qualified as serious, but the moral nerve of this constraint as a prohibition such against an act of a particular type is that one must not *aim* to inflict harm on others.[1] Some hold this to be an absolute or near-absolute prohibition such that if it admits of exceptions, it does so only in rare or extreme circumstances. Others regard the force of this weighty constraint somewhat less strictly. To allow for differing views about its stringency, I shall sometimes refer to the constraint as a moral presumption against acts that aim to inflict harm on others. (My use of 'presumption' is not meant to imply that the restriction is weak.)

The moral rights in focus are among those that are called basic human rights. We are held to possess such rights equally in virtue of our humanity or personhood; they are said to include the right to life and the right to liberty. Philosophical disagreement about the nature of basic rights is familiar enough, particularly on the question of whether they are only rights of non-interference or whether they also entail duties of positive action or assistance on the part of others. (Is your right to life simply a right not to be killed, or does it also require that others rescue you from danger if they can do so without incurring significant cost or risk themselves? Do I, a passer-by, violate your right to liberty in declining to free you from a serious impediment when I could easily do so, or is my conduct a gross failure of benevolence?)

In urging the importance of normative context to a central moral constraint and its corresponding right, I shall take rights such as the right to life and the right to liberty as rights of non-interference. This is not meant to suggest that such rights are always only rights of non-interference, but it does imply that such rights are, and must be, at least rights of non-interference. If the right to life means anything, it must provide moral protection against being killed; similarly, a right to liberty must morally protect against coercion. As rights of non-interference, the right to life and the right to liberty are distinguishable. Obviously to kill someone against his will is also to violate, indeed to extinguish his liberty; but a person's liberty can be violated to a very great extent short of actually taking his life. However, having noted this distinction, it will serve my present purpose to combine these two rights under a more general description that emphasizes their relationship, as rights of non-interference, with the general moral constraint against aiming to harm others that I identified earlier. This moral constraint prohibits or restricts certain types of interference with other people: we must not aim to harm them by, for example, killing or enslaving them. The constraint can be coupled with a right on the part of other persons not to have harm aimed at them.[2] Rights of non-interference possessed by persons are themselves moral constraints on the conduct of others.

The above exposition is intended to be relatively uncontroversial amongst both adherents and critics of the general ethical position outlined. What might be problematic for the following discussion, however, is that in addressing *ad hominem* those sympathetic to this position, what I urge could seem to have an air of preaching to the converted. There is a sense in which I would welcome this impression, since if what I maintain about the importance of normative context is right then I think it should be obvious. Moreover, the importance of normative context to the moral constraint and corresponding right in focus is in fact quite commonly implicitly accepted or invoked. The perplexing question is why this acceptance and its deeper theoretical significance are so seldom taken up in an explicit fashion.

The most effective way both to identify what I mean by normative context and to highlight its importance is to address an appropriate issue of practical ethics. The issue that I have selected for this purpose is the ethics of retaliation. The existence of a moral presumption against acts that aim to inflict harm on other people, together with a corresponding right of non-interference on the part of others, would usually be taken to have direct bearing on the question of the ethics of retaliatory action. The obvious approach to questions about the ethics of retaliation would then be to ask whether any such acts can be justified despite this presumption and corresponding right. Nevertheless, in this chapter my argument will go in the other direction. In my view, the relationship between normative moral theory and reasoning in practical ethics is two-way, and my argument here aims to show how the issue of the ethics of retaliation highlights the normative context in which we should understand a presumption against aiming to harm others and a corresponding right on the part of others not to have harm aimed at them.

The presumption against the intentional infliction of harm on others, and its corresponding right of non-interference, are frequently invoked in practical ethics, since both can be interpreted very broadly to encompass any interference that aims negatively to impact on a person's interests or welfare, including (harmful) coercive acts and deprivations of liberty. However, coercive acts and deprivations of liberty are arguably not always harmful to the subject's interests or welfare or intended as such. (Questions of paternalism attest to this.) Similarly, other prominent moral constraints, such as a presumption against deception, are not reducible in their rationale or their content to a general presumption against aiming to *harm* others. This makes it appropriate to ask whether what I shall maintain about the importance of normative context to the presumption against aiming to harm others can be generalized to other, distinct moral constraints. It is an important question, but not one that I have space to address in this chapter.[3]

3   The ethics of retaliation

Retaliation is a type of response – a reaction, typically to another person's conduct. I say typically because it is possible to retaliate against non-personal agents (e.g. by hitting the dog that bites you) and even against non-agents (the urge to strike photocopiers isn't unfamiliar). Perhaps there is also a notion of self-retaliation that involves self-imposed penalties for various lapses on our own part. Further, in characterizing retaliation as a response to conduct, I am using 'conduct' very loosely so as to include voluntary and involuntary actions (e.g. someone could retaliate against an injury that was either deliberately inflicted or accidental) and also what a person does as well as what happens to her (e.g. a loser might retaliate against a rival whose success is through her own efforts or is purely down to luck). Often, perhaps most often, retaliation is against conduct that has been directed at us or such that we are on the receiving end of it. Vicarious retaliation, however, taken on behalf of another person with whose cause the retaliating agent identifies, is familiar enough.

Retaliation differs from other responsive action in virtue of what retaliation is *a response to* and the *type of response* it is. We retaliate against conduct that we perceive, rightly or wrongly, as negative or bad. (We say that she repaid kindness with hostility but not that she retaliated against kindness with hostility.) Retaliation is *intended* as a response to conduct perceived as negative or bad. Here I use 'intended' in a weak sense to make a point about the explanation of retaliatory conduct even when it is spontaneous or unreflective. ('Why did you hit her?' 'She hit me.') A retaliatory response is hostile, meaning that it is unfriendly or opposed. (To repay cruelty with kindness or to turn the other cheek is *not* to retaliate.[4])

On the basis of these central features of retaliatory action, I use 'retaliation' in a fairly broad sense that includes as forms of retaliation some acts of self-defence, together with acts of revenge and retributive punishment. Revenge and retribution are clearly retaliatory, but perhaps we are unaccustomed to regarding self-defence as a form of retaliation. Admittedly not all self-defence involves retaliation: for instance, I might successfully defend myself by using an object as a barrier against attack. Nevertheless, self-defence can be and often is retaliatory where it involves counter-attack or striking back at an aggressor. Self-defence is retaliatory where the repulsion of a threat requires the return of force aimed at the infliction of harm on the aggressor. It is the fact that self-defence can require retaliation that raises the issue of the moral justification of self-defence. (There is no moral question about using a shield harmlessly to deflect an attack. However, the use of force that is aimed at inflicting injury on someone is morally significant – something that calls for moral justification.[5]) 'Retaliation' can of course be used in a narrower, backward-looking sense in which its rationale is always a payback or penalty for a past injury or wrong.[6] In this narrower sense, self-defensive action, which aims to repel or ward off an imminent threat, is not retaliatory even when it involves striking back; acts of revenge and retributive punishment would be paradigmatically retaliatory. I interpret 'retaliation' more broadly, however, to include any hostile act that aims to inflict harm on another person where the normative context of this act is that it is a response to negative conduct or treatment. These are the features of retaliatory action that are significant for my discussion.

To speak of 'the ethics of retaliation' suggests that there is something about retaliation itself that raises ethical concerns. Many would consider that retaliatory action requires moral justification in virtue of one or more of its inherent or characteristic features. As outlined above, retaliation is inherently hostile and characteristically aims to inflict harm of some kind on another person. Thus, retaliation *qua* retaliation would seem subject to a general presumption against acting with hostility towards others and aiming to inflict harm on them. A presumption against retaliation could be defeasible: on this view retaliation is morally wrong in the absence of an overriding justificatory reason. That is, I think, the standard view. I shall nevertheless maintain that we should reject it.

At this point I must stress that in the following discussion I am not urging the relatively uncontroversial claim that there is no single answer to the question of whether retaliation is justified. 'Retaliation' applies to diverse conduct, including: individual and collective speech and action; self-defence and defence of others; revenge; retributive punishment; and warfare. The motivation and rationale of the various forms of retaliation differ. Retaliation can be emotional or dispassionate; defensive, vindictive, or punitive; it can be a response to setbacks or injuries, or to wrongs or offences. The moral standing of those who are retaliated against varies across instances of defence, revenge, and punishment. For example, defensive force might be used against an insane attacker; members of a jury might become the subjects of revenge; punishment can be imposed on someone guilty of a heinous offence. These variations and others, for example in the effects of retaliation on the agent, on those retaliated against, and on others, can bear on the overall justification of particular retaliatory acts. That last claim is compatible with the view I will be rejecting, namely that retaliation always requires moral justification in virtue of its inherent or characteristic features. This is the view that there is a general presumption against hostile acts that aim to harm others, including a presumption against retaliation *qua* retaliation.

Shortly I shall question whether there is a general presumption against hostile acts that aim to harm others. But first, by way of contrasting presumptions I want to focus critical attention on what a presumption against retaliation *qua* retaliation might imply. Consider a presumption against speaking falsely with the intent to deceive. This is a presumption against lying *qua* lying. In this respect we can contrast such a presumption with, for example, a presumption against self-defensive homicide that would usually be said to arise from its being an instance of homicide. (On this view, there is a general presumption against killing *qua* killing; self-defensive homicide requires justification as an instance of killing.) Here self-defensive homicide does not require justification *qua* self-defence, but rather in virtue of the fact that it kills someone. Force used in self-defence is retaliatory, and the fact that homicide is committed in self-defensive retaliation is an important part of the justification of homicide in these circumstances. The salient features of retaliation that give rise to the purported presumption against it are that it is hostile conduct that aims to harm others. But then reference to *a particular form of retaliation*, such as self-defence, grounds the *justification* of an act with those features.

Consider also retributive punishment. Punishment is usually held to require moral justification as the intentional infliction of suffering on someone. But just as an appeal to self-defensive retaliation can ground the justification of hostile conduct that aims to harm another person, so the theory of punishment as retribution is a widely accepted justification of punishment. This problematic point – the justificatory role of some forms of retaliation – obviously bears on whether there is a general moral presumption against hostile acts that aim to harm others.

Is there a general moral presumption of this kind? Given the justificatory role of some forms of retaliation, it could be objected that my statement of the relevant moral presumption has been oversimplified. In particular, it might be said that as stated the presumption wrongly extracts conduct under the description 'hostile act that aims to harm another person' from the different normative contexts in which such acts occur. Such a presumption does not discriminate, for instance, between on the one hand, the use of defensive force and, on the other, an aggressive act that aims to inflict harm on someone else. This objection deserves to be taken seriously. Nevertheless, it must be said that the relevant moral presumption *is* typically expressed in a widely inclusive, non-discriminatory way: as a principle of non-maleficence, or as a general moral prohibition against the intentional infliction of harm. T.M. Scanlon's claim that, '...except for a few very unusual kinds of cases, we can accept a prohibition against intentionally inflicting serious harm on others' can be taken as representative.[7] But for the reasons outlined above self-defensive retaliation and hostile retribution, as justifications, are deeply problematic for this purported general presumption. Furthermore, the use of force in self-defence and the imposition of retributive punishment are not unusual kinds of cases; they are not the kinds of rare exceptions to a general prohibition against aiming to inflict serious harm on other people that Scanlon and others who cite this presumption have in mind.

If, as I maintain, the normative context in which a harmful act occurs is relevant to the role of a presumption against acts that aim to inflict harm on others, how should this context be explained or specified? One suggestion that arises from the objection canvassed above, that as stated the presumption wrongly extracts hostile acts from the different normative contexts in which they occur, would take the distinction between aggressive and retaliatory acts as pivotal. Aggressive and retaliatory acts are hostile and aim to inflict harm on others. However, it might be claimed that whether there is a presumption against an act with such features depends on whether the normative context of the act is aggressive or retaliatory: while aggressive acts that aim to inflict harm on others require moral justification, retaliatory acts do not. On this view, there is no presumption against the hostile infliction of harm that is a response to a harm received. (Such an act could, nevertheless, be unjustified if, for instance, the harm inflicted were disproportionate.)

That particular view is unsatisfactory. The normative context of all retaliation – the fact that retaliation is a response to (perceived) injury – is not itself sufficient to counter a moral presumption against hostile acts that aim to harm others. This is because 'retaliation' itself spans a wide range of morally significant normative contexts, both across different forms of retaliation and also within some forms of retaliation. For example, the threat that a particular act of self-defence aims to repel by striking back might be unjust, or it might be a just threat or one that is not unjust. Revenge is the return of injury with the intention of making someone suffer because she has made us suffer. People can resent and take revenge against justified setbacks or injuries; for example, they can persecute rivals who have won fair and square. Both vengeance and retribution are forms of retaliation for the commission of a wrong or an offence. Vengeance aims to pay someone back for a perceived wrong; where retribution is exacted from an offender, its rationale is to make the offender pay on account of her wrongdoing. Other forms of retaliation include angry reactions to various types and degrees of provocation.

The varied normative contexts across and within what can be classified as acts of retaliation undermine a claim that the normative context of retaliation itself – the mere fact that a hostile act is retaliatory – is sufficient to exclude it from a presumption against the intentional infliction of harm on others. But in questioning whether there is always a moral presumption against retaliation we needn't maintain that there never is. Arguably a satisfactory specification of the relevant presumption against aiming to inflict harm on others would be sensitive to the normative contexts of *some* forms of retaliation, such as self-defence against an unjust threat or retribution imposed for an offence, placing them outside the presumption. This could then allow retaliation to carry *positive* moral weight in some contexts, as indeed it does in widely accepted justifications of both self-defensive retaliation and retributive punishment. In both of these cases the purported justification of conduct that is aimed at harming another person, in the sense of imposing an injury, suffering, or deprivation on her, is a positive one (something we are entitled or required to do), as opposed to a justification that characterizes harmful conduct as a forced choice of the 'lesser of two evils'.[8] Where a form of retaliation, such as self-defence or retribution, is held to carry positive moral weight, the implication is that the object of the retaliation, although harmed, is not thereby wronged.

4   Harming, wronging, and retaliation

The distinction between harming someone and wronging her is familiar in some contexts. It is important, for example, to Joel Feinberg's interpretation and defence of J.S. Mill's 'harm principle' as articulated in *On Liberty*. Feinberg expresses the distinction between harming and wronging in terms of different senses in which we might be said to harm someone. To harm a person in the first of these two senses is to invade, and thereby to thwart, damage, or set back his interests or well-being. We can harm someone in this sense by inflicting physical, psychological, financial or other forms of damage on him, with or without his consent. Significantly, one can harm someone in this sense irrespective of whether the interest that is damaged is a legitimate one. (For example, a thief harms those from whom he steals; the thief is harmed by having his identity revealed to the police.) However, harm in the second of the two relevant senses *does* depend on the damaged interest being legitimate: to harm someone in this sense is to infringe her rights, to wrong her, to treat her unjustly.[9] (In this sense, a thief harms those from whom he steals, but the thief is not harmed by being identified to the police.) Obviously there is a good deal of overlap in practice between harming in these two senses. Nevertheless, the distinction between harming someone in the sense of damaging her interests or welfare, as opposed to harming her in the sense of wronging her or treating her unjustly, can be morally very important (independently of whether or not we accept the use to which Feinberg puts this distinction in respect of the 'harm principle'). In urging the importance of this distinction below, I shall myself refer to harming someone (in the first sense distinguished above) as opposed to wronging him, and not (as I think, confusingly) to two different senses of 'to harm'.

The distinction between harming a person as opposed to wronging her is crucial to the ethics of some forms of retaliation and to an appropriate understanding of the relevant moral presumption and corresponding right. For instance, the distinction helps to dispel what J.L. Mackie calls the 'paradox of retribution' that, he claims, arises because 'on the one hand, a retributive principle of punishment cannot be explained or developed within a reasonable system of moral thought, while, on the other hand, such a principle cannot be eliminated from our moral thinking'. The principle of punishment that gives rise to this purported paradox maintains that wrongful acts *require* a hostile response.[10] (On this view *not* to engage in hostile retaliation, for example to repay cruelty with kindness or to turn the other cheek, would require justification, and not the other way around.) Mackie then asks how this positive principle of retribution can be reconciled with the fact that 'a wrong action is intrinsically forbidden because it is harmful'.[11] He claims, more generally, that principles that require us to do harm cannot be integrated into a moral system that generally forbids harming.

Even if we accept Mackie's principle of positive retribution, the purported paradox arises, it seems to me, only if we agree that 'a wrong action is intrinsically forbidden because it is harmful'. An alternative view is that the relevant moral presumption is sensitive to normative context inasmuch as what it intrinsically forbids are acts that wrong others, that treat them unjustly, that violate their rights, as opposed to acts that harm them in the sense of interfering with their interests or welfare.[12] And while the object of intended harm is often thereby wronged, in *some* normative contexts to aim to inflict harm on someone is not thereby to wrong her. Two widely accepted such contexts are self-defensive retaliation against unjust aggression and hostile retribution as a response to wrongdoing.

Nevertheless, retribution is a controversial justification of punishment in the form of the infliction of suffering or deprivation, as opposed, say, to a rebuke or reprimand. If, as Mackie claims, it is integral to the concept of wrongdoing that it requires a hostile response, then that may leave open the type of hostile response required. For these reasons, something like a principle of self-defence against unjust aggression provides a more secure basis from which to challenge a purported general presumption against hostile acts that aim to inflict harm on others.[13] Provided retaliation (striking back) is necessary for self-defence and the degree of force used is not disproportionate, there is a widely accepted presumption *in favour* of this form of retaliation: the presumption is that the use of necessary and proportionate force in self-defence against unjust aggression is morally permissible.[14] Say we accept this presumption. Does this undermine a *general* presumption against hostile acts that aim to inflict harm on others? I think it does. However, the obvious alternative view to consider is that in a case of self-defensive retaliation there are two conflicting general presumptions that apply to one and the same action and that must somehow be resolved: on the one hand, there is a permission (right) of self-defence; on the other, there is a general constraint against acts that aim to harm others.

Can there be such conflicting moral presumptions for and against one and the same action? An easy affirmative answer would point out that an action can have more than one morally significant feature and can thus be characterized under different morally relevant descriptions.

In the case of self-defensive homicide, for instance, one *is saving one's own life* and also *killing another person*. There is a presumption in favour of the act of saving one's own life, under that isolated description; described as an act of killing another person, the presumption is against. (Philosophical discussions of the moral justification of self-defensive homicide are typically configured in this way: they accept that there are such conflicting presumptions and require that, for self-defence to be justified, these presumptions must be resolved by appeal to some consideration in virtue of which saving one's own life is overriding.) However, when we describe the act in question more appropriately and fully as killing in self-defence, the question resurfaces: If self-defence requires retaliation, does this generate a moral presumption against it? Such a presumption seems inconsistent with a principle of self-defence: if there is a right of self-defence against an unjust aggressor that includes the use of necessary and proportionate force, then the fact that an act of self-defence is retaliatory cannot also generate a presumption against it.

I do not think there is a presumption against genuinely self-defensive retaliation against an unjust aggressor. On the contrary, this form of retaliation is something to which we have a positive right: it is something that we are positively entitled to do. In this highly significant respect, the justification of self-defensive retaliation is unlike, for example, the justification of lying from benevolent motives or of breaking a promise in an emergency. If I lie or if I break a promise, say, in order to prevent suffering, then these instances of lying or promise breaking would need to be justified (if at all) as permissible infringements or violations of general presumptions against lying *qua* lying and of promise breaking *qua* promise breaking. But if we have a right of self-defence that *authorizes* the use of necessary and proportionate force against unjust aggression, then self-defensive retaliation cannot be a permissible infringement or violation of a presumption against retaliation *qua* retaliation or of a more general presumption against hostile acts that aim to inflict harm on others.

Nevertheless, I must acknowledge that retaliation is a contingent feature of self-defence. An act of self-defence aims to ward off or repel a threat, and if self-defence is possible without retaliation, for example by using a protective shield, then the presumption is against the use of retaliatory force (defending oneself by striking back). Hostile retribution, by contrast, is *essentially* retaliatory: its rationale is that it is a negative response to wrongdoing that (in the case of retributive punishment) aims to inflict suffering on the offender. So it can make sense to ask whether an act of self-defence is justified *despite* its requiring hostile action that aims to inflict harm, whereas it makes no sense to ask whether an act of retributive punishment can be justified *despite* its having these features.

Here, though, I question whether the fact that an act such as self-defensive retaliation *calls for* justificatory explanation means that it *requires* justification in the sense that implies that there is a moral presumption against it. To say that an act *requires* justification means that it is normally wrong, on some grounds or for some reason, but given the presence of countervailing considerations it can, under some conditions or in some circumstances, be morally permissible or right. Say I forcibly take something from your possession. In this case it is appropriate to *call for* justificatory explanation. Such an act *requires* justification if, for example, I was taking your car keys. (Perhaps I was doing this to prevent you from driving while intoxicated.) But if I was, say, doing what was necessary to retrieve my own wallet (or my medication or my child), then this can establish that there was no presumption against my acting in that way. In this case the normative context of my hostile action, the fact that I was retrieving something from your wrongful possession, can reveal that I had a positive right to act as I did. And this is so also with the use of necessary and proportionate force in self-defence against unjust aggression.

It is a mistake to think that the fact that any hostile conduct that aims to inflict harm on others calls for justificatory explanation implies that there is a moral presumption against all such acts irrespective of the normative context in which they occur (whether they are, e.g., acts of warding off unjust aggression or of retrieving something wrongfully taken). Furthermore, consider that we might decide against retaliating in self-defence against unjust aggression, or that we might let the thief make off with our wallet, preferring instead not to engage in hostile conduct that aims to harm another person. Here, in declining to inflict harm on someone in circumstances where non-maleficent treatment by us is not this person's due (we would not wrong her in acting otherwise), the *principle* on which we act is not that of non-maleficence but rather that of benevolence: we are being merciful, magnanimous. If this is right, then a presumption against hostile acts that aim to inflict harm on others must be shaped by reference to normative context; in particular, it must be shaped by particular normative relationships in which we stand to each other. While the mere fact that an act is retaliatory is insufficient to exclude it from a moral presumption against aiming to harm another person, the fact that such an act *prevents* or *remedies* an injustice can be sufficient to *reverse* such a presumption. (Significantly, a key concept in retribution as a positive justification of hostile treatment is the idea that it *counteracts* or *annuls* an injustice. Whether it does so, and how, is debatable. Nevertheless, central to retribution is the idea that, as Mackie says, wrongdoing calls for a hostile response. Not to respond to wrongdoing with hostility is, according to the positive principle of retribution, to let the injustice stand.)

5 The importance of normative context

It will be said that the importance of normative context is satisfactorily accommodated where the relevant moral constraint is held to prohibit acts that aim to inflict harm on *innocent* people. The constraint in focus is sometimes stated in this somewhat less inclusive way. But then how 'innocent' is to be interpreted is debated. The view that would appear to have the most currency is that 'innocent' in this context means 'currently harmless' (as opposed, say, to 'morally innocent').[15] The qualification 'innocent' does invoke a normative context to which the constraint against intended harming is held to apply: one must not aim to inflict harm on a person who is not currently harming (others). If we interpret 'harm' in the first of the two senses distinguished earlier (where to harm someone is to damage or set back her interests), then the qualification 'innocent' would place self-defensive retaliation, and also action against enemy combatants engaged in fighting, outside the constraint. However, so specified, the constraint against hostile acts that aim to harm others would apply to retributive punishment. (Even if a particular offender can be regarded as an ongoing threat to others, the rationale of retribution is that it is a hostile response to past wrongdoing.)

On the other hand, to interpret 'innocent' in the first sense (not currently harming) excludes too much. Consider, for example, a person engaged in self-defensive retaliation against unjust aggression: such a person *is* currently harming someone else (the aggressor). But surely someone engaged in self-defence against an unjust aggressor must be regarded as innocent in the relevant sense: it is his right of non-interference that is being violated by the unjust aggression, and it is on this basis that he can permissibly use necessary counter-force to defend himself. For this reason, 'innocent' is more plausibly interpreted as matching the second of Feinberg's two senses of 'harm', so that an innocent person in the relevant sense is someone who is not currently engaged in wronging another, that is, in violating another's rights or treating another unjustly. On this view, the normative relationship that underpins the permissibility of retaliatory force in self-defence is that the object of the hostile act is an unjust aggressor who, as someone presently engaged in violating another person's rights, does not have a right of non-interference that he would otherwise have as an innocent person.[16] This interpretation of 'innocent' could also extend to cases of retrieval or reversal of injustice (such as forcibly regaining one's medication or one's wallet). However, thus interpreted, the constraint would leave retributive retaliation as problematic.

As justifications, both retaliatory self-defence and hostile retribution maintain that although harmed, the object of the conduct is not thereby wronged. The context relevant to self-defence as a justification is strongly normative and evaluative: the hostile conduct is retaliation against an unjust threat. (Both 'retaliation' and 'threat' are normative; 'unjust' is evaluative.) The normative context that would be necessary to place hostile retribution outside a constraint against conduct that aims to harm others is not captured by the qualification 'innocent' under either of the two interpretations identified above (currently harmless/not currently wronging). Is there a plausible alternative interpretation of 'innocent' that would be sufficient to exclude both retaliatory self-defence and hostile retribution from the constraint? Not that I am aware of. For this reason, a general constraint that forbids aiming to harm other people must, I think, be interpreted as a constraint against wronging them, against violating their rights or treating them unjustly. And as such, it must be derived from a complex set of normative relations between persons that both reflect and explain who has the various rights of non-interference against others, and why. This is consistent with the non-consequentialist view that regards rights as reflecting considerations of justice, and which holds that as *legitimate* claims, rights are not reducible to considerations of interests or welfare, however multi-layered such considerations might be.

The specification of the set of normative relations in which constraints against interference, and corresponding rights, operate is a difficult task. Nonetheless, I am not convinced that when John Finnis says that 'there is no alternative but to hold in one's mind's eye some pattern, or range of patterns of human character, conduct, and interaction in community, and then to choose such specification of rights as tends to favour that pattern, or range of patterns', this is the best that can be said.[17] For instance, much contemporary non-consequentialist thinking about the nature of moral constraints and rights has lost sight of key aspects of traditional natural law thinking that could very usefully be revived. Particularly significant is the view that as rights of non-interference, so-called basic human rights such as the right to life and the right to liberty are conditional on conduct. (Is there a right that we can plausibly be said to possess unconditionally, irrespective of conduct, simply *qua* persons? Arguably the only such right is a right not to be treated merely as a means of promoting the welfare of others. Substantive rights implied by this more general right would include the right not to be enslaved, tortured, subjected to vicarious punishment, or treated merely as an object.)

It is important here to address two objections to what I have said about the importance of normative context to a presumption against aiming to harm others. The first objection is that I have outlined a vacuously circular position, whereby there is a moral constraint against wronging people, and people have a right not to be treated unjustly. My argument is, however, that the relevant moral constraint must be one that prohibits acts that wrong people. And for this reason, it must specify, defend, and take into account the normative relations that determine those whose moral status is such that they are wronged by having harm aimed at them, and those who are not. The second objection is that in questioning a general presumption against acts that aim to inflict harm, I have ignored the fact that harming something can be morally wrong even when the object of the harm has no corresponding right of non-interference. (Perhaps because it is not the kind of being or thing that can have rights.) However, nothing I have said implies that to inflict harm is not intrinsically a bad thing, or that harming something of positive value is permissible provided one violates no one's rights. What I have maintained is, rather, that whether or not there is a constraint that intrinsically forbids aiming to inflict harm on someone, such that to do so is to violate her rights, depends on normative context. It depends on whether, in the context of the act, the relation in which the object of the harm stands to others means that she has a right against this type and degree of harmful interference.

The distinction I drew earlier between acts that call for justification, as opposed to acts that require it, might seem like a fine one. Nevertheless, it is both theoretically and practically significant. To say that an act of a particular type requires justification is to maintain that there is a presumption against it. But, as I have argued, whether there is a presumption against a hostile act that aims to inflict harm on another person can depend on the normative context in which the act occurs. Failure to recognize this has led, for example, to unsatisfactory arguments that maintain that the use of force in self-defence against unjust aggression needs to be justified (somehow) as the 'lesser of two evils', or that such force is wrong but excusable, as opposed to permissible.

The last point leads me back to what I said at outset about the two-way relationship between normative moral theory and practical ethics. In this chapter I have addressed an issue of practical ethics in order to oppose a widely accepted *general* moral constraint against acts that aim to inflict harm on others. In conclusion, it would seem appropriate to ask what impact the rejection of this general constraint might have in practical ethics for the justification of particular acts that aim to harm others. For instance, would it have a significant bearing on the justification of such an act that there is a presumption against it if, as many maintain, such a presumption is defeasible? I think that it would. More generally, it is important to a judgment about the justification of any act whether or not there is a moral presumption against acts of that type. If there is a moral presumption against acts of a particular type, then this has a strong bearing on the nature and the weight of the considerations that are necessary, and that might be sufficient, to overcome or outweigh the presumption, and hence to justify such an act in particular circumstances. The considerations that might justify such an act are far more onerous and restrictive than would be the case were there no such presumption, were there no weighty moral barrier against the act to be overcome. Where there is a (defeasible) presumption against a particular type of act, then *not* to do that act is always a significantly stronger option, morally speaking, than were there no such presumption. And to refrain from doing that act is a stronger option still, than would be the case if there were a moral presumption in *favour* of that type of act. It matters to practical ethics whether there is an onus or burden morally to justify an act as an act of a particular type, or no such presumption, or a presumption in favour of that type of act.

Notes

1. Foreseen but unintended harm is morally significant and requires justification, but it can be permissible under certain conditions. The principle of double effect is relevant here.
2. This does not imply that any moral constraint necessarily entails a corresponding right on the part of the objects(s) of the constraint, but rather, that for this particular constraint against aiming to inflict harm on persons there is a corresponding right.
3. Significantly, problems of normative context arise for constraints such as those against deception and coercion that are said to derive from the conditions of rational autonomy. Is it permissible to lie to a murderer? Is it permissible to coerce a tyrant?
4. Retaliation is usually hostile, not simply opposed. However, some non-hostile responsive conduct is arguably, although at best marginally, retaliatory. Consider,

for example, a response that aims to demean someone on account of her rudeness, by taking the high moral ground against her. Is this retaliation? (I owe this question and the example to Mark Sacks.)

5. Some maintain that the use of genuinely self-defensive force never aims to inflict injury, its aim being to repel or ward off an attack, foreseen injury to the aggressor being unintended. This is implausible in my view. Someone acting in self-defence intends to use the type and degree of force necessary in the circumstances to repel or ward off the attack. This can mean, for example, intending to disable the attacker by injuring him. For a detailed discussion of intention and self-defence, see Suzanne Uniacke, *Permissible Killing: The Self-Defence Justification of Homicide* (Cambridge: Cambridge University Press, 1994): ch. 4.

6. The *OED* defines 'retaliate' as repayment of (injury, insult, etc.) in kind, as casting something untoward or bad back upon a person, as returning evil, as making reprisals.

7. T.M. Scanlon, *What We Owe to Each Other* (Cambridge, MA: Belknap Press of Harvard University Press, 1998): 209.

8. Some maintain that the use of (lethal) force in self-defence against an unjust aggressor must be justified, if at all, as the lesser of two evils (harming the aggressor being a lesser evil than suffering harm oneself). I argue against this view, and in favour of self-defence as a positive right, in *Permissible Killing*.

9. Joel Feinberg, *Harm to Others* (Oxford: Oxford University Press, 1984): ch. 1. The consent of the victim can also be relevant to the question whether to inflict harm in the first of these two senses is also to inflict a wrong. Feinberg distinguishes the second of these two senses of harming (wronging) as normative. However, any notion of harming is normative, since the notion of harming something invokes a standard (e.g. a *status quo* or an expected course of events) that the object of the harm is taken below by the (harmful) interference. Feinberg's notion of harming as wronging is not simply normative but evaluative.

10. J.L. Mackie, 'Morality and the Retributive Emotions', in his *Persons and Values*, ed. Joan and Penelope Mackie (Oxford: Clarendon Press, 1985): 207.

11. Ibid: 213.

12. Mackie states something like this view himself in the course of the same article (ibid: 211) when canvassing the argument that a person 'has the right not to be made to suffer as long as he commits no wrong...If he has unfairly invaded the rights of others, he cannot reasonably complain at what would otherwise be a corresponding invasion of his own rights'.

13. A principle of self-defence against unjust aggression would be more like Mackie's principle of permissive retribution that permits a hostile response to wrongdoing, as opposed to his principle of positive retribution that requires such a response; ibid: 207.

14. Some might maintain a stronger view, more akin to Mackie's principle of positive retribution, that self-defensive retaliation against an unjust aggressor is morally required in the absence of sufficiently weighty countervailing considerations. This stronger presumption could flow from a claim that we have a duty to prevent the infliction of unjust harm, even to ourselves. Usually, however, self-defensive retaliation is regarded as something that we are not morally obliged to engage in. The right of self-defence is a permission that

we can waive or choose not to exercise. Defensive retaliation against an unjust aggressor might be more widely thought to be morally required in cases of defence of a third party, where we are in a position to come to the aid of someone who is incapable of defending herself, especially where this person is someone for whom we have a special responsibility of care.

15. See, for example, G.E.M. Anscombe, 'Mr. Truman's Degree', reprinted in her *Ethics, Religion, and Politics: Collected Philosophical Papers*, Vol. 3 (Oxford: Blackwell, 1981); Philip E. Devine, *The Ethics of Homicide* (London: Cornell University Press, 1978); Thomas Nagel, 'War and Massacre', reprinted in M. Cohen *et al.* (eds), *War and Moral Responsibility* (Princeton NJ: Princeton University Press, 1974).

16. See Uniacke, *Permissible Killing*: ch. 5.

17. John Finnis, *Fundamentals of Ethics* (Oxford: Clarendon Press, 1983): 128.

8
Law, Liberalism, and the Common Good

Jacqueline A. Laing

1 Introduction

There is a tendency in contemporary jurisprudence to regard political authority and, more particularly, legal intervention in human affairs as having no justification unless it can be defended by what I shall call the principle of modern liberal autonomy (MLA). According to this principle, if consenting adults want to do something, unless it does specific harm to others here and now, the law has no business intervening. Harm to the self and general harm to society can constitute no justification for legal regulation or prohibition. So pervasive is this understanding of legal intervention in human affairs, that it is common now to encounter arguments in favour of permissive laws on, for example, private drug use, pornography, and sexual and reproductive choice, based on the idea that to intervene in these areas would constitute a breach of the liberal ideal.

The only alternative to MLA is assumed to be radical oppression, in which the State intervenes in the individual's life to impose unwarranted measures designed to further its own ends. The legacy of Stalin, Hitler and other modern tyrants has undermined conceptual appeals to the common good. So widespread is this liberal assumption in the Western, English-speaking world that critics of the outlook embodied by MLA are customarily regarded with suspicion and charged with paternalism, narrow-mindedness, and intolerance. Given those unbecoming epithets, one will probably be reluctant to identify oneself as a critic of the prevailing ethos. Nonetheless, highlighting contradictions inherent in the modern liberal tradition is precisely the kind of thing I want to do here. I will be arguing that there is a certain reliance on the notion of the common good within the natural law tradition that may be instructive.

According to this view, the common good constitutes a mean between two extremes: on the one hand, contemporary liberalism's over-insistence on radical individual autonomy and, on the other hand, totalitarianism's over-emphasis on collective social benefit. There is, I will argue, substantial terrain between the conceptual excesses of modern liberalism and oppressive tyranny that needs to be acknowledged and discussed.

Although there are numerous examples of legal prohibition that (at least implicitly) challenge MLA – such as laws imposing taxation, or prohibiting incest and bigamy between consenting adults, or laws prohibiting drug use and controlling pornography – this chapter will concentrate for the purposes of simplicity on matters surrounding sex, family, and reproduction. I will be arguing that moral and political debates surrounding the family throw up the sorts of question that challenge the very foundations of modern liberalism.

In what immediately follows, two opposing views are outlined. First considered are the claims of liberalism throughout the nineteenth and twentieth centuries. Then I discuss an older outlook, namely the natural law tradition, that depends on the idea that authority is exercised legitimately if it is committed to the common good of society but that to attain this it must employ morally acceptable means. I examine some central trends in that tradition.

I then consider the implications of prohibitions on mass human cloning, incest, bestiality, necrophilia, drug possession, and a number of other activities. An important dilemma facing defenders of MLA is laid bare. Either our commitment to modern liberal versions of individual autonomy will drive us to deny the legitimacy of laws even the fiercest defender of MLA accepts, or we drop our commitment to the contemporary liberal outlook and admit that modern liberalism, at least in its most widely accepted form, fails.

Finally, the roots of self-destruction implicit in the ideology itself are considered. Insofar as liberalism erodes the mechanism of its own survival, the ideology contains the principles that ensure its collapse. It is, I argue, an unsustainable doctrine, if not actually incoherent.

2 Historical foundations of modern liberal autonomy

The father of modern liberalism is generally thought to be John Stuart Mill. In his essay *On Liberty*, Mill formulates what is generally known as the Harm Principle thus:

The only purpose for which power can be rightfully exercised over any member of a civilised community, against his will, is to prevent harm to others. His own good, either physical or moral, is not a sufficient warrant. He cannot rightfully be compelled to do or forebear because it will be better for him to do so, because it will make him happier, because in the opinion of others, to do so would be wise, or even right.[1]

Liberalism has, in modern times, come narrowly to construe harm and, with it, the role for legal prohibition and regulation. It has been applied to break down a number of social and legal taboos surrounding sex and reproduction. Let us take pornography or homosexuality as examples. The idea is that as we have no evidence of any connection between social or individual harm here and now and pornography, there can be no prohibiting it. Certainly the 'harm to others' principle has been influential in a number of twentieth-century reforms. In 1957 Sir John Wolfenden published his committee's report recommending retention of the offence of soliciting and living off the earnings of prostitution, but decriminalisation of homosexual acts in private. Paragraph 61 of the Report sums up the committee's fundamental philosophy thus:

Unless a deliberate attempt is to be made by society, acting through the agency of the law, to equate the sphere of crime with that of sin, there must remain a realm of private morality and immorality which is, in brief and crude terms, not the law's business.[2]

There is an undeniable truth in this. After all, there are a great many sins or wrongs that go unpunished by the criminal law. I may seethe with murderous thoughts about my neighbour. I may fantasise about bringing about his demise, but if I do not engage my will, if I do not intend and take steps to carry out my desires, either myself or by conspiring with another, my black imaginings will go unpunished by law. I may entertain all manner of arrogant thought. If I do nothing to incite others to crime, then these thoughts will be of no interest to the law. Entertaining these thoughts, although not illegal, may well be regarded as evidence of an underlying vice – pride, perhaps. There is, however, no crime of pride, or anger, or envy, or covetousness simpliciter, at least not until these vices find their expression in some intention to commit a crime together with preparatory acts geared to achieving that end. Wolfenden was surely right to point out that there is a realm of private morality and immorality that is simply not the proper business of the law.

There are sound reasons why the law should not punish thoughts alone. Punishing immoral thought fails to recognise and reward the self-control that ensures that these thoughts are not acted upon. I may know that I have a tendency for envy or covetousness, and along with them dark fantasies, and I may be trying to control these poor characteristics in myself. To punish me for my thoughts, without giving credit to me for my self-control, fails to recognise worthwhile efforts to avoid immoral action. Moreover, the law has other public interests that morality does not. The means of supplying evidence of these vicious thoughts necessarily involves problematic techniques. The evidence would be purely confessional. There would be few if any public acts to confirm the charge; and so on. Getting evidence of thought crime would be licence for police brutality since confessions would be the sole source of evidence.

There may be good reason not to punish thoughts that are purely private. But it is clear that thoughts that are given public expression in the form of, say, conspiracy, complicity, and attempt are nonetheless routinely regarded as of interest to the criminal law and subject to criminal sanction.

There is then a fundamental truth behind the Wolfenden idea that there must remain a realm of individual vice (whether performed in public or private) 'which is, in brief and crude terms, not the law's business.' To recognise this fact, however, is not to acknowledge the greater claims made by Mill and those who follow him. Nor is it necessarily to accept without qualification the self-regarding/other-regarding distinction traditionally used to promote MLA.

The principle of MLA has been used in the twentieth century to widen the scope of that which is regarded as 'not the law's business.' And so in the West there is a continuing process of decriminalisation and legal accommodation of activities that, at other times and in many other places even now, are thought of as 'undermining the social fabric' and adversely affecting future generations.

The Wolfenden Report generated much public discussion and led to an important ideological exchange now known as the Hart–Devlin debate. In *The Enforcement of Morals*,[3] Patrick Devlin argued that '[t]he structure of every society is made up of politics and morals'[4] and more particularly that '[s]ociety is not something that is kept together physically; it is held by the invisible bonds of common thought...The bondage is part of the price of society; and mankind, which needs society, must pay its price.'[5] He was of the view that '[t]he suppression of vice is as much the law's business as the suppression of subversive activities.'[6]

He argued that 'there must be toleration of the maximum individual freedom that is consistent with the integrity of society'[7] but that tolerance should cease 'where there is a deliberate judgement that the practice is injurious to society.'[8]

Professor Herbert Hart's reply in *Law, Liberty and Morality*[9] argued that '[r]ecognition of individual liberty as a value involves, as a minimum, acceptance of the principle that the individual may do what he wants, even if others are distressed when they discover what it is that he does – unless, of course, there are other good grounds for forbidding it.'[10] He also suggested that Devlin's argument that maintaining moral bonds is essential to preserving society itself, rests on 'an undiscussed assumption...that all morality – sexual morality together with the morality that forbids acts injurious to others such as killing, stealing, and dishonesty – forms a single seamless web, so that those who deviate from any part are likely or perhaps bound to deviate from the whole...But there is no evidence to support, and much to refute, the theory that those who deviate from conventional sexual morality are in other ways hostile to society.'[11]

Finally, Hart urged that any society's views about morality will change from time to time, and that it is 'absurd'[12] to say, as Devlin does, that this means that one society has ceased to exist and another one has taken its place. Changing views about morality may more accurately be compared not with 'the violent overthrow of government but to a peaceful constitutional change in its form, consistent not only with the preservation of a society but with its advance.'[13] Of course, views about morality cannot be infinitely mutable if liberalism is not to amount to an inherently self-contradictory ideology. After all, there are ideologies that are opposed to liberalism. In order to accommodate these differences it is important to understand what liberalism is not. Liberalism cannot be all things to all people if it is not to degenerate into incoherence. The issues raised by Hart in his reply to Devlin will be discussed later in this chapter.

But let us return now to Hart's point about sexual morality. Hart distinguishes between 'sexual morality' and the 'morality that forbids acts injurious to others.' He criticises those who would regard these distinct categories as forming 'a single seamless web' on the ground that he sees 'no evidence to support, and much to refute, the theory that those who deviate from conventional sexual morality are in other ways hostile to society.' Hart's special concern for freedom, then, appears to take matters of sexual morality as primary.

This is the first assumption contained in Hart's critique: the harm-to-others principle should be construed narrowly to refer to harms 'here and now,' not in terms of broad-ranging notions such as the public interest and the interests of the next generation. The second is that there can be no social harm arising out of sexual activities performed by consenting adults in private. It is in this way that Hart is able to conclude that the law should not interfere with the private acts of consenting homosexuals.

Hart was likewise keen to point out that sexual morality is a matter of convention in a way that other kinds of morality are not, since there is no evidence to suggest that those people possessing what he regarded as unconventional sexual mores were likely to be 'in other ways hostile to society.' It should be understood that defenders of MLA customarily extend the idea of harm 'here and now' to permit legislation prohibiting that which causes *shock* or *offence*, here and now, by virtue of being witnessed (e.g. indecent behaviour, offensive billboards, soliciting, and so on). Accordingly, because the immediate offensiveness element is present in the case of soliciting, indecent behaviour, and the like, it falls within the Harm Principle whereas sexual activity in private between consenting adults does not. This element of immediate offensiveness is what distinguishes that which happens 'behind closed doors' between consenting adults from acts that imply a legitimate public interest.

Thus Hart's analysis mirrors what can only be regarded now as mainstream thought in the West. If it makes you happy, and you are consenting adults, and your proposal relates to matters defined by Hart to be private matters, then there should be no legal intervention, indeed possibly there should even be legal accommodation of the chosen activities and lifestyles. The 2004 Civil Partnership Bill, for example, allows same-sex couples to register their partnership and qualify for new rights and privileges. Both the present UK government and the Conservative opposition leader support the proposal, with the latter announcing that permitting same-sex civil partnerships 'recognises and respects the fact many people want to live their lives in different ways. And it is not the job of the state to put barriers in their way.'[14] Despite the dearth of political opposition in the UK, there has been spirited debate about the issue across the Atlantic. In *Romer* v. *Evans*[15] (the case more commonly known as the Colorado Amendment 2 Case), there were vigorous apologetics by defenders and critics of MLA in a case challenging the constitutionality of an amendment to the Colorado Constitution. Amendment 2 aimed to prohibit state and local governments from enacting, adopting, or enforcing 'any statute, regulation, ordinance or policy whereby homosexual, lesbian, or bisexual orientation, conduct, practices or relationships [would] constitute ... or entitle any person or class of persons to have or claim any minority status, quota preferences, protected status or claim of discrimination.' This proposal was adopted in November 1992 by a vote of 53.4 to 46.6 per cent.

John Finnis was called as an expert witness on behalf of the defendants, the Governor and the State of Colorado, arguing that the state's position was a secular one that traced its roots to the ancient Greeks. Finnis argued that 'all three of the greatest Greek philosophers, Socrates, Plato and Aristotle, regarded homosexual conduct as intrinsically shameful, immoral and indeed depraved ... all three rejected the modern linchpin of modern "gay" ideology and lifestyle.'[16] Martha Nussbaum, in her testimony, urged on behalf of the plaintiffs – homosexual activists, civil liberties groups, and representatives from some Colorado municipalities – that 'prior to the Christian tradition there is no evidence that natural law theories regarded same-sex erotic attachments as immoral, "unnatural" or improper.' A debate then ensued on whether homosexual acts were regarded by the Greeks, and in particular Plato, as an outrage, a shameless act, or as an adventure, enterprise, or deed of daring.[17] In the final analysis the majority of the Supreme Court (Scalia J. dissenting) found that Amendment 2 did discriminate against an identifiable class of people and violate their rights to due process and equal protection of law.[18]

In like fashion, the UK's proposals for same-sex civil partnerships assume that it is discriminatory to prevent same-sex partners enjoying the same kinds of privileges open to biologically unrelated heterosexual partners. In so doing, they pave the way for the legal and routine creation of children for same-sex partners using asexual techniques such as *in vitro* fertilisation. This class of children, needless to say, will be knowingly and deliberately created asexually to live without the love and support of at least one and sometimes both of their biological parents. Where surrogacy is involved, the children will sometimes be removed from their birth mother. Separation from one's blood (and birth) parents, once regarded as a 'damage limitation exercise' (e.g. in cases of extreme danger to the child), in no way chosen when avoidable, will become a legally recognised, chosen, and state-acknowledged way of life. Such separation, already recognised in law on an *ad hoc* basis with donor insemination and similar techniques, would be logically necessitated and, importantly, guaranteed by the State's recognition of the new family arrangement.

Hart did not make explicit reference in his discussion to reproductive autonomy. His technique, however, of separating sexual matters from matters in which the state has an interest, can and has been extended to the reproductive realm. Accordingly, the notion of reproductive (as distinct from sexual) privacy has been used to defend a raft of activities now regarded as standard, for example donor insemination, surrogacy, the freezing of gametes and embryos, and so on. Whether or not Hart would have supported reproductive liberty in the eloquent way in which he defended sexual liberty is a matter of speculation. What can be said with some certainty is that the debate in respect of reproductive liberty and autonomy is conducted in precisely the same way.

Indeed, the concept of sexual and reproductive autonomy is now one of the central and defining features of modern Western liberal society. Moreover, MLA with respect to the sexual and reproductive is a philosophy that fits neatly with a consumer mentality, if for no other reason than that if it does make someone happy there is usually substantial business in it. Whether the industry is in pornography, sex itself, abortion, or fertility, there is usually no small financial incentive involved as well.

That it has come to be widely thought that issues regarding family life, sex, and reproduction are wholly private matters in which the State has no business cannot be doubted. What Hart thought of as unconventional morality – fornication and adultery, *de facto* 'marriage,' asexual reproduction, and a host of activities once thought irregular – is now regarded as perfectly acceptable. Those who would raise any objection are generally regarded as 'moral fascists', Luddites, or, to put it bluntly, are forgiven as ignorant, first-generation immigrants yet to see the liberal light. Attempts at legal control of these areas of human activity are thought to be aimed at regulating private morality in the same objectionable way as penalising thoughts would be. Accordingly, it is supposed that these areas remain largely within the realm of the self-regarding and so implicitly non-harmful, rather than the other-regarding and therefore potentially harmful. This domain of human behaviour is generally thought to be properly immune from any legal regulation and prohibition deriving from consideration of the common good.

Because taboos surrounding sex, family, and reproduction are regarded as without rational foundation, a host of laws once thought justifiable, and indeed a necessary feature of the law's communicative function, are now thought to be wholly unjustifiable. Laws upholding monogamy and preventing polygamy or punishing bigamy are now beginning to be thought to impinge unnecessarily upon the private. Indeed Hart himself noted that opponents of the bigamy law might 'plausibly urge, in an age of waning faith, that the religious sentiments likely to be offended by the public celebration of a bigamous marriage are no longer widespread or very deep and it is enough that such marriages are held legally invalid.'[19] Further, it might now be argued that because in other societies polygamy is permitted, only outmoded Christian taboos, insupportable by liberal values, could explain traditional Western practice. Reproductive and sexual liberty, as we have said, are thought to be an essential feature of MLA. Indeed the prospect of multiple-party same-sex civil partnership arrangements might well constitute the future of the new family. In this intellectual climate so imbued with the assumptions of MLA, only the demand for incest between consenting adults gives the modern liberal pause.

Before concluding this section on the historical foundations of MLA, it is worth remembering that in most other societies now and in the past, it would have seemed most peculiar to assume that the mere characterisation of an activity as one that relates to the sexual or reproductive would be sufficient to take it outside the public sphere and into the domain of the purely private, there to be regarded as an inappropriate subject of restriction or regulation. Behaviour in this realm would have been (and continues widely to be) regarded, on the contrary, as the right and proper subject of restriction if only because the interests of the next generation, of children, of family, and of the tribe were at stake. The very character and spirit of the group or society would have been thought to be involved. Accordingly it would have been unthinkable to hive off the sexual and the reproductive from other areas of legitimate social or political intervention.

It is also worth remembering that, on any view of the matter beyond the familial, there are vast numbers of laws, even now, that interfere with the activities of consenting adults. These laws appear to exist irrespective of whether they are undertaken in private, and irrespective of whether they are thought to involve any direct harm to others here and now. Accordingly, any cursory examination of current English law will yield up offences of incest, bestiality, necrophilia, grave robbery, non-dangerous road traffic offences, non-dangerous forgery and counterfeiting, customs and excise offences as well as a host of non-dangerous offences against public justice such as making false statements as to births and deaths, and so on. These offences, appear to exist despite what consenting adults might want to do in private and despite the fact that no harm can be discerned immediately, here and now. We discuss some of these matters in the next section.

3   The natural law tradition and the common good

The classical natural law tradition has had little difficulty with the anxieties of modern liberalism. This is so for a variety of reasons.

Modern liberalism stresses the propensity of individuals to value different things differently, and often aligns itself with both individual and social relativism. The classical natural law tradition generally rejects this understanding of the world. Humans, by use of their reason, are able to understand the natural order inherent in the universe. The natural law tradition also stresses that there is a law that is the same for all people, that is at a certain level of generality, and that can be discerned by proper understanding of our nature. This is so even if there is a substantial portion of human law that is quite properly regarded as different for different peoples and at different times, such laws governing the side of the road on which citizens might travel, laws governing corporations, taxation, planning, and so on.

A second important reason why the supporter of the natural law tradition does not share the worries of the modern liberal is that, in the main, it is a tradition that has a developed sense of the common good. The writings of Plato, Aristotle, Cicero, Augustine, and Aquinas bear this out. Plato writes of the common good as embodied primarily in the virtue – justice – which with temperance, courage, and wisdom permit fellowship between heavens and earth, gods and men. He considers

> the mark to which a man should look throughout his life, and all his own endeavours and those of his city he should devote to the single purpose of so acting that justice and temperance shall dwell in him who is to be truly blessed. He should not suffer his appetites to be undisciplined...a mischief without end. For such a man could be dear neither to any other man nor to God, since he is incapable of fellowship, and where there is no fellowship, friendship cannot be. Wise men, Callicles, say that the heavens and the earth, gods and men, are bound together by fellowship and friendship, and order and temperance and justice, and for this reason they call the sum of things the 'ordered' universe, my friend, not the world of disorder or riot.[20]

For Plato, of the two choices of inflicting and suffering wrong, the greater evil is to inflict it, the lesser evil to suffer it. This is because good and evil are not even secondarily understood in terms of individual bodily pleasure, but in terms of 'the ordered universe' in which 'heavens and the earth, gods and men, are bound together by fellowship and friendship.' Of societies built on injustice or jealousy, Plato writes that 'such societies...are no constitutional states, just as enactments, so far as they are not for the common interest of the whole community, are no true laws.'[21] There should be 'no intention of conferring an office in ... society on anyone for his wealth, or his possession of some similar advantage, such as physical strength, stature, or family.'[22] It should be for the 'man who is most perfect in obedience to established law, the man whose victory over his fellow citizens takes that form, to whom we should give the function of ministry to the gods, the highest post to him who stands first, the second to him who is next in the contest.'[23] Indeed, Plato says, 'the preservation or ruin of a society depends on this more than on anything else. Where the law is overruled or obsolete, I see destruction hanging over the community; where it is sovereign over the authorities and they its humble servants, I discern the presence of salvation and every blessing heaven sends on a society.'[24]

Plato's common good is that which is one with God's law and opposed to 'vanity ... pride of riches or rank or foolish conceit of youthful comeliness.' He who 'needs neither governor nor guide, but is fitted rather to be himself a guide to others ... such a one works general confusion by his frantic career.' Although he is thought by some to be great, he is 'left alone, forsaken of God.' It is God 'who ... holds in his hands beginning, end, and middle of all that is, moves through the cycle of nature, straight to his end, and ever at his side walks right, the justicer of them that forsake God's law.'[25] In other words, it is God who is the guarantor of justice.

The common good, then, is conceived in eternal terms, not solely in terms of what might produce most satisfaction either to those who would rule or to those who would be ruled. The common good is conceived in terms of the fellowship of heavens and earth, of God and men.

For Aristotle, the political community and public authority are based on human nature and likewise belong to an order established by God. The understanding of this order is to be gleaned from the nature of things, the kinds or species to which individuals belong and the ends proper to them. As Aristotle's well-known proposition at the beginning of the *Nicomachean Ethics* has it, 'every art and every inquiry, and similarly every action and pursuit, is thought to aim at some good; and for this reason the good has rightly been declared to be that at which all things aim.'[26] All things aim at the good but the good of the community is regarded as the more godlike to attain. This is because 'even if the end is the same for a single man and for a state, that of the state seems at all events something greater and more complete whether to attain or to preserve; though it is worth while to attain the end merely for one man, it is finer and more godlike to attain it for a nation or for city-states. These, then, are the ends at which our inquiry aims, since it is political science, in one sense of that term.'[27]

But for Aristotle, the art of politics does not rule over the gods any more than virtue presides over philosophic wisdom. This is because politics derives from the gods and virtue derives from philosophic wisdom:

> But again [virtue] is not supreme over philosophic wisdom, i.e. over the superior part of us, any more than the art of medicine is over health; ... [f]urther, to maintain its supremacy would be like saying that the art of politics rules the gods because it issues orders about all the affairs of the state.[28]

And good government is neither tyranny, oligarchy, nor democracy, as Aristotle conceives it, because this would amount to corruption of the common good.[29] Furthermore, the common good is for Aristotle, as for Plato, a matter of friendship between men and God (or the gods) and not confined merely to the transient world of human convention. For Aristotle, the friendship of children to parents, and of men to God, is a relation to them as to something good and superior, 'for they have conferred the greatest benefits, since they are the causes of their being and of their nourishment, and of their education from their birth; and this kind of friendship possesses pleasantness and utility also, more than that of strangers, inasmuch as their life is lived more in common.'[30]

For Aquinas, the common good is that for which human society exists, it is the purpose of the human community.[31] Aquinas believes that human society, like everything else, exists to glorify God. Relative to the members of human society, it exists for the sake of the full flourishing of all of those members. That flourishing, the good of each individual, is dictated by the natural law. It is dictated by what reason determines to be the end or ends toward which God has determined every human to be directed according to his or her rational nature.

For Aquinas, the common good and justice are closely related. Laws are either just or unjust and laws may be said to be just according to their end when they are directed at the common good. These laws are neither excessive nor disproportionate. If indeed laws are just, they have the 'power of binding in conscience, from the eternal law whence they are derived, according to Proverbs 8:15, *By Me kings reign, and lawgivers decree just things.*'[32] Laws are said to be just 'both from the end, when, to wit, they are ordained to the common good, – and from their author, that is to say, when the law that is made does not exceed the power of the lawgiver, – and from their form, when, to wit, burdens are laid on the subjects, according to an equality of proportion and with a view to the common good. For, since one man is a part of the community, each man, in all that he is and has, belongs to the community; just as a part, in all that it is, belongs to the whole . . . .'[33]

Laws may be unjust, that is more like acts of violence, by being opposed to the human good in that they are over-burdensome or are not directed at the common good but at the good of the lawmaker, or are disproportionate. These laws do not appear to bind the conscience. Accordingly, Aquinas believes laws are unjust in two ways: 'first, by being contrary to human good, through being opposed to the things mentioned above: – either in respect of the end, as when an authority imposes on his subjects burdensome laws, conducive, not to the common good, but rather to his own cupidity or vainglory; – or in respect of the author, as when a man makes a law that goes beyond the power committed to him; – or in respect of the form, as when burdens are imposed unequally on the community, although with a view to the common good.' All laws of this sort are 'like are acts of violence rather than laws; because, as Augustine says (*De Lib. Arb.* i.5), "a law that is not just, seems to be no law at all." Wherefore such laws do not bind in conscience . . . .'[34]

Those who understand the individual good properly will also understand that the common good of the family, and of the state or the kingdom, is implied. In other words, seeking the good of the many is precisely seeking the good of the individual since the individual who does not harmonise with the whole of which he is a part offends the principle of unity. Thus Aquinas writes that '[h]e that seeks the good of the many, seeks in consequence his own good.'[35] This is so for two reasons: 'First, because the individual good is impossible without the common good of the family, state, or kingdom . . . Secondly, because, since man is a part of the home and state, he must needs consider what is good for him by being prudent about the good of the many.'[36] For Aquinas, 'the good disposition of parts depends on their relation to the whole; thus Augustine says (*Confess.* iii, 8) that "any part which does not harmonize with its whole, is offensive".'[37]

Accordingly, for Aquinas, the common good is not understood in purely relativist or subjectivist terms. It is understood as that which allows the destiny of men to be achieved, namely knowledge, love, and service of God. It is a theory that has little difficulty accommodating inter-generational concerns or seeing the need for taboos and prohibitions surrounding sex, family, and reproduction because 'the individual good is impossible without the common good of the family, state, or kingdom . . . .'

The classical natural law tradition appears, then, to reject some of the central driving forces behind MLA. It does not regard value as entirely a matter of individual or socially relative preference. On the contrary, it regards value as a mind-independent reality. A substantial part of human law may indeed be different for different people at different times (road rules, planning laws, etc.). But that part does not exhaust the totality of human law. This is so because there is a part of the law that is the same for all people at all times. This part is eternal and unchanging and is closely related to reason and truth. Examples of laws that are eternal and unchanging are those which prohibit the persecution, violation, or destruction of the innocent, and those principles within human law that demand proportionality and equity. For Plato and others in the classical natural law tradition, the common good is conceived in eternal terms, not solely in terms of what brings about, say, the greatest sensory satisfaction either for the ruler or those ruled. The common good is conceived in terms of the fellowship of the heavens and the earth, of gods and men.

In what follows I want to challenge popular versions of MLA. We will see how various examples challenge the principle of sexual and reproductive liberty or autonomy outlined earlier. Liberals will be faced with a dilemma. Either the commitment to this autonomy will prohibit laws purporting to interfere with, for example, mass human cloning (or the creation of animal–human hybrids, consensual incest, bestiality, or consensual cannibalism) or the liberal will have to drop his commitment to sexual and reproductive liberty and admit that MLA, in its most potent form, fails.

4 Autonomy and its limits

When Aldous Huxley wrote *Brave New World*,[38] he described the 'glass and nickel' and the 'bleakly shining porcelain' of the Central London Hatchery and Conditioning Centre. *Brave New World* painted a fearful picture of a place where human gametes and embryos were screened for flaws, destroyed if imperfect, quality-controlled and mass-produced in incubators. It was clean, clinical, and carefully calculated – and it was utterly inhuman. Huxley's vision of the future was, at the time, a disturbing one. We were invited to contemplate the dehumanised process of reproduction described, as well as the inhuman values that would regard it as normal. Reading the first chapter now, Huxley's imagined world is reminiscent of our own. Ectogenesis (gestation of children outside the womb) is not yet reality, but mass human cloning is virtually upon us. It is now commonly thought that so long as the clones are not gestated, there is no inhumanity in the process.

What, it might be asked, have asexual reproduction and the biotechnological reproductive revolution got to do with the Hart–Devlin debate? It is that Huxley's vision challenges the assumption that sex and reproduction are and ought to be somehow immune from public scrutiny because these are purely private matters between commissioning parties or sole reproducers,[39] as they are now called, and service providers. We cannot regard sex, family, and reproduction as purely private matters when they are entered into by consenting adults, and therefore as being immune from questions relating to the common good.

A man may indeed wish to clone himself one thousand times over. Or he may want to create a group of animal–human hybrids for useful service. Or he may be a doctor motivated by charity and so pleased also to create hundreds of children for consenting, infertile women – using his own sperm. MLA gives us no way of explaining why these desires ought not to be accommodated. If we are to say these kinds of acts are impermissible we need to go beyond the MLA and reach out for other general principles.

Why, it might be asked, should we balk at the prospect of mass human cloning, animal–human hybrids, and remote multiple parenting? After all, is it not mere moral squeamishness that leads us to deny the legitimacy of such developments? Are these not the intuitions of the Luddite or the 'moral fascist'?

The answer to these fundamental questions must be given in terms of the public interest in general and the interests of the next generation in particular. These wider concerns go well beyond those Hart assumed legitimate in *Law, Liberty and Morality*. They also challenge the two basic assumptions Hart used to question Devlin's argument, namely that (1) the harm-to-others principle should be construed narrowly to refer to harms 'here and now,' rather than broad-ranging notions such as public interest and the interests of the next generation; and (2) there can be no social harm arising out of sexual activities performed by consenting adults in private. On the contrary, I argue, public interest *can* include such things as the integrity of the individual and the dignity of all human life, respect for women and their dignity as mothers, and other vulnerable groups such as the disabled.[40] It might also involve recognition of the right to know one's genetic heritage.

Cases are currently being brought in the UK by children born of the fertility industry who want to know fundamental information about themselves. In *Rose and Another* v. *Secretary for Health and Human*

Fertilisation and Embryology Authority[41] two claimants, Joanna Rose, an adult and E.M., a child represented by her mother, sought any available information about their biological parents. In the course of the case Joanna Rose was, catastrophically for her, advised that this crucial information about herself had been destroyed by the clinic involved.

In a preliminary hearing before the High Court, Mr Justice Scott Baker, himself one of the architects of the Human Fertilization and Embryology Act 1990, concluded that 'Article 8 of the ECHR [European Convention on Human Rights, article protecting private and family life] is engaged in the circumstances of these claimants.'[42] Whether there has been any breach of the convention has, at the time of writing, yet to be determined. In the course of his judgement, Mr Scott Baker outlined the need of one of the plaintiffs, Ms Rose, to know her true identity. Joanna Rose, in her affidavit, described the position of the child born of donor insemination. This class of individuals, unlike all other people in the UK, has no right to fundamental information about themselves, their parents, relatives, medical inheritance, and race. Fertility clinics often have control of such information and are unwilling to release it despite the significance of that information to the children they have created. Whereas it is an offence to falsify the birth certificate of every other child in the UK,[43] children born of the fertility industry are offered no such protection. Joanna Rose, in her affidavit, suggests that there can be no resolution of her grief as she can only assume that her relatives are still alive. There is no comfort for her since there is no social recognition of the depth of her loss; rather, it has been assumed that this class of people has no right to complain because they owe their very lives to these techniques. Rose points out that she lives with the uncertainty of reunion, the very real possibility of passing her father or siblings on the street and indeed marrying one of them. She wonders whether they would recognise one another. She wonders whether her relatives think of her and whether they could meet. She describes the business of having used her social father's medical history as her own when in fact it has no conceivable relevance to her at all, and discusses the danger involved in medical misinformation.

> I have a strong need to discover what most people take for granted. While I was conceived to heal the pain of others (i.e. my parents' inability to conceive children naturally) I do not feel that there are sufficient attempts to heal my pain.[44]

Whilst it appears the case concerns the right to information, it is clear from Joanna Rose's evidence, and the nature of the whole case, that much more is at stake. One issue concerns the implications of permitting techniques that *systematise* asexual reproduction, particularly when the technique deliberately fragments the child's origins from conception. When the state legitimises these reproductive methods, it arguably creates arbitrary and irrational exceptions in respect of certain classes of people. Accordingly, this class could be systematically deprived of information about themselves, unlike all others. Moreover, this class could be created in ways, chosen and avoidable from the outset, that took it for granted that they would not need the love and support of their blood or birth parents. (The deliberate and avoidable nature of the activity is important.) This class could be created asexually and frozen (cryo-preserved), with multiple siblings involved. Such a class of people could be expected, unrealistically, to feel neither loss concerning their asexual beginnings nor any sense of confusion about multiple, unknown siblings, lost family, and separation by time, space, and cryo-preservation. This class of people might be created of parents long dead and yet be expected to suffer no loss, anger, or grief. Such people would be expected to suppress complaint on the grounds that they owed their existence to these artificial reproductive techniques and that many other people are also separated from their blood families by circumstance or necessity.

Nevertheless, the argument that the child born of these techniques has no right to complain since she owes her existence to them contains a profound non sequitur. A child born of abusive reproductive techniques, such as incest (where there is legislative prohibition), need feel no moral indebtedness to incest as a means of reproduction nor feel obliged to agree that incest is morally acceptable. Moreover, of fundamental importance to these reproductive developments, now routinely justified on the basis of MLA, is precisely that they are chosen (though avoid-able), deliberate, systematised, and permitted routinely by the state. The argument that many children are separated from their blood families by circumstance or necessity, hence children born of donor gametes should not feel aggrieved, holds little sway. Homicide is not the same kind of loss as natural or accidental death: one suffers an extra kind of grief and loss when one learns, not merely that a loved one has died, but that they have been murdered. Systematic homicide involves even a further dimension of wrongdoing. Likewise, loss of one's biological parents through death or necessity is unlike the same loss that is avoidable yet *chosen* for a child, and moreover systematised and legally sanctioned by the state.

Let us return to our examples of the man who wants to clone himself several times over, or create animal–human hybrids, or father hundreds of children. There may be a number of *social* reasons why permitting these acts would be an imprudent path for society to adopt: it might inhibit genetic diversity and thwart the useful mechanisms of natural selection, or perpetuate certain kinds of defects, and so on. But one of the most significant reasons for doubting the good of permitting these kinds of action relates to the interests of the people so conceived. One of the problems for clones derives from the fact that they will have been created *precisely* to be a genetic replica of another. Replication undermines the sense of uniqueness of the cloned person and creates in the mind of the client clone-creator expectations not ordinarily had of children by parents conceiving naturally. A further problem derives from the societal and family expectation, once they have been created, that clones suppress any identity problems that might arise for them in virtue of the fact that their genetic origins were fragmented from the beginning by never having had any genetic father (a sperm-free conception) or genuine biological mother (the relevant characteristics of the egg are absent). Another arises out of the questions of domination and control exercised over the child's genetic future by the very act of cloning. And problems also arise in virtue of their asexual beginnings, dehumanised in the way Huxley so eloquently described, and the profound fragmentation of their family and kin.

Clones would, after all, be living in the shadow of their prototypes and, to further undermine their uniqueness and individuality, in the case of mass human cloning, they would have to live in the knowledge that they had to establish their uniqueness against a multitude of other clones. If we consider the identity of any particular clone, let us for the sake of argument call her Eve, we see her origins have been quite literally scrambled. If Eve were to be brought up by the woman whose clone she was, her mother would be her genetic 'twin sister,' her social grandparents in a sense her 'genetic parents.' Her social uncles and aunts would be her genetic 'brothers and sisters,' and all because she was the genetic replica of another person. Not only would she have been asexually created, she would be a replica of an existing individual. (Contrast the case of identical twins, where although they might be genetic replicas of one another, the element of domination and control of the their future is ordinarily absent and the time at which replication takes place is limited to the early days after conception. Replication is not 'made to order' for the purpose of satisfying another's desire; it is, rather, a random process that does not occur within a technological framework in which children are used as means to ends.)

It is a familiar point that we cannot assume human cloning to be entirely safe, since similar experiments in animals[45] have resulted in gross disability, heart defects and malfunction in growth. But even if we do assume, for the sake of argument, that such physical malfunction can be overcome, there are still sound reasons to suppose that the child created by these means has been created in a wrongful or abusive way. We can see that even the clone has an interest in the manner and mode of her origins. Moreover, these interests cannot be set aside just because she owes her existence to her prototype or to those who asexually replicated her.

The point to be understood from the use of the example of mass human cloning is this. If we are to hold on to the idea that the law ought to intervene to prevent this kind of abuse, we will need to jettison MLA. It is hard to see what version of MLA could perform the conceptual work necessary to demonstrate why legal intervention is desirable. After all, there appears to be no immediate harm or offence done 'here and now' by permitting a man to clone himself a hundred times over where he is able to find consenting parties to assist him in his plan. Whatever conceptual apparatus we use to conclude that legal prohibition is appropriate will, I would argue, need to be derived from a moral world well beyond MLA.

Likewise, if we are to understand why we might balk at the prospect of routine creation of animal–human hybrids, we are going to need to appeal to moral generalities surrounding the interests of the class of children so created, their health, identity, family, and kinship. These generalities will emerge from a moral hinterland well beyond that traversed by MLA.

These paradigm cases of identity fragmentation place in sharp focus the issues concerning people conceived by donor gamete and other asexual reproductive techniques. Although not suffering the same number and kinds of loss as those suffered by clones, there are certain similar questions that arise for children born of both kinds of procedure. Very often, modern intuitions are so affected by notions of reproductive liberty that there is an unwillingness to hear of the concerns, loss, and grief of people conceived by the fertility industry. Their outrage is discounted as unwarranted and unjustifiable. It is often assumed that their sense of loss is best suppressed. So pervasive in contemporary Western society are the dogmas of MLA that they seem to obliterate ordinary human sympathy.

In fact there are, even in Western nations, familiar limits on both sexual and reproductive liberty. There are offences of bigamy[46] and incest even where the parties to the offence are consenting adults.[47] There are offences of bestiality (whether or not this causes immediate offence to anyone)[48] and there are offences of sexually interfering with a corpse, again whether or not the dead person would have agreed in life to such interference and whether or not the act causes offence to anyone.[49] The point of these examples is to challenge the notion adopted by Hart, and developed further in recent times, that sexual morality does not raise matters that imply harm to others in which the law has any business interfering, where the individuals involved are consenting adults.

If there is to be any recognition of the above examples as genuine offences, there will need to be an admission that MLA does not supply the necessary conceptual foundation for legal intervention in these areas. Whatever else is true, MLA cannot be the sole operative principle in determining the proper limits of the law in relation to sex and repro- duction. We cannot assume that matters relating to sex and reproduction are intrinsically private, self-regarding matters that are 'not the law's business.' Nor can we assume that in such matters the desires of con- senting adults, here and now, are the only relevant factors to be taken into consideration. There are societal interests, of which Devlin spoke so eloquently, and there are the interests of the next generation to be considered.

It is perhaps a little easier, then, to see why other cultures and other peoples have found strange the view that there should be no taboos or legal restrictions surrounding sex and reproduction: these involve the well-being and capacity to flourish of the people or culture, as well as, potentially, its very survival. This touches on Devlin's statement, so jarring to the modern ear, that the 'suppression of vice is as much the law's business as the suppression of subversive activities.' The statement sounds crude to us now, but implies a fundamental truth about the need to consider both the common good and the interests of the next generation in public matters surrounding sex and reproduction. If we are to be able to explain why we need to restrict the desires of the multiple cloner, we need to jettison our commitment to MLA. If we cling to MLA, we have no way of explaining what is wrong with mass human cloning and other abusive ways of creating people, such as incestuous reproduction.

The sexual and reproductive realms are not, however, the only ones that challenge MLA. It is worth remembering that there are a great many other areas of law which appear to contravene the principle. There are offences prohibiting the possession of controlled drugs (such as heroin, cocaine, and a multitude of other substances) whether or not the parties in possession are consenting adults, whether or not the harm caused by their use is solely done to the self, and whether or not this possession would allow the adult involved greater freedom to express himself in the manner he, as an individual, thinks fit. The rationale behind criminalising possession of drugs will be framed, if at all, in terms of the common good and the interests of society. Rational debate about whether a substance ought to be regarded as 'controlled,' and how it should be classified, must revolve around the immediacy and scope of the impact of the substance, the propensity of the substance to cause long-term illness whether mental or physical, the likelihood that widespread availability of the substance will interfere with the ordinary life of fellow citizens, as well as the cost to the nation of long-term, freely available use. All of these questions presuppose a realm of rational discussion that is well beyond the scope envisaged by MLA.

Again, a large part of the criminal law is dedicated to non-dangerous road traffic offences. Not only are there offences that do not immediately raise the spectre of danger or harm, such as parking offences, but there are also offences that prohibit driving without a seatbelt or riding a motorbike without a helmet. There might well be rational debate about whether these regulations intrude too deeply into the individual's life in defence of the common good. But such debate, insofar as it accepts the in-principle legitimacy of such laws and regulations, takes it for granted that *some* intervention is warranted to promote the common good, whether or not such intervention limits the individual's freedom to express himself.

There are, in addition, offences against public justice, whether or not these offences cause any actual harm or affront to others, and irrespective of whether the offender's interest in freedom of expression is thereby limited. False statutory declarations;[50] concealment of evidence;[51] contempt of court;[52] false statements about births, marriages, and deaths;[53] and perjury[54] are offences whether or not there is any third-party victim. It is generally assumed that there is a legitimate category of offence dedicated to the defence of the common good of public justice.

Indeed there are a great many offences relating to the vice of dishonesty which do not depend on the existence of any victim before they take effect. Certain kinds of fraud, counterfeiting, tax offences, forgery: none of these depend essentially on the notion of a victim of harm, whether actual or threatened.

In English law, at least, there is also the contentious offence of assisting suicide whether or not the victim consented.[55] Likewise, a German court recently convicted self-confessed cannibal Armin Meiwes of man-slaughter, sentencing him to eight-and-a-half-years in prison.[56] Meiwes admitted killing and eating Bernd Juergen Brandes after sex and hours of sadomasochism, but insisted his victim had volunteered. The com-puter technician killed and ate Brandes, whose body parts he froze, after placing an advert on the Internet. He told the court in Kassel that it was the realisation of an ambition he had had since his youth, when he fan-tasised about consuming classmates. The conviction and punishment of a defendant accused of killing his albeit-willing victim demonstrates that violation of a person's consent is not the only rationale for the pro-hibition on killing.

Those who hold that such prohibitions are appropriate, despite the victim's consent, will point to the interests of society in criminalising the relevant behaviour. They will make the same kinds of points as those made by Lord Templeman in *R* v. *Brown*, a case of conviction for assault between consenting sadomasochists, when he asserted that '[s]ociety is entitled and bound to protect itself from the cult of violence. Pleasure gained from the infliction of pain is an evil thing. Cruelty is uncivilised.'[57] Even the dissenting judge, Lord Slynn, did not dispute that 'if society takes the view that this kind of behaviour, even though sought after and done in private, is either so new or so extensive or so undesirable that it should be brought . . . within the criminal law, then it [would be] for the legislature to decide.'[58] In other words, society might well have an interest in criminalising such behaviour (since it promoted a cult of violence, threatened the vulnerable, and was generally det-rimental to the social fabric) whether or not the adults involved consented to the behaviour and undertook it privately.

In defence of MLA, it might be argued that individuals value things differently and that because one man's virtue is another man's vice it is neither for the courts nor for parliament to judge. On this view, there is no moral objectivity in the virtues or the vices: a life dedicated to consensual cannibalism is equal in value to a life dedicated, for example, to music or medicine. Each to his own, it might be thought. Accordingly, it might be argued, there should be the promotion of genuine autonomy. Laws imposing prohibitions should be limited to those that violate a person's freedom to consent. Since no one's consent is violated in cases such as Brown or Meiwes, and no harm done to anyone else, there should be no state persuasion either way. On this view, there is no moral objectivity except that which attaches to individual consent.

The trouble with this kind of rationale is that it seeks to insist on moral objectivity when it promotes MLA but at the same time denies that there can be any genuine moral objectivity at all. Even the proponent of MLA must insist on the moral objectivity of his own position if it is not to degenerate into incoherence. Proponents of MLA, for example, regard the creation of so-called victimless crimes as unjustified and oppressive to the human spirit and are loath to permit offences that entrench traditional conceptions of marriage. They press for moral reform, arguing against this alleged oppression and injustice. It is by meditating upon the details of particular moral positions that we begin to see how moral objectivity is presupposed. This is a familiar objection and one that has been considered at greater length elsewhere.[59] For our purposes it serves to highlight the inconsistency inherent in MLA, which leads its supporters to attempt arbitrarily to privilege certain moral conclusions at the expense of coherence.

As to consensual acts and the common good, one reason it might be thought proper to prohibit consensual cannibalism is simply that its legalisation licenses homicide, one of the most serious kinds of criminal offence. On this view a market in intentional homicide is contrary to the common good. It endangers the innocent, the vulnerable, and the system of justice itself in significant ways. Since life is necessary for human flourishing of any sort, the deprivation of it constitutes a loss to society, to the family, and to the individual whose life is cut short. The fact that the victim consents to the bringing about of his own death for a cannibalistic or, indeed, any other purpose does not detract from that grave loss. Moreover, the institutional recognition of intentional killing creates dangers to the innocent that a legal system, with its limited powers of detection and proof, cannot eliminate. Favouring the interests of the intentionally homicidal interferes with the interests of the law in protecting its vulnerable members and ensuring injustice can be detected at all. Consent is easily manufactured – where in writing, forged – and acquired by duress or unconscionable means. Where there is state-sanctioned medical killing, for example, the opportunity for systematic and wholesale homicide of the vulnerable, the elderly, or the young – whether for pleasure, monetary gain, spare hospital beds, or organs – becomes a reality. A climate is created in which those who were once professionally obliged to care for and cure vulnerable individuals become instead the very same people who seek out the consent to kill and perform the practice of killing these same vulnerable individuals.

Once a homicide conviction is made to depend on the issue of the victim's consent, the principal means of investigating wrongdoing, namely forensic evidence such as lethal doses of drugs in the body, bodily harms, and the like, disappear as a ground for suspicion in their own right. Whilst searching for consent might be an appropriate way of dealing with lesser matters, like criminal damage, theft, and assault, it is a less prudent way of dealing with grave matters which currently attract, proportionally speaking, the most serious penalties. Homicide, all things being equal, attracts graver penalties than non-fatal and property offences.

Accordingly, it would be appropriate to protect the innocent from abuse, and to safeguard the legal system against systematising injustice, precisely by limiting the autonomy of those whose desires threaten these goods. On the position I am defending, the gravity of the offence – the taking of innocent human life – would be a sound reason to regard even consensual homicide as a thing that ought nonetheless to constitute a legal taboo, with all its associated prohibitions. Nothing less than the combined values of life and justice would be at stake. The same might not be said of other forms of vice in which the common good was not threatened. For example, it might be a vice for two consenting adults to meet to enjoy conversations steeped in envy of another's goods, or to engage in conversations that were grossly racist in nature. It would not, however, be appropriate to create legal prohibitions to prohibit such activity. Public goods would not be at stake, in the way that they would be in the case of systematised consensual homicide (whether for cannibalistic or other purposes). In the latter case, the vulnerable, the psychologically unstable, the morally weak, the young, the foolish, and the easily suborned would be the first to find their very lives endangered. As in many other walks of life, a permissive mentality would endanger those least capable of defending themselves.

The recognition that prohibitions are appropriate in the case of consensual homicide (in a way that they are not in the case of racist gossip) arises out of a proper understanding of principles of proportionality, moral similarity and difference of kinds, and of the fundamental human goods. To apply principles of MLA to prohibit legal intervention in respect of consensual homicide on the grounds that 'one man's virtue is another man's vice' suffers from several defects. First and foremost, it disallows proper discussion of the very rational principles that allow us to see individual freedom and consent as fatally undermined by recognition of consensual private homicide in a way they would not in the case of vicious private gossip. We can no longer see how grave a threat is involved, or how difficult it would be to prove any kind of wrongdoing. We blind ourselves to the threat to the vulnerable and, in our effort to protect the freedom of the suicidal, we are prepared to sacrifice the innocent and indeed our very system of detecting injustice and doing justice.

At the beginning of this chapter it was made clear that there is some truth to Wolfenden's idea that 'there must remain a realm of private morality and immorality which is, in brief and crude terms, not the law's business.' Hart's supposition that the sexual is precisely the limit at which the law's interest should expire, however, is doubtful. There are sound reasons to regard a proper legal approach to the sexual, the reproductive, and other areas of public life as challenging MLA. Furthermore, an understanding of individual and common flourishing allows us the conceptual resources with which to undertake rational debate in the first place.

5   The self-destructive and totalitarian aspects of liberalism

> The preservation or ruin of society depends on this more than on anything else. Where the law is overruled or obsolete, I see destruction hanging over the community; where it is sovereign over the authorities and they its humble servants, I discern the presence of salvation and every blessing heaven sends on a society.[60]

In the course of his discussion, Lord Devlin argued that there must be 'toleration of the maximum individual freedom that is consistent with the integrity of society,' and that tolerance should cease where 'the practice is injurious to society.'[61] One of Hart's objections to Devlin's worries about societal breakdown was that any society's views about morality will change from time to time, and that it is 'absurd' to say, as Devlin does, that this means that one society has ceased to exist and another one has taken its place. It will be remembered that Hart was of the view that changing opinions about morality may more accurately be compared not to 'the violent overthrow of government but to a peaceful constitutional change in its form, consistent not only with the preservation of a society but with its advance.'[62] This argument in itself is compelling. We change. Society changes. The thought that societal change necessarily entails societal decline cannot be supported logically. Hart was surely right to point out that change is not necessarily deleterious.

There is, however, one matter that neither Devlin nor Hart expressly considered in their respective essays on liberalism, perhaps because the problem did not present itself as starkly in those days as it does now, and perhaps too because they were not concerned with matters of fertility and reproduction.

Hart's liberalism is now establishment ideology but there are grounds for suspecting that this once-unconventional perspective is running into difficulty. One interesting feature of liberalism is that it appears to go hand in hand with native populations' decline. This may be the result of the fragmentation of what is left of the tribe, viz. the nuclear family, as well as of widespread contraception, abortion, infertility, and the greater atomisation of individuals. Whichever way we look at it, Western liberal societies appear not to be in the business of replacing themselves. One obvious problem with any prevailing ideology in a society that fails to replace itself, is that the society may well be replaced by people who do not adopt the same ideology as those establishmentarians, liberal or otherwise, within it.

That native population decline is a feature of modern Western liberal society cannot be doubted. There has been continuing population decrease, both absolute (leaving aside immigration) and relative, in all Western liberal countries. One U.N. publication, *World Population at the Turn of the Century*, reports that 'Europe is literally melting away like snow in the sun, slipping from 15.6 per cent of the world population in 1950 to 10.2 per cent in 1985 and 6.4 per cent [projected] in 2025.'[63] The United Nations method of choice for addressing the declining population and creating the numbers necessary for economic survival is replacement migration.[64] It recommends one million replacement immigrants a year to make up the shortfall in the skilled workforce of the UK and to pay the pensions of an ageing population. Hart spoke with equanimity of changing morality, never explicitly recognising that a potential volte-face in the outlook of Western countries' inhabitants might be entirely at odds with his own liberal ideals. Not all ideologies are logically compatible with liberalism. It cannot be assumed that replacement societies will adopt modern liberalism as their preferred ideology. It is in this environment that the oppressiveness of liberalism is bound to become manifest.

If liberalism can be regarded as containing within it the seeds of its own native population decline, a dwindling liberal establishment will need to cling to power with the use of greater and greater intolerance. Demographic decline and replacement migration is one thing. Ideology replacement, however, is quite another. In order to sustain itself in its death throes there will need to be a powerful use of propaganda and the domination of legal, political, and educational institutions to oust dissent by suppression of alternative views. Universities will not be prepared to entertain legitimate debate. Significant posts in government, media, and in universities will be advertised to liberals, in liberal establishment organs, for candidates who are sufficiently liberal ideologues. Schools will teach MLA as a fundamental quasi-religious dogma, all the while observing the destruction of the central pillars upon which all society is founded, namely, family and religion. The ruling elite will increasingly suppress alternative viewpoints and, ironically, those very alternatives to liberalism will all the while exist in ever greater supply by virtue of its need for replacement populations.

What might not have been any problem for a society whose fundamental structures were strong will prove the undoing of a liberal society in decline. And so, for example, public symbols of rejection of MLA will be banned in desperate attempts to entrench a failing ideology. Thus we see in France and Germany the banning of headscarves in schools. This simple item of apparel, a symbol of Islamic feminine modesty and public testimony to the wearer's ultimate allegiance to religion and family, incites sufficient fear in the minds of the declining French liberal establishment that it has thought fit to ban it from schools. Such oppression would never have been considered in a flourishing France whose fundamental structures were intact and whose population was burgeoning. Humanity's need for religious expression would have been respected and understood. In a decaying liberal France, on the other hand, this kind of prohibition constitutes an answer of sorts, albeit an oppressive one, on behalf of an ideology in retreat. Paradoxically, what may have had its origins in a respect for freedom will become a parody of freedom. A false ideology bent on liberty at any cost will take liberty hostage and ransom it as it self-destructs.

In section 3 it was suggested that the classical natural law tradition has within it the conceptual apparatus that allows us properly to understand freedom in society. It rejects the relativist idea that there can be no rational debate about morality because each man has his own value and each culture different customs. It highlights the inherent self-contradiction of such an outlook, for even liberalism seeks to entrench itself as a moral norm. Natural law permits an account of law for human beings that is eternal and unchangeable (whether or not the ruler, ruling elite, or the majority recognise it). It supplies an analysis of morality and law that allows us to regard tyranny and oppression as timelessly and unchangeably unjust extremes. Equally it supplies the mechanism by which we are able to recognise self-destructive ideologies such as MLA for what they are. Individual flourishing is to be found in the common good and this latter, in turn, depends on the true nature of humanity which can be discovered via the use of human reason.

In the classical tradition, the natural law does not become law because or when it is written down, any more than physical laws become laws when they are understood or published in textbooks . The natural law derives from the eternal source of all things. It is this that allows us to understand oppression and tyranny for what they are.

We noted that there was some truth to the idea that '[u]nless...the sphere of crime [can be equated] with that of sin, there must remain a realm of private morality and immorality which is, in brief and crude terms, not the law's business.' Oppressive regimes seek to create thought crimes, to intrude upon the genuinely private, destroying human modesty, constantly monitoring human words and deeds – even those of the innocent – as well as suppressing art and originality, and allowing police extensive powers to watch, intervene, and arrest citizens on the basis of supposition. This kind of oppression is a familiar characteristic of a number of tyrannies of the twentieth century. It would be edifying, if somewhat implausible, to believe that it was these kinds of concern that motivated the Wolfenden reforms.

As suggested early in this chapter, there are good grounds for believing that the law should not punish private vice, such as wicked thoughts alone. Punishing immoral thoughts fails to recognise and reward the self-control that ensures that these thoughts are not acted upon. Law is bound up too with questions of evidence, detection and prevention in a way that morality is not. The means of supplying evidence of individual vice, for instance private racist thoughts, necessarily involve problematic techniques (such as obtaining confessional evidence in the absence of public acts) that can endanger the innocent.

To agree that there should be no laws punishing thoughts alone is not, however, to agree that there is no such thing as vice. On the contrary, it presupposes a realm of private vice in which there should be no legal intervention. The reason for this is not that morals are relative or the desires of consenting adults paramount, but that the form of intervention necessary would itself pose a grave threat to the innocent and to the system of justice. It was Augustine who asked: 'What are states without justice but robber bands enlarged?'[65] It is precisely the recognition that the state itself may become the wrong-doer that suggests the need for legislative restraint. A much-admired feature of English law is its protection of the innocent by means of principles such as *habeas corpus*, the presumption of innocence, and the high standards of proof characteristic of criminal cases. The power of the state and its officials to abuse the innocent and perpetrate injustice upon them is appreciated. Permitting state punishment of private vice allows the state to intrude upon the lives of the innocent in novel and unjust ways.

It is by understanding the potential threat to the innocent and to justice itself by the recognition of thought crimes, that we begin to discern two opposing excesses. The first is that of MLA (with its false supposition that the sexual, the reproductive, and a host of other activities now argued to be beyond the law's legitimate interest, cannot bear on the public good). The second excess is that of totalitarianism (with its preparedness to sacrifice the innocent in its determination to root out threats to the state). If legal intervention to protect the common good is indeed a mean between two extremes, the idea that certain sexual activities are more akin to 'thought crimes' than to genuinely subversive behaviour is at least, on the face of it, plausible. By contrast, the recognition of homosexual 'marriage', with its promise of systematised means of reproduction that deliberately deprive children of their blood parents, albeit with the consent of all parties to the 'service contract,' unfairly privileges the interests of this generation over those of the next. It does so also with the complicity of the state. It is this sort of concern that fuels existing prohibitions on human cloning, incest, and other abusive means of bringing children into the world.

Elevating the interests of consenting adults at a cost to later generations, on the assumption that these new people will owe their existence to their forebears and thus have no right to complain, is rationally unsustainable. The argument that children born of incest or rape have no ground to reject the legitimacy of the way they were created simply because they owe their very existence to this means is a *non sequitur*. It is often the case that good emerges from evil. To say so implies neither that the evil means used was not evil to begin with, nor that the innocent beneficiaries of such unjust acts must agree to their moral permissibility. The same idea, that from wickedness and wrongdoing much good may come, is contained in an enchanting and ancient Christian hymn[66] marvelling that Adam's taking of the forbidden fruit led to the creation of the 'Lady Queen of Heav'n.'

6 Conclusion

We have seen a number of ways in which the principle of MLA is challenged by existing English law. Drug possession laws, traffic laws, laws protecting public justice and government, are examples of laws that defend the public interest irrespective of whether the acts regulated or prohibited do harm to others here and now. Likewise, laws preventing human cloning and animal–human hybrids demonstrate that there are undoubtedly limits on reproductive liberty in the interests of generations to come. Laws punishing incest, bestiality, and necrophilia (never mind more contentious laws entrenching Christian values such as monogamy) whether or not undertaken behind closed doors challenge the principle of sexual liberty. All threaten MLA. We have observed that many of these laws, in different ways, seek to protect the interests of the vulnerable, the next generation, and the very fabric of society (implicit in institutions such as that of the family, public justice, or government itself).

Modern liberalism prides itself on having secured certain rights and freedoms – to destroy one's self, one's offspring, and collectively to destroy one's culture. Built on the empty rhetoric of relativism and blind to its own *de facto* subservience to illicit industries, MLA promises the good life and then drives us to individual and collective self-destruction. A suicidal ideology that scorns the very means of its own survival is destined to encounter difficulty. An increasingly atomised and alienated life for a steadily ageing population, desperate for the material security for which it paid by life-long service, will quite literally be supplanted by more robust, life-loving theories and cultures. It is in this context that the tyranny of liberalism with its thought crimes, ceaseless monitoring, persecution of the innocent, and attempts to manufacture and control its own citizens is bound to become manifest.

It might be asked whether scientific and commercial techniques such as cloning and asexual reproduction offer liberalism a safe haven against the self-destruction implicit in its modern embodiment. All the signs are that human cloning, conception using donor gametes, and artificial reproduction in general cannot solve that problem. First and foremost, nurture of a child is a lifelong commitment. It also implies a financial cost that the state could not undertake by itself. The very tenets of liberalism erode the desire, the will, and even the rationale to undertake those kinds of life-altering commitments. As long as there are no privileges that attach to the obligations surrounding child rearing, as long as marriage is regarded as one among many partnership options and marital fidelity, the *sine qua non* of child support, ridiculed as otiose, as long as sex is routinely separated from babies by contraception, the commitment and labour associated with child rearing will simply not be undertaken by liberal ideologues or those millions of us who have grown up with liberalism's legacy.

By contrast, certain strands of thought within the classical natural law tradition, the earliest articulation of which can be found in the thought of Plato and Aristotle, supply the conceptual mechanism that enables us to discover a place of equilibrium between the dual excesses of liberalism and totalitarianism. It is here that a proper understanding of both common and individual flourishing is to be discovered. It is from within the natural law perspective that the self-destructiveness of liberalism and the injustice of totalitarianism may be discerned. As we move into an era of mass human cloning, animal–human hybrids, routine freezing of young human life, and children conceived asexually of parents long dead, it will be vital to turn to the wealth of understanding contained in the classical natural law tradition.[67]

Notes

1. J.S. Mill, *On Liberty* (London: Penguin, 1974): 68–9. For an opposing view, see Sir James Fitzjames Stephen, *Liberty, Equality, Fraternity and Three Brief Essays* (Chicago: University of Chicago Press, 1991 [1873]).
2. *Report of the Committee on Homosexual Offences and Prostitution*, 1957, Cmd. 247, Par. 61.
3. P. Devlin, *The Enforcement of Morals* (Oxford: Oxford University Press, 1965).
4. *Enforcement*: 9.
5. Ibid: 10.
6. Ibid: 13–14.
7. Ibid: 16.
8. Ibid: 17.
9. H.L.A. Hart, *Law, Liberty and Morality* (Oxford: Oxford University Press, 1963) (quotations from 1975 edition).
10. *Law*: 47.
11. Ibid: 50–1.
12. Ibid: 51.
13. Ibid: 52.
14. *The Independent*, 10 February 2004: 'Howard in U-turn Over Gay Marriages'.
15. *Evans et al.* v. *Romer, Governor of Colorado et al.* 882 P. 2d 1335 (1994).
16. John Finnis, '"Shameless Acts" in Colorado: Abuse of Scholarship in Constitutional Cases', *Academic Questions* 7 (1994): 10.
17. John Finnis and Martha Nussbaum, 'Is Homosexual Conduct Wrong? A Philosophical Exchange', in Alan Soble (ed.), *The Philosophy of Sex* (Lanham: Rowman & Littlefield, 2004; 4th edn), originally in *The New Republic* (1993); Finnis, '"Shameless acts" in Colorado'; Martha C. Nussbaum, 'The Use & Abuse of Philosophy in Legal Education', *Stanford Law Review* 45 (1993): 1627–45; Nussbaum, 'Platonic Love and Colorado Law: The Relevance of Ancient Greek Norms to Modern Sexual Controversies', *Virginia Law Review* 80 (1994): 1515–1651; Gerard V. Bradley, 'In the Case of Martha Nussbaum', *First Things* 44 (1994).
18. *Romer, Governor of Colorado et al.* v. *Evans et al.* (94–1039), 517 U.S. 620 (1996).
19. Hart, *Law*: 43.

20. Plato, *Gorgias*, 507e–508a, in *The Collected Dialogues of Plato*, E. Hamilton and H. Cairns (eds) (Princeton: Princeton U.P., 1961) (see *Dialogues* for notes up to and including 25).
21. Plato, *Laws* IV, 715b.
22. Ibid., 715b–c.
23. Ibid., 715c
24. Ibid., 715d.
25. Ibid., 716a–b. Also 'For the good man 'tis most glorious and good and profitable to happiness of life, aye, and most excellently fit, to do sacrifice and be ever in communion with heaven through prayer and offerings and all manner of worship, but for the evil, entirely the contrary', *Laws* IV, 716d.
26. Aristotle, *Nicomachean Ethics* I.1, 1094a, trans. W.D. Ross: *The Works of Aristotle*, vol. IX, ed. Ross (Oxford: Clarendon Press, 1925).
27. *Ethics* I.2, 1094b.
28. *Ethics* VI.13, 1145a.
29. Aristotle, *Politics* III.7, 1279b, trans. Jowett, *The Works of Aristotle*, vol. X, ed. Ross (Oxford: Clarendon Press, 1921): 'Of the above-mentioned forms, the perversions are as follows: – of royalty, tyranny; of aristocracy, oligarchy; of constitutional government, democracy. For tyranny is a kind of monarchy which has in view the interest of the monarch only; oligarchy has in view the interest of the wealthy; democracy, of the needy: none of them the common good of all.'
30. *Ethics* VIII.12, 1162a.
31. St Thomas Aquinas, *Summa Theologica* I–II, q. 92 a. 1 ad 3: 'The goodness of any part is considered in comparison with the whole; hence Augustine says (*Confess.* iii) that "unseemly is the part that harmonizes not with the whole." Since then every man is a part of the state, it is impossible that a man be good, unless he be well proportioned to the common good: nor can the whole be well consistent unless its parts be proportionate to it' (trans. Fathers of the English Dominican Province; London: Burns, Oates and Washbourne, 1927 (2nd edn, vol. 8).
32. *Summa Theologica* I–II, q. 96 a. 4, resp.
33. Loc. cit.
34. Loc. cit.
35. *Summa Theologica* II-II, q. 47 a. 10 ad 2.
36. Loc. cit.
37. Loc. cit.
38. Aldous Huxley, *Brave New World* (London: Flamingo, 1994 [1931]): ch. 1.
39. Julian Savulescu, 'Procreative Beneficience: Why We Should Select the Best Children', *Bioethics* 15 (2002): 413–26. See also John Harris, 'Rights and Reproductive Choice', in John Harris and Soren Holm (eds), *The Future of Human Reproduction: Choice and Regulation* (Oxford: Oxford University Press, 1998): 5–37.
40. A similar list is suggested by Maureen McTeer in 'A Role for Law in Matters of Morality', *McGill Law Journal* 40 (1995): 893–903.
41. *Rose and Another* v. *Secretary for Health and Human Fertilisation and Embryology Authority* (2002) EWHC 1593 (ADMIN).
42. Article 8(1) states: 'Everyone has the right to respect for his private and family life, his home and his correspondence.'

43. Perjury Act 1911, ss. 3–4.
44. See note 41.
45. Dolly, the first sheep to be cloned by scientists, was put down because of her severe disability: 'Dolly the Sheep is dead', *The Daily Telegraph*, 15 February 2003, p. 1.
46. Offences Against the Person Act 1961, s. 57.
47. Sexual Offences Act 2003, s. 64.
48. Ibid., s. 69.
49. Ibid., s. 70.
50. Perjury Act 1911, s. 5.
51. Criminal Law Act 1967, s. 5.
52. Contempt of Court Act 1981.
53. See note 43.
54. Perjury Act 1911.
55. Suicide Act 1961, s. 2.
56. See global press, 30 January 2004.
57. *R v. Brown* (1993) 97 Cr. App. R. 44 at 52; (1994) 1 A.C. 212 at 237.
58. Ibid. at pp. 89 and 282. The emphasis is mine. Cf. *R v. Wilson* (1996) Cr. App. Rep. 241, in which branding one's consenting wife with a hot knife within the confines of the marital home was not regarded as proper matter for criminal investigation or prosecution. Perhaps what distinguished the two cases despite the manifest element of violence was precisely the 'cult' element in the case of *Brown*.
59. On the inconsistency inherent in moral relativism, see David S. Oderberg, *Moral Theory* (Oxford: Blackwell, 2002): 19–20, where he also quotes W.V. Quine's remark: 'He [the cultural relativist] cannot proclaim cultural relativism without rising above it, and he cannot rise above it without giving it up' ('On Empirically Equivalent Systems of the World', *Erkenntnis* 9 (1975): 313–28 at 327–8).
60. See note 24.
61. See notes 7 and 8.
62. See note 13.
63. *World Population at the Turn of the Century* (New York: United Nations, 1989): 8.
64. 'Immigrants Needed to Save West from Crisis', *The Guardian* 22 March 2000. See also: *Expert Group Meeting on Policy Responses to Population Ageing and Population Decline*, Population Division, Department of Economic and Social Affairs, United Nations Secretariat, New York, 16–18 October 2000.
65. *City of God* IV. 4: 'Remota itaque iustitia quid sunt regna nisi magna latrocinia?'
66. 'Adam Lay Y-bounden' (c. 1450), in *The New Oxford Book of Christian Verse*, ed. D. Davie (Oxford: Oxford University Press, 1981): 21. 'Ne had the apple taken been . . . Ne hadde never our Lady / A been heaven's queen.'
67. Previous versions of this chapter have been given at the Oxford Jurisprudence Discussion Group and at the Society of Legal Scholars seminar at the University of Birmingham. I would like to thank the participants for their helpful comments, in particular Stephen Shute, John Finnis, and John Gardner. I would also like to thank Hugh Henry and Ian McLeod for lively and profitable discussion of the subject matter.

9

'Double Effect' or Practical Wisdom?

Gerard J. Hughes

1   Aim

The Principle of Double Effect (PDE) traditionally has had two related functions: the primary function has been to explain why an action which apparently contravenes some absolute moral principle is after all not wrong; and the secondary function to provide a kind of test matrix into which any permissible action must fit, and hence to offer a decision procedure for dealing with complex cases. PDE, occurring perhaps only once in the writings of Aquinas,[1] associated with the Jesuit casuists in Louvain and lambasted by Pascal, is still a source of controversy.

Unsurprisingly, the traditional uses of PDE are for the most part concerned with difficult situations involving human life, since a principle of fundamental importance is obviously involved. Thus we have Aquinas's views on killing in self-defence, and other medieval discussions of such actions as destroying a bridge for urgent reasons of military strategy while knowingly killing refugees who are still trying to escape across it. In more recent times, PDE has been appealed to in connection with the termination of an ectopic pregnancy, or the use of lethal injections to alleviate pain in cases of terminal illness. To kill an innocent human is surely one of the clearest instances of wrongdoing, yet this apparent moral commonplace is called into question by the demands of public good, or care for the needs or the rights of others. To some, the casuistic use of PDE has seemed to offer a coherent and humane way of dealing with difficult situations involving moral conflict; to others such as Pascal, PDE has seemed to be little more than a licence for laxity.

I shall not in this chapter comment on all the issues raised by several contemporary commentators. Many of these issues have been sufficiently set out and dealt with in different though not unrelated ways by both Timothy Chappell and Sophie Botros.[2] I am broadly in agreement with their analysis of the ways in which many criticisms of PDE are either beside the point or unsuccessful. Chappell and Botros are nonetheless willing to defend the principle in one form or another. It will be my contention that, on the contrary, PDE cannot provide any decision procedure at all that would be a useful means to dealing with difficult cases, nor can it provide a satisfactory *post factum* explanation and defence of what was done, nor can it explain why the agent should be exonerated from full responsibility for the adverse effects.

I set out the classical statement of PDE in the form in which Botros gives it:

1. The action in itself, as specified by its object, must be good or at least indifferent.
2. Only the good effect may be intended.
3. The good effect must not be produced by means of the evil effect.
4. There must be a proportionately grave reason for permitting the evil effect.

The first and third of these conditions in the classical formulation were essential in order to avoid the charge that the end could justify the means. Such a charge would be sustained if the action in itself were wrong, a possibility that is excluded by 1; similarly, if perhaps less obviously, the charge would be justified if the means to the good effect were itself wrong. Putting the two together, PDE set out to exclude any causal chain in which an earlier member was wrong, no matter how good the final outcome might be. It is not the case that PDE sought to absolve the agent from all accountability for the bad outcomes of what was done, as 4 makes clear; but it does imply that foreseeably permitting a bad outcome does not in itself entail that the agent is morally blameworthy, whereas the agent is morally blameworthy whenever such an outcome is intended.[3]

Plainly, then, PDE depends upon being able to formulate a clear view of what is to count as the action in itself as distinct from its consequences and circumstances, and on having a clear account of intending as distinct from foreseeing. I hope to show that neither of these requirements can be fulfilled without begging the key questions. Hence I shall spell out why PDE fails as a decision procedure and has severe limitations even as an explanation of decisions taken. I will then outline the obvious alternative, an account which, I hope, will satisfactorily avoid the charge of the end justifying the means without making any dubious assumptions about intending and foreseeing.

2 'The action in itself'

Confusion in this debate is sometimes caused by unacknowledged differences in the use of the term 'action'. Many writers will speak of the same action under different descriptions; others will individuate actions by their descriptions. Both ways of using the term are entirely legitimate, but to avoid confusion in what follows I shall take it that actions are individuated by their descriptions. I shall use some neutral term such as 'behaviour' or 'what was done' to refer to what happened without categorising it in any further way. Thus, which action was performed might be a matter of dispute, even if there is agreement on some other description of what happened.[4]

The first clause of PDE requires that the action in itself should be morally good or morally neutral. The reference to 'the action itself' is often implicitly or explicitly related to Aquinas's criteria for determining whether or not an action is morally wrong.[5] Now, Aquinas claims that while a type of action can be morally neutral, an individual action cannot.[6] Hence the first clause in the traditional formulation of PDE was probably intended to refer to types of action rather than to individual actions. Types of action can be more general or more specific: killing an animal, killing a human being, killing the innocent, and killing the innocent in self-defence are all types of action. Individual pieces of behaviour can instantiate several morally significant types (feeding a child, caring for a child's welfare, looking after someone in need even at one's own expense, and refusing to feed some starving people, for instance, might all be instantiated by one piece of behaviour in a refugee camp); and the moral qualities of these types may be conflicting.

Two key problems arise in this area. The first is how action-types are to be assessed morally. It might be argued, for instance, that walking down the road is morally neutral, or that killing a human is morally wrong, or that curing someone's illness is morally right. Even in simple cases like these it is perhaps not entirely clear how the assessment is arrived at. Be that as it may, Aquinas claims that while a type of action can be morally neutral, an individual action cannot. Other examples of action-types are much more difficult: killing innocent humans while saving a city from rape, murder, and pillage (to take a traditional example); punishing parents for the misdemeanours of their children (to take a more modern one). It may be the case that whatever assessment of an action-type is reached, it will still be true to say that any action instantiating just that type and no other morally significant type will have the same moral quality as the type itself does. The difficulty arises from the fact that we have so far no instructions on how to take an overall view of the morally conflicting elements involved in the action-type.

There is a second and even more serious problem, that of identifying which type of action an individual piece of behaviour instantiates. Obviously, this will depend on the facts of the individual case; but it will crucially depend also on which of those facts are taken to be morally relevant. This is true, though trivially so, even in the case of murder since, if a particular piece of behaviour is truly describable as murder, there will not in fact be any other morally significant features to be taken into consideration. But similar considerations arise in other instances as well: it was once put to me that in saying to my hostess that her meal had been lovely, I was not merely being polite, I was also lying, and even that I was wrongfully ignoring the interests of future guests. In my view, such moral considerations as truth and the needs of future generations were simply irrelevant at that point in time, important though either might be in other circumstances. If the view is controversial, then that serves to make my point. It is a matter of dispute which action I did in fact perform that evening, and the answer to that question is often not obvious. I would not accept that I lied, nor even that I lied in a good cause, and certainly not that I was heedless of the comfort of future guests. I was being polite, grateful, and trying not to undermine the confidence of a young woman. To this point we shall return later.

While the texts are not entirely clear, I believe that what Aquinas means by the 'object' of an action just is the (perhaps complex) action-type which that individual piece of behaviour instantiates, whatever that might be. That such complexity could in his view arise is evident from his comment that the circumstances in which the agent acts sometimes have to be taken into account in determining the object of an action itself. This is the case whenever it is not the degree of goodness or badness involved in an action that is affected by the circumstances, but rather when its moral quality is changed from permissible to wrong, or the reverse.[7] This is tantamount to claiming that the circumstances sometimes make a difference to which action was in fact performed.[8] It is also, as we shall see, significant that it seems to be a judgement about the particular case which determines the way in which the object of the action is defined, and not the other way round.

The first clause in the traditional account of PDE requires that the action itself as specified by its object, and as distinct from the consequences of that action or its end, must be in itself morally permissible. This is the requirement that excludes any suspicion of the end justifying the means. But the clause provides no method for deciding when the requirement is fulfilled. How is one to identify the action itself as distinct from its consequences, in a manner that is not *ad hoc* and arbitrary? A moral theologian writing in the 1930s defended the following views about the 'action itself': that Captain Oates's action was not to commit suicide but simply to leave more food for the other members of the stranded expedition; that a maid who leapt to her certain death to avoid being violated did not commit suicide either (as he put it, 'The distinction between the jump and fall is obvious. In this case, the maid wishes the jump and puts up with the fall'); and that in order to preserve confidentiality, a person may say something that is strictly speaking true, but which he foresees will be misunderstood by the hearer. The intention is to say something true, and the deceit is foreseen but not intended.[9] Whatever one thinks of the rights and wrongs of these cases, it is surely important to know how the action in itself is supposed to be determined.

Is there a non-arbitrary way of determining what is included in the action itself? There is one which, though it is unlikely to commend itself, is instructive to consider. Some American jurists have proposed to define an action as a mere voluntary bodily movement, and to say that everything else is either consequence or circumstance.[10] Mr Justice Oliver Wendell Holmes puts it as follows: 'An act is always a voluntary muscular contraction, and nothing else. The chain of physical consequences which it sets in motion or directs to the plaintiff's harm is not part of it, and very generally a long train of such consequences intervenes.'[11]

Up to a point, this suggestion would suit the advocates of PDE well enough, implying as it does two of the requirements they would be looking for. In the first place, it might seem plausible to suppose that we have here a perfect example of an action-type that is morally neutral, and hence indefinitely many examples of individual actions-in-themselves that are also morally neutral. Hence, as PDE requires, the individual action in itself is not morally wrong. So even if the first condition of PDE is almost trivially fulfilled, at least it is fulfilled. Moreover, it could also be said that although individual actions in themselves would, on this proposal, be morally neutral, individual pieces of behaviour would not be, since behaviour will involve not merely the action in itself, but an end, and perhaps some accidental circumstances as well.

Flexing a finger, if voluntarily done, would be a beckoning, or the pulling of a trigger, or exercising to help one's arthritis or whatever, and, as Aquinas would argue, would have some moral quality in consequence. The second advantage is that on this account the difficulty in separating an action in itself from its consequences seems to be solved, and solved in a non-arbitrary way. The advocates of PDE wish to avoid any suggestion of endorsing the view that the end justifies the means. If the means – in this case the action in itself – is a mere bodily movement, it will be morally neutral, and will need no justification. And since the means–end relationship is surely a causal relationship, to take as the action in itself the first link in the causal chain seems to be the obvious solution.

Nonetheless, the Holmes proposal has found few supporters outside the legal profession. It is a very long way indeed from ordinary usage, and, for that very reason, points to a problem with PDE. For it might encourage people to exculpate themselves by an outlandish and all too easy use of the 'But all I did was...' manoeuvre, relegating the undesirable features of what took place to the level of consequences or circumstances. For then they can put the weight of the decision onto the proportionate reason clause, which is flexible in a way in which the action-in-itself clause is not. But if the proposal is rejected, as it should be, it is no longer clear where else the line between the action in itself and its consequences and circumstances is to be non-arbitrarily drawn.

3 Intention

From the way in which PDE is formulated, it is clear that there must be a distinction between intending, on the one hand, and merely foreseeing on the other. The traditional view of PDE took it as a necessary truth that the agent intends the action in itself; but it is not a necessary truth that they intend all the consequences of that action in itself. It is also clear that the tradition holds the agent to be in some way accountable both for what they intend and for the foreseen consequences of what they intend. But, as Chappell rightly argues, this accountability, without which the fourth requirement would be quite pointless, must be different from the liability to moral praise or blame which accompanies intending.

Some version or other of these assumptions underlies the traditional examples that I mentioned above, involving such issues as the treatment of ectopic pregnancy, the administration of lethal analgesics, the use of mental reservation in preserving confidentiality, the maid escaping from the rapist, and killing someone in self-defence. The majority view in each of these cases was that what was done was morally permissible. The actions in themselves (treating a malfunctioning fallopian tube, giving an analgesic, saying something true, jumping out of a rapist's reach) are intended, and the bad effects, though foreseen, are tolerated but not intended.

Perhaps. But might not each of these cases be read quite differently? Consider the administration of the analgesic known to be lethal.[12] Exactly which is the 'action in itself' that the doctor – let us call her Dr Nightingale – performed? There surely are several possible answers, even if we discount the Holmes view that her action consisted in moving her thumb. Did she simply alleviate her patient's pain? Did she administer a lethal dose to her patient? Did she administer a lethal dose as the only way of alleviating his pain? We may suppose that she has no ulterior motive – hastening an expected legacy, for instance. She regrets his death, and in this respect she would be utterly different from an unscrupulous colleague – let us call him Dr Crippen – who also expected a legacy and was delighted that the opportunity of ending his patient's life had presented itself in the ordinary course of things; for in other circumstances he would never have taken the risk of ending his patient's life.

Advocates of PDE might try to distinguish between administering a dose that would be sufficiently analgesic and administering a dose that would kill the patient. Dr Nightingale might point out that if the patient's pain could have been reduced by a lesser dose, she would have administered the lesser dose. But the counter to this suggestion surely is that in the circumstances it is implausible to claim that all she actually did was administer an injection that then had two effects – one analgesic, the other lethal. *In those circumstances* to administer an analgesic injection just is to administer a lethal injection. The crucial difference between the two doctors is not in what they proposed to do, which was to alleviate severe pain by administering an injection which they knew to be lethal. For suppose that what Dr Nightingale did was permissible. I think it is then clear that what Dr Crippen would have done in the same circumstances would also be permissible, for in both cases their behaviour would conform to accepted good practice. This point might be contested by the claim that they did different things: but that claim needs an independent justification if it is to stand up at all. There is of course an important difference between the two doctors. Dr Crippen is delighted that best practice will lead to the patient's death; Dr Nightingale regrets this fact. But it is not at all obvious that that is a difference in what they *do*.

Can the notion of intending not be used to explain the traditional distinction between the action in itself and its consequences? If so, we might hope to explain why it is morally permissible to treat an ectopic pregnancy, for instance, by distinguishing between the intended removal of a section of the fallopian tube and the unintended bringing about of the death of a foetus. Other examples are given similar treatment in the tradition. It is alleged that all Captain Oates actually did was go out for a walk; all that the person who equivocates actually does is utter some ambiguous words; all the threatened maid actually does is jump. Yet if the notion of 'the action in itself' is unable to bear the weight of this distinction, does 'intention' do any better?

Chappell, following Michael Bratman, accepts that one intentionally acts under that description which gives the reason why one does it. On this view, a defender of the traditional version of PDE could argue that the doctor does not intend to kill the patient, nor Oates to commit suicide, nor the equivocator to deceive. The plans and hence the intentions would then not be 'to relieve pain by killing the patient', 'to give my fellow explorers a better change of survival by committing suicide', 'to preserve confidentiality by deceiving'. But what is it to intend? Chappell insists that is not a matter of somehow 'pointing one's internal act of intending' as he puts it, citing Pascal's satirical remark.[13] So let it be agreed that the separation is not to be achieved by an effort of intellectual concentration. The idea of a plan which is central to Bratman's and Chappell's account must therefore be more than what the agent might say to him- or herself at the time. 'I am not setting out to ... (by killing the patient, by committing suicide, etc.)' is not a strong enough account to escape Pascal's censure.

Perhaps the key point consists in the regret that such a decision has to be taken because this regret points to the fact that had the circumstances been different the person would have chosen to act differently. But this argument can be countered by insisting that what we are interested in is what is actually chosen at the time, not what might have been chosen in some less fraught situation. To be sure, there is indeed a difference between the doctor who regrets what she has to do, and the one who is pleased at what he has to do. There is a difference between Captain Oates being sorry that the only way to save his companions is for the weakest person to walk out, and a Captain Oates who reflected that at least he would not have to face going home as a member of a failed expedition. But these differences need not even involve any difference in the motivation for what the agents did, let alone a difference in what was done. The doctor who is pleased at the prospect of bringing about an early death for his elderly patient may nevertheless administer the injection because to do so is the recognised procedure for pain relief in the circumstances. Were it not, he certainly would not contemplate doing so, on grounds both of professional ethics and ordinary prudence. Captain Oates might well, for all we know, have believed that his sad trek into the snow was not an unmitigated disaster even from his own point of view. But that is not to say that this belief would make all the difference to what he could be properly said to have intended or done.

4 Intention and moral conflict

In contrast to this whole approach stands Aristotle's treatment of the case of the captain who jettisons his cargo in order to lighten his ship when it would otherwise sink in a storm. Aristotle distinguishes between the moral quality of a type of action considered in the abstract, and the quality of what was done at the time. Nobody would throw the cargo overboard just like that, but any sensible person would do so if it were the best means of saving the ship and its passengers. There are two sides to what was done, he admits ('actions of this kind are mixed'), but 'on balance they are willingly done, because they are chosen at the time of acting, and the aim (*telos*) of an action depends upon the situation at the time'.[14] Aristotle does indeed distinguish between unloading the cargo ('in itself' a perfectly legitimate type of action, and just what the captain would normally have done upon reaching port) and losing the cargo (which no decent captain would do, just like that). The captain, on Aristotle's account, does not argue that losing the cargo was not part of his plan merely by pointing out that in a flat calm he would never have intentionally thrown it overboard. Aristotle insists that what the captain plans to do and does willingly is what he chose to do there and then in the situation that faced him. As things are, the captain simply has to lose the cargo in order to save the ship; he cannot deny that he intentionally did just that merely by appealing to what he would have wished had things been different. To reply that his plan is what explains why he acted as he did is of no avail unless one identifies what it was that he did; and what he did, as Aristotle rightly says, is what he did in the circumstances obtaining at the time. What explains his willingness to lose the cargo is his desire to save the ship.

Suppose that at a subsequent inquiry into the loss of the cargo the captain were accused of intentionally losing it. He would be most unwise to defend himself by invoking PDE to the effect that all he intended, and hence all he did, was to jettison the cargo; he would of course have been delighted had some other ship been able to pick it up. Certainly, some defence is called for, but not, I suggest, this one. Aristotle's own solution is not at this point to invoke the perfectly intelligible distinction between unloading the cargo and losing it. Common sense leaves it beyond all doubt that in the circumstances, to unload the cargo just is to lose it. Aristotle admits that losing the cargo by throwing it overboard is at least one part of what in the crisis was willingly done (*hekousion*). The proper description of what the captain did is complex: he chose to lose the cargo by throwing it overboard as the only way to save his ship. That is the action which the captain performed, and which Aristotle believes to be right, whereas intentionally losing the cargo, without further qualification, is wrong. In my view this is the best approach, and it involves conceding that the complex action just mentioned, as well as each of its parts, was intentionally performed. It takes the relevant circumstances into the identification of what the captain did on that particular occasion.

There is indeed the other distinction that I have already mentioned and to which Aristotle draws attention: the important difference between a captain who regrets having to lose the cargo, and another one who was glad that his employers were damaged by what happened. But the difference is one of moral character, not between one captain who acts rightly and the other who does not, nor in what they intentionally do. Each of them performs the same action which in the circumstances was the right thing to do.

If one now reads this treatment back into the cases concerning ectopic pregnancy, lethal injections, Captain Oates, and equivocation, one arrives at a much more realistic picture of how such cases ought to be analysed. Moreover, it emerges that what the person did – the action in itself – was complex, was morally right, was intended and was done for a good end. On the other hand, the solution to the dilemma of the threatened maid is surely not to defend her by making a distinction that has no relevance to what was done at the time, but to say that, while in panic and confusion she was intent only on avoiding the man, she was no doubt entirely blameless. Indeed, if she was panicked enough it is not clear that she performed the final action at all in any responsible sense. Be that as it may, the type of action 'jumping to death to avoid being raped' is (I suppose) wrong; and if that is what she did, she was mistaken in believing it to be for the best, because her life was in the end more important than avoiding rape. To put the same point in Aquinas's terms, one has to distinguish between types of action in the abstract and individual actions that may, according to circumstances, instantiate various morally significant types with conflicting moral qualities. What is done and intended is the particular action, and the circumstances obtaining at the time may very well determine some of its essential features.[15]

5 Causal connections

I can now make explicit an assumption that was already present in my discussion of the relationship between the action in itself and its consequences. The means–end relationship is surely a causal relationship. If one is going to escape the charge of claiming that the end justifies the means, one does so, on the traditional account, by making sure that nothing which it is morally wrong to intend is the cause of anything else which is intended. This move is clear in the case of the relationship between the action in itself and its consequences; and it is also clear in the traditional requirement that the intended good effects must not be caused by anything that is bad. *Qui vult finem vult media*, as the maxim had it. To intend to achieve an end is to intend to take some steps to attaining that end. To intend that something should happen is more than just wishing for it; one has to be prepared to take some steps to bring it about. Conversely, if something is a means to an intended end, it will itself be intended.

The way to deny that there is any means–end relationship is to deny that there is any causal relationship. Now causation is a relationship between individuals – individual entities, or individual events. It is the sun that causes the earth to move in the orbit it does. It is the striking of that match which caused that petrol to catch fire. It may indeed be the case that to discover the cause one uses one's knowledge of the regular patterns in which things of a given kind interact with other things; and causal laws may express such general regularities. But causal laws are not causes; such laws are universal statements whereas causes are individual entities. It follows, I believe, that whereas statements identifying causal laws must be referentially opaque, statements identifying some entity as the cause of some event or state of affairs can be referentially transparent. There is no lawlike relationship between being six feet tall and infecting me with flu, but the six-foot man might still be the cause of my getting flu. Similarly, in the circumstances of an ectopic pregnancy it might well be that the event which could be described as killing the foetus is identical with the event of saving the woman's life. In which case, the distinction between those two events cannot be sustained on causal grounds even though there is no lawlike relationship between killing foetuses and saving a mother's life. And so with the other examples. The maid's fall, Oates's death, the death of the foetus, and the loss of the cargo are, given the situation at the time, the necessary causal outcomes of the jump, the walking out into the snow, the removal of the damaged fallopian tube. If there is a means–end problem, it cannot be solved merely by redescribing the terms of the relationship involved.

6   Practical wisdom

The general tenor of my argument so far has been against the tendency of PDE to divide up what is done into small discrete parts, to each of which a different mental attitude can be taken. The principal reason for what I take to be the failure of PDE to work as advertised, whether as a decision-making procedure or as a *post factum* explanation, is that PDE gives no satisfactory rationale for drawing the dividing lines in one place rather than in any of several others.

But even in PDE there is a large hint that a quite different approach is also required. The last of the traditional requirements, calling for a proportion between the good effects intended and the bad outcomes permitted, clearly assumes that the agent is in some way accountable for all the foreseeable outcomes of their action. There is no hint in the tradition that this proportion is in any way a quantitative utilitarian calculation involving commensurable values. All that is required is an overall judgement that the desired outcomes are reason enough to permit the regrettable outcomes. 'Reason enough' is not defined, and, I shall argue, is not definable either. Quite generally, outside mathematics and logic, what counts as a good reason for something is not a precise notion.

It should come as no surprise that the larger, one might say holistic, approach that appears in this part of PDE is characteristic of what both Aristotle and Aquinas have to say about practical wisdom. For my present purposes, there are just four features of practical reasoning I would wish to highlight:

1. *Phronēsis* (=*prudentia*) is the intellectual ability to make morally good practical decisions. In so doing the agent will make an assessment of the situation in the light of their past experience.
2. The act of discernment itself is essentially a judgement about a particular situation.
3. A particular judgement may or may not involve an alteration in the way in which a universal principle has hitherto been understood or applied.

4. The particular judgement consists simply in seeing what needs to be done there and then. There is nothing more basic than this insight to which appeal can be made.

Whereas PDE involves an analysis of the content of the various judgements that have to be made in difficult situations, these four aspects of practical wisdom analyse a process, relating it at once to reasoning and to sheer insight. One can indeed predispose oneself to grow in practical wisdom, but there are no direct instructions on how to make the practical judgements involved in a way that is more accurate rather than less.[16] The act of making a moral judgement, though a rational act, is not one of discursive reasoning, nor of the application of principles quasi-deductively to a particular situation. It is what Aristotle terms an *aisthēsis* and Aquinas a *sensus*, whereby we perceive a particular action as an instance of some principle(s). Here is Aristotle:

> Everything which is done is a particular, that is to say, an ultimate. So the person of practical wisdom needs to recognise particulars just as understanding and judgement too are concerned with things that are done, and so with ultimates. Now insight [*nous*] is concerned with ultimates in both directions; it is insight rather than argument which gives us both the initial definitions and ultimates as well. In scientific proofs it provides the unchanging definitions from which they start, and in practical matters it provides a grasp of the particular which could be otherwise and is given by the minor premise. These [particular insights] are the origins of the end one has in view, since universals are derived from particulars. Of these particulars, then, we must have a perception, and that is insight.[17]

The context in which Aquinas discusses this passage and other similar passages is in answering the question whether *prudentia* concerns universals or particulars. The problem he sees is that the intellect knows only universals whereas particulars as such are known by the senses. Yet surely practical wisdom is an intellectual virtue and deals with particular cases? Aquinas's comments are as follows:

> [What Aristotle describes as] 'this particular ultimate' is a particular end, as he says; so the 'understanding' which is considered as a part of practical wisdom is a right estimation of some particular end.[18]

Practical wisdom involves not only rational consideration but also the application of [this consideration] to a task; for to do that is the point of practical reason. But nobody can apply one to the other appropriately unless they have knowledge of both, that is to say, of what has to be applied, and what it has to be applied to...

Reason is in the first place and principally concerned with universals. However, it is able to apply universal reasons to particular [instances], which is why syllogisms can have particular as well as universal conclusions...

As Aristotle says in *Ethics* VI, 8 practical wisdom is not one of the external senses whereby we come to know what is proper to those senses. It belongs to an internal sense which is perfected by memory and experience to the point that it can judge immediately about particular cases. It does not belong to the internal sense as to its principal subject; its principal subject is reason, but by a kind of application it extends to this kind of sense.[19]

This perception of what to do in a particular situation involves reading the situation in terms of the principles we have formulated in the light of our past experience. Sometimes in so doing we will be led to refine our understanding of those principles in the light of the present case, either by seeing that the principle should be understood to cover the present case, or by seeing that it should not. Neither the process by which such principles are formed nor the process by which individual cases are judged in the light of those principles can be justified by anything more primitive or basic. Both are known on the basis of the facts of the case by a non-discursive and non-deductive insight into those facts.

So, according to both Aristotle and Aquinas, there is just no way of spelling out a universal method to be followed for discovering how the present action should be seen, or by what description it is to be identified. Nor is there any independent proof of how a particular action is to be distinguished from its consequences, or why this particular action, seen in these terms, is to be done rather than some other action that involves reading the same situation in another way. Of course, Aristotle's doctrine of the practical syllogism spells out the agent's coming to view what they were doing in a certain way. What it does not do is explain the process by which the agent came to that view.[20] The insight into the particular situation is an act of reason, but it is not the outcome of a process of reasoning. Of course the explanation of any moral decision will invoke principles and will identify what was done as falling under the principle(s) invoked. So in a sense the explanation sets out the criteria which the agent in fact used in choosing to act as they did. But it does not justify the use of those criteria, and especially does not justify the way in which they have been adjudged to apply in this case.

It would therefore be quite contrary to Aquinas's intentions, as it seems to me, to regard PDE as the method whereby we discover whether some proposed course of action is permissible or not. Similarly, it does not describe a method for assigning responsibility. Which is just as well since, if I am right, these are functions it simply cannot perform. What PDE tries to do is to explain what might at first sight seem to be a surprising or even counter-intuitive moral conclusion to which one has come by the exercise of practical wisdom. To my mind at least, the required conclusion has in each of these cases already been accepted: PDE is intended as offering a rationale for that conclusion, rather than an account of how that conclusion is in fact arrived at.

But even as a *post factum* explanation, I do not think PDE is entirely successful. It rightly retains the principle that the action the agent actually performed must not be morally wrong, because that action must be part of the agent's intention. It also rightly retains the principle that the end does not justify the means. Where it is less successful is in its failure to accept that the action the agent performed might well be such that partial descriptions – each correct as far as it goes – of what was done might categorise it in ways which, abstractly speaking, are of conflicting moral value. Rather than accept this, it resorts to unrealistic and indefensible attempts to ensure that the action itself has only one simple moral quality, which is either that of being morally neutral, or morally good. The idea of an all-things-considered moral assessment of a complex action in itself is not considered by PDE, and method it has usually been taken to embody opens the door to absurd justifications appealing to claims of the form 'All I did was...'.

7 Action and responsibility

There are two further issues to be addressed. Does PDE presuppose, as Chappell suggests, that there are degrees of 'actionhood'; and are such degrees of actionhood paralleled by degrees of responsibility?

I suppose that there are degrees of actionhood, in so far as it makes sense to speak of degrees of control that agents might have over their behaviour. A person who deliberately drops a vase is exercising a greater degree of actionhood than a clumsy person who tries to pick up the vase and drops it; and this person in turn is exercising a greater degree of actionhood than someone who stumbles and upsets the vase in passing. The test here is the amount of control that the person was able to exercise at the time. It is, of course, true that we ascribe degrees of responsibility in parallel with degrees of actionhood. The clumsy person was not being careless, it is only that they could not at that moment fully control what happened; and the stumbler (I am assuming) simply could not control himself at all. No doubt similar considerations, even if they are difficult to measure, apply in the case of sleepwalkers, the mentally handicapped, and those suffering from compulsive illnesses such as kleptomania or alcoholism. I suggest, though, that in these latter cases there is no doubt about which is the action in question: breaking the vase, stealing the pullover from the shop, or having another gin. The question is not which action the person did, but whether the agent can properly be said to have performed any action at all.

I claim, however, that things are quite different in the case of what is intended and foreseen. The question here is not one of degrees of actionhood, but which action it is that the agent can properly be said to have performed. Whichever it is, they performed it with all their wits about them, and in control of what they did. If such agents are criticised, or if they are sued or accused of a crime, their defence will consist in spelling out all the relevant features of what was done, and arguing that that action, so identified, was justified. The captain will not argue that the loss of the cargo was irrelevant, nor the doctor that the death of the patient was irrelevant. Rather they will argue that, in precisely those circumstances in which it was causally impossible to prise apart the various relevant elements in the situation, these unfortunate aspects of what was done do not in themselves determine what the action was, nor whether what they did was right. Of course they would have preferred to have been in a situation in which such stark choices did not have to be faced. Of course they took all these unfortunate considerations fully into account; and of course they knowingly and deliberately performed the action which consisted of all those elements.

In conclusion, the following contrasts can be made. PDE is designed to show that, for instance, the captain's action in jettisoning the cargo was not wrong, given all the other features of the situation. In my view that is not what the captain did; hence I believe that what has to be shown is that the action that was right was the complex action of saving the ship by taking the only step which, in that storm, would have saved it. PDE achieves this by singling out one good and causally prior element as primary. I believe that to do this is morally arbitrary, and that the attempt to isolate the relevant causal element is often impossible.

Further, PDE, in considering the acceptable proportionality between good and bad outcomes, allows for a process of evaluation that need not be further analysed, and indeed cannot if some form of incommensurability thesis is true. I believe that this non-discursive process of evaluation is involved in *all* the elements of the situation, and indeed in the assessment of which elements in the situation are the relevant elements.

Moreover, PDE relies upon a notion of intention that is either a disguised way of evaluating the situation as a whole, or else relies on hypothetical facts about what the person would have wanted in different circumstances. I prefer the view that what the agent intentionally does is whatever they would describe themselves as doing precisely in the circumstances with which they are faced: the captain would accept that he intends to save the ship by throwing overboard and thereby losing the cargo; the doctor intentionally administers a lethal analgesic as the only way of relieving pain; Captain Oates intends to sacrifice his life for the sake of his companions. They do not intend criminal damage, murder, or suicide.

In the last analysis, neither PDE nor practical wisdom provides a method for settling complex moral problems, and some of the criticisms of both seem to be based on the assumption that some such method – deontological clarity, utilitarian calculation, Rawlsian justice – is both possible and required. I believe that we have to be content with the experienced and emotionally well-balanced judgement of a well-informed and intelligent agent. Practical wisdom is an ability; it cannot be understood as a precise criterion, nor as itself resting on something more fundamental. Pascal, I suppose, would take this line to task for laxity, just as he did the early casuists who used PDE. I see no reason to suppose that a reliance on practical wisdom need lead to laxity. But that is another story.

Notes

1. *Summa Theologiae*: II-IIae, 64.7. That this really is PDE is not universally agreed, however.
2. Sophie Botros, 'An Error about the Doctrine of Double Effect', *Philosophy* 74 (1999): 71–83. She cites J.T. Mangan in *Theological Studies* 10 (1949): 41–61. Also Timothy Chappell, 'Two Distinctions that Do Make a Difference: The Action/Omission Distinction and the Principle of Double Effect', *Philosophy* 77 (2002): 211–33.
3. For the sake of simplicity, I shall not here consider cases in which someone's behaviour at the time was beyond their control, for instance if they were driving and had a totally unforeseen heart attack. Similarly, I shall not consider cases

of recklessness or negligence. So nobody should have been driving if their sight was severely impaired, or they were subject to epileptic fits.

4. The idea is to provide an agreed description while leaving it open which elements in that description might require us to put some moral construction on what happened.

5. See *ST*: I-IIae, 18.4: 'It follows then that in a human action there is a fourfold goodness which can be considered: a) the generic goodness which comes from it being an action, since, as has been said it is good just in virtue of being an action, an existent; b) specific goodness, which depends upon the suitability of its object; c) goodness deriving from the circumstances, as from accidents of some sort; and d) goodness deriving from the end, as from a relationship to the cause of its goodness.' In reply to the third objection he goes on to say that if the action is to be morally good overall, it cannot be bad in any of these four respects.

6. For the first part of the claim, see *ST*: I-IIae, 18.8; for the second, ibid., 18.9. Even if an action in itself instantiates no morally significant type, it will, he believes, at least have a moral quality according to its end. The suggestion is that even an action (walking along the street, perhaps) which is in itself of no moral significance must, if it is to be chosen at all, be chosen as a means to some end; and to take steps to achieve this end will necessarily be either morally permissible or not.

7. *ST*: I-IIae, 18.5 ad 4, and I-IIae, 18.10.

8. It seems that the *finis*, the end of the action, is in Aquinas's view a yet further element in the overall assessment.

9. H. Davis, S.J., *Moral and Pastoral Theology*, Vol. II (London: Sheed and Ward, 1946): 144. For lying, see 413–14.

10. The American Law Institute, in *Restatement of the Law of Torts* (Philadelphia, 1934), Vol. I: 8.

11. *The Common Law* (Boston, Little, Brown: 1881): 91.

12. I am using this description as a morally non-committal account of what happened which might be agreed by all parties, whatever they then wish to say about intention or responsibility in the light of these facts. See note 4.

13. Chappell, op. cit: 224–7. In his contribution to this book, Chappell suggests that the crucial test is one of 'normal causal separability'. I regard this, too, as unsatisfactory. As I shall argue, what one might claim to be doing *in other circumstances* (let us say, 'normal' circumstances) is beside the point. The question is what one can properly be said to be doing in the circumstances obtaining at the time. Chappell concedes that there is a problem about the relevant description.

14. *Nicomachean Ethics*: III.1, 1110a4–26.

15. Chappell makes it clear that while he accepts Aristotle's analysis of the sea-captain case, he does not believe that this case is parallel to the others, since it does not, and they do, illustrate PDE. It seems to me that all of these examples *could* be analysed in either way, but that one way is much more realistic than the other in every case, as well as being less arbitrary.

16. Aristotle and Aquinas outline the prerequisites for the exercise of *phronēsis* (*prudentia*) in terms of emotional balance, experience, and correct information.

17. *Nicomachean Ethics*: VI.11, 1143a32–b5.
18. *ST*: II-IIae, 49.2 ad 1. Aristotle elaborates the same point in *NE*: VI.11, 1142a23–29.
19. *ST*: II-IIae, 47.3 *respondeo*, and replies to first and third objections.
20. Similarly in scientific proofs: the syllogisms of theoretical reason exhibit knowledge achieved; they do not explain *how* that knowledge was achieved.

10

Beyond Double Effect: Side-Effects and Bodily Harm

Helen Watt

1 Introduction

Much attention has been devoted by philosophers to the Principle (or Doctrine) of Double Effect (PDE) for which various formulations have been offered. While I believe that PDE is defensible – at least in some formulations – I want to argue that the relationship between intentions and side-effects needs some further thought. It is commonplace for defenders of PDE to point out that it does not give carte blanche for causing side-effects that are disproportionately harmful. It is less often noted that there are side-effects which, while remaining unintended, nonetheless have a central role in the description of certain kinds of act. Rather than being just a factor to be weighed against the good effects at which we are aiming, bad side-effects can generate an independent moral conclusion[1] in conjunction with the long- or short-term intentions with which they are connected.

The causing of such morally conclusive side-effects may be physically indistinguishable, at every stage, from the causing of intended effects, whether these are good or bad. Take the following example, from the area of deliberate homicide. It is unlikely (though not, of course, impossible) that a murderer intends to kill an innocent person precisely *qua* innocent person.[2] In most cases, the murderer will be intending to kill the person under some other description (e. g. 'my business rival' or 'the heir to the throne'). The victim is no more killed *qua* innocent person than he or she is killed *qua* middle-aged person or member of a local library.[3] While murder – at least in its central case – involves an intention to kill, the intention connects to the killing itself, rather than to the innocence of the victim. Nonetheless, the innocence of the victim[4] is surely central to the definition of murder: it is not a 'mere' side-effect like (for example) the risk of getting caught. Rather, it is a side-effect that is a necessary part of the intrinsic wrong of murder. In contrast, the wrong of risking prosecution, as a 'mere' side-effect of committing murder, is *dependent on* (*inter alia*) the intrinsic wrong of murder, since it is not always wrong to risk prosecution if what we are doing is otherwise morally blameless.

In this chapter, I will focus not on homicide where death is intended, but on what I see as a distinct phenomenon – the case where a person's body is deliberately affected in a way foreseen to cause death, but without this intention. Such cases are often discussed in the context of killing in self-defence. St Thomas Aquinas,[5] and many since Aquinas, have argued that it is permissible for a private person to use foreseeably lethal means of self-defence against an aggressor, but not to intend death as such. Intuitively, such lethal means seem more appropriate in the case of genuine aggressors (by which I mean deliberate, morally unjustified aggressors[6]) than in that of innocents, to whom we feel inclined to grant a higher level of bodily immunity. What is this higher level, and how does it relate to the intentions of those who harm the innocent, without intending harm as such?

2 Deliberate affecting

Warren Quinn has suggested a reformulation of PDE, giving attention to the wrong involved in 'using' people – that is, deliberately affecting them in ways which, in effect, do harm. This reformulation, he suggests,

> distinguishes between agency in which harm comes to some victims, at least in part, from the agent's deliberately involving them in something in order to further his purpose precisely by way of their being so involved (agency in which they figure as *intentional objects*) and harmful agency in which either nothing is in that way intended for the victims or what is so intended does not contribute to their harm.[7]

Quinn further distinguishes between what he describes as 'direct opportunistic agency' (agency which benefits from the presence of the victim, who is made to serve our plans) and 'direct eliminative agency' (agency which 'aims to remove an obstacle or difficulty that the victim presents'[8]). An example of the latter would be a craniotomy or crushing of the skull of an unborn child who is stuck in the birth canal and thus endangering its mother. An example of the former would be a doctor who leaves a particular group of patients untreated so as to observe the progress of a serious disease. Quinn sees 'opportunistic' affecting of this kind as more difficult to justify than 'eliminative' affecting – at least in the absence of consent on the victim's part to be so used. On the question of deliberate affecting in general, he observes:

> What seems specifically amiss in relations of direct harmful agency is the particular way in which victims enter into an agent's strategic thinking. An indirect agent may be certain that his pursuit of a goal will leave victims in its wake. But this is not because their involvement in what he does or does not do will be useful to his end. The agent of direct harm, on the other hand, has something in mind for his victims – he proposes to involve them in some circumstance that will be useful to him precisely because it involves them. He sees them as material to be strategically shaped or framed by his agency.[9]

2.1 Deliberate bodily invasions

Quinn's reworking of PDE can, no doubt, be criticised in some respects. However, there is surely much of value in the general line Quinn is taking on intentional involvement or affecting. The intention to affect – particularly (I will argue) if the effect is internal to the victim's body – is itself morally significant, even in cases where harm or aspects of harm such as death or disablement are not intended.[10]

Take another example: the case of the human shield, the criminal, and the police officer (Crook and Cop, as one writer dubs them[11]). In this case, Crook grabs a passer-by (Shield) and Cop (or Cop 1) shoots through the body of Shield in shooting at Crook. While, admittedly, Cop 1 does not bring Shield into the situation (he has already been 'opportunistically involved' in this way by Crook), Cop 1 nonetheless is, or probably is,[12] intending *something* vis-à-vis Shield – that the bullet pass through his body in order to get to the body of Crook. In contrast, Cop 2, who shoots from *behind* Crook, foreseeing that her bullet will pass into the body of Shield after Crook has been shot, need not intend *anything* vis-à-vis Shield, since nothing in regard to his body is needed to affect that of Crook.

Is Cop 1 intending that Shield die, in shooting through his body? There seems no reason why she should be: such a death would not advance her goals, and she is unlikely to believe that it would. Cop 1 need not intend anything more for Shield than she would intend if Shield were already dead. Nonetheless, she is aware that Shield is alive and this awareness has, I want to argue, an important moral significance. The fact that she intends to invade the body of what she knows to be an innocent person, in a way she knows will do that person only lethal harm is, I think, sufficient for her action to be morally unjustified. (The issue of culpability is, of course, a different question: Cop 1 may blamelessly believe that her action is morally permitted or even morally required.)

2.2 Logical and causal closeness

Some will object that intentionally shooting through a person's body is logically or causally impossible to distinguish from intending to bring about death. However, it is an empirical question whether Cop 1 is intending death: the answer may well be no, particularly as Shield's death will not assist in disabling Crook. Causally, shooting may have death as a certain consequence, but giving morphine for palliative reasons – a paradigm case of unintended killing – may have an earlier death for the patient as an equally certain consequence. It is worth noting that death and shooting through a body are not merely *conceptually* distinct: they are *physically* distinct,[13] in that shooting causes death (and not the other way around[14]). The causal relationship between these two events makes it easier, not more difficult, to separate intending the shooting from intending its lethal results.

As regards logical connections: there is no such connection between causing death and shooting through a person's body. Even if there were, this would not imply that Cop 1 was motivated in acting by both (or all) the factors that are logically connected. I can intend to buy a car with my lucky number on the number plate without intending to buy a car whose number on the plate is divisible by five. Logical and causal 'closeness' can, however, affect what we are, in practice, likely to be able to separate in our minds: the claim not to be intending one of two connected factors may be psychologically implausible.[15]

There is another way in which logical or causal or other 'closeness' can matter morally. As J.L.A. Garcia has noted, sometimes p and q will be so connected that intending p will be vicious for largely the same reasons that intending q is.[16] Bodily integrity (i.e. the absence of internal effects of a kind that bullets cause) and life itself would seem to have this kind of close connection as components of human well-being. To invade the boundaries of an innocent person's body in a lethally harmful and non-beneficial way is therefore harder to justify than non-invasive interventions that cause harm.

2.3 Relocation and bodily invasion

Another example: imagine that we are on an overcrowded raft that will soon capsize if the fattest member of the crew (or two thinner members) are not thrown overboard. It is, I think, morally acceptable to throw the fat crew member off the raft:[17] he does not have an inalienable right to remain in his current place of safety, given what this means for others.[18] If, however, the crew member is thrown overboard not (or not only) to keep the raft from sinking but to feed a hungry shark, this is unacceptable, even if death itself is not intended by his crewmates. What they *are* intending – an effect on his body which they foresee will do him no good, but only lethal harm – is quite bad enough for their act to be morally excluded. The act not only involves an intention that their crewmate's body be internally affected in a way known to be lethally harmful, but has the additional defect of constituting, in Quinn's terms, 'opportunistic' and not merely 'eliminative' agency.

In contrast, imagine that sharks are not in question: however, the crew member is wearing a bright yellow lifejacket that will soon attract the attention of enemy aircraft. A deep sea diver on the raft proposes to swim underneath the crew member and hold him underwater for 10 minutes until the planes have passed. I would argue that this is morally acceptable: neither death nor harm nor an effect internal to the crew member's body which is known to result in death or harm is intended by the diver. Admittedly, the diver does intend that the crew member be surrounded by an element foreseen to be hostile to life over the relevant period of time. However, this is a 'location' intention, not an intention relating to the bodily integrity – the bodily boundaries – of the victim.

We can also imagine a case of 'relocation' which is nonetheless immoral as involving opportunistic agency – say, where the diver drags the crew member away from the raft and along the surface of the water to attract enemy fire. Here it is not essential that the enemy *hit* the crew member's body for them to be usefully distracted; however, the 'opportunistic' element makes (or helps to make[19]) this action immoral, though the body is merely moved by the diver, and not deliberately invaded. The crew member is used precisely as a target, as if he were a subhuman object – something barely (if at all) preferable to using him as food for a shark.

However, there is, I would argue, no general right not to be moved into (or forced to stay in) hostile environments. The intention to move someone from one environment to another relates to something – the physical world – that people share in a way they do not share their bodies. With regard to environment, we may go ourselves, and send others into harmful environments without necessarily exploiting ourselves or others in the process. Sometimes consent will be required from the subject: it is soldiers, rather than 3-year-old children, who should be asked to perform dangerous manoeuvres that are non-beneficial to themselves. However, it is expected that adults will consciously take certain risks of an environmental kind, as part of their responsibility for protecting others at a time of common danger. While respecting a person's 'location' rights is, of course, part of respecting that person, respect for his/her bodily integrity involves respect for the person in a more immediate sense, since the body is what we are. It is therefore easier for people to lose their right to extrinsic, instrumental goods such as a favourable location than it is for them to lose their right to intrinsic goods such as bodily integrity.

2.4 Respect for bodily integrity

Indeed, certain rights 'internal' to our bodies do not disappear, I would argue, even if we ourselves seek to waive them.[20] The body is the person, and must be respected as much in oneself as in one's (innocent) neighbour. Take the case of a surgeon who removes a heart from a living and consenting donor to use in transplantation. This act need not involve the aim to kill (or otherwise harm): the donor's death does not advance the surgeon's goals,[21] which will be met by the retrieval and transfer of the heart and its good effect on the recipient. While the surgeon may, as a matter of fact, see himself as involved in intentional homicide, it would, or might, be psychologically possible for the surgeon to see the patient's death as outside his plan of action. The surgeon is, however, failing to respect the integrity of the donor's body by treating it simply as a source of useful transplant material.[22] In the same way, the donor is failing to respect the integrity of his own body by treating it in this way. Both the surgeon and the donor are involved in 'opportunistic' and not merely 'eliminative' agency: the donor, like the surgeon, is exploiting his body in treating it as a mere resource.[23]

Some qualification may need to be made here, since certain interventions may be harmless to the great majority of people, and harmful only to those who are already very ill. If some great good, even for others, depended on parting the lips of someone at the point of death,[24] with the foreseen result that death would be hastened, this might be justified, as it would do no harm – whether immediate or longer-term – to someone in a normal state of health. While we must, of course, have regard for each other's special vulnerabilities, there is surely a limit to the kind of restraint these vulnerabilities require.

To be avoided are bodily invasions that do significant harm in themselves (and would harm even a healthy person of the relevant age) and especially invasions that, in practice, do serious and permanent harm. Sometimes immediate harm[25] can be subsequently reversed, in a way that makes causing it morally permissible: a donor of a paired organ is immediately harmed by the extraction procedure, but this is a harm from which he or she is normally expected to recover. However, to make a deep wound in someone's body will constitute serious and permanent – and not merely immediate – harm if that person will not be stitched up (e.g. if he or she will die at once, due to some pre-existing illness). The wound itself would harm even a healthy person, though its most serious and permanent effect is in practice restricted to those who will not have a chance to heal, given their medical condition. Innocent people have a right to bodily integrity which is unjustly thwarted by bodily invasions of this kind.

3 Pregnancy and bodily harm

3.1 Abortion as lethal bodily invasion

In the remainder of this chapter, I will seek to apply these principles to one area where double-effect reasoning has traditionally been applied – that of pregnancy in general, and maternal–foetal conflicts in particular.[26] Assuming that the foetus has full human status (an assumption I will not defend here[27]), lethally invading the body of the foetus to benefit the mother would seem, on the face of it, no more permissible than lethally invading the body of the mother to benefit her child. The case of pregnancy is interesting, since the unborn child is within the pregnant woman's 'outer' boundaries, but nonetheless outside her 'inner' boundaries: it is a separate organism within her body, with its own boundaries which need to be respected. Some implications of this unique situation are explored below.

I have mentioned the case of craniotomy (more common in philosophy than in modern medicine) where the skull of the foetus is crushed in order to extract it from the body of a woman giving birth. It is easy to see why a doctor might be tempted to do such a thing, particularly if the unborn child was, in any case, doomed to die. Nonetheless, there is a right at stake – the child's right[28] not to have its body lethally invaded – which, I would argue, deserves the same respect as the right of a dying woman not to have her own body harmed to save her child.[29] As an innocent human being, incapable of aggressive intentions, the foetus has a right not to have its body invaded in ways that do it only lethal harm. This is so even if the aim of the procedure is not (as many think it must be[30]) to cause the child's death.

That the aim is not necessarily to cause death seems clear when we consider that the surgeon would crush the skull whether or not the foetus was still alive. The death of the foetus is immaterial as far as its extraction from the mother is concerned. Perhaps the skull will need to be crushed beyond the point at which the foetus will die. Alternatively, perhaps the foetus will die after the point at which its skull is sufficiently crushed for it to be extracted from the mother. Even if the foetus dies at the precise point at which the skull is sufficiently crushed, this does not mean that the death of the foetus is included in the surgeon's intentions. His intentions may rather be to alter the shape of the foetus, solely for the purpose of enabling the foetus to be extracted from the body of the mother, whose life is endangered by its presence. These aims will be satisfied not by the death of the foetus, but by its crushing and subsequent removal. (Of course, the surgeon will be intending the death of the foetus if he does not distinguish in his own mind between the aim of crushing and that of causing death.)

The wrongness of craniotomy is secured not by the intention to cause death, which need not be present. It is secured by the intention to perform a bodily invasion of a kind foreseen to do only lethal harm to the (innocent) human being whose body is invaded. As in the case of the homicidal transplant surgeon, this is quite sufficient to categorise what the doctor is doing as seriously immoral.[31]

If the account just given of lethal bodily invasions is correct, we have a reason to object to abortion (or to many abortions) which is independent of the aim of causing foetal death. If a doctor wants to terminate a pregnancy, but does not want, in the sense of intend, to end the life of the foetus, the fact that an abortion – say, by D&C – involves a lethal bodily invasion of the foetus will be morally conclusive in itself. The same can be said about inductions of labour before viability, on the assumption that the placenta and amniotic sac (which the foetus develops and which support its life) are organs of the foetus. If this is so, a harmful attack on these organs in order to bring about miscarriage must be regarded as a harmful attack on the unborn child, and thus as morally unjustified. The fact that the foetus might have survived if these organs had been somehow repaired and reconnected to the mother is not relevant, any more than normal hospital Caesarians[32] are relevant to the cutting open of pregnant women where this will lead to their deaths. In the context in which early labour is induced – that is, a context in which repair and reconnection are not envisaged – breaking up the placenta and amniotic sac constitute the infliction of a lethal wound on the foetus,[33] and are thus an impermissible invasion of its body.

This will also apply to some ways of treating ectopic (i.e. extrauterine) pregnancy – for example, when the embryo has implanted in the fallopian tube. An attack on the trophoblast, or layer of cells connecting the embryo with the tube, by using the drug methotrexate (MTX), will constitute a lethal bodily invasion – though in this case, there will be an additional intention to thwart the bodily function of the embryo by thwarting the activity of the trophoblastic cells.[34] Again, if the embryo or foetus is squeezed out of the tube, and the foetal membranes are deliberately and harmfully invaded in the process, this can be judged along similar lines. The objection will not, however, apply to cases where squeezing the foetus out of, or along, the tube may benefit the foetus, such as cases where it is 'milked' towards the uterus to give it a chance to reimplant.

3.2   Abortion as relocation/withdrawal of support

What should we say about cases – whether in relation to ectopic or to uterine pregnancy – where the aim is one of mere relocation or withdrawal of support? There is surely a possibility of a deliberate 'termination of pregnancy' which is not a deliberate, harmful invasion of the body of the foetus. The 'morning after' pill, for example, would fall into this category, if the intention of the woman who took it was neither to kill (by any means) nor to invade the body of any child conceived, but 'merely' to change her own body so the embryo would be unable to implant.

However, we need to ask if such withdrawal of support is morally defensible, given the mother–child relationship and the kind of support that pregnancy involves. The support of the uterus, in particular, is support of a kind that all (or almost all[35]) adults have received; moreover, it involves no technology, but the exercise of normal human functions. The uterus is the natural home of the unborn child: it is functionally geared to support it. *Qua* withdrawal of bodily support, abortion seems similar to refusal to breastfeed when one is living in an isolated area, and the child will die if not fed. Imagine a case where one refuses to take responsibility for one's newborn baby, who is left in a cold room, rather than fed and cared for in the warm part of the house. Just as an infant has a right to basic shelter and bodily support, so an embryo has a right to implant and remain within the mother's uterus. (The focus here is on moral obligations in pregnancy, not on culpability for failures to meet those obligations. Given the uncritical support for abortion in many social circles, it can be very difficult for women with unplanned pregnancies – especially those under other forms of pressure – to refuse what is offered as an obvious solution.)

Uterine support in standard cases is basic support of a kind that is morally required of the gestating mother. It is more like breastfeeding than like giving a stranger the use of one's kidneys (to use a somewhat strained example of Judith Jarvis Thomson[36]). More difficult are cases where abnormal, ectopic support is in question, and generally cases where the pregnant woman is at serious risk. Looking back at the case of the fat crew member who is thrown overboard, could we perhaps justify terminating pregnancy in a similarly dire situation – assuming this could be done without a lethal bodily invasion, or an aim to kill? Admittedly, we have a parental relationship here, but could we not imagine cases where a newborn child could be lethally evicted by its mother from a place of temporary safety? Imagine, for example, that a mother is on a raft with three children, which will sink if one child is not thrown overboard (and the mother is needed to protect the other children).

3.3 The pregnancy relationship

Here I want to argue that pregnancy is a special case: the duty not to evict or withdraw support in pregnancy is, uniquely, absolute. At this stage in the mother–child relationship, it is crucial that this relationship be seen as literally unconditional: 'till death [or birth] do us part'. Such unconditionality enables the mother to bond effectively with the child she is carrying, whose life is accepted as inextricably bound up with her own. While later on, parenthood is a matter of a gradual 'letting go', introduction to other carers, and encouragement to independence, it is important that both women and children feel that there was one time at which the child was unconditionally supported. Pregnancy should involve a unique commitment to the child, whose presence is accepted as a 'given': any deliberate removal of the child, or willingness to do so in certain circumstances, goes against that unconditional commitment.

Having said this, the pregnancy relationship has another unique feature, in that harmful side-effects for the child may be caused in pregnancy where this would be morally more questionable if the child were already born. The mother entirely surrounds the child: she is its 'nearest neighbour', as well as its parent. However, this cuts both ways:

neighbours should support each other but may also inflict harms on each other as a side-effect of choices they make. A 'surrounding' neighbour might perhaps be seen as having special rights and duties.[37] While the mother must accept certain side-effects of the presence of the foetus – particularly if there is no other option than attacking or expelling the foetus – the foetus must 'accept' side-effects of certain maternal activities, if these are sufficiently important. A woman who needs medicine to save her life, or even to prevent some other serious injury, may be given such medicine by a doctor, even if death of her child will result. In contrast, it is not clear that a doctor would be justified in giving the woman medicine if the lethal result would be for some other member of her family (say, a breastfeeding baby). The difference lies in the fact that in pregnancy the bad unintended, as well as the good intended effects of treatment take place within the outer boundaries of the woman's body – and so, in a sense, within her rightful 'sphere of influence'.[38]

How, then, should doctors respond to a case of ectopic pregnancy? It is worth stressing that it is deliberate removal, rather than removal as a side-effect of something else, which I am claiming is proscribed. In the case of uterine pregnancy, miscarriage is sometimes foreseeably but permissibly caused by life-saving treatment of the woman, as when a woman miscarries after treatment for cancer. In the same way, a pregnant woman with cancer of the womb may have a hysterectomy, despite the fact that her unborn child will be removed together with the womb. While it is not always wrong to do what 'indirectly' – that is, non-intentionally – terminates prenatal support, this is very different from aiming precisely at such a termination.

This also applies to ectopic pregnancy: if the fallopian tube, or part of the tube, is damaged to such an extent as to pose a serious threat to the woman, the intention of the surgeon may simply be to take out the tube, or the affected part of it. By this stage, the foetus is likely to be very close to death, if not already dead. It is the tube, not the foetus, that is causing the current threat necessitating treatment. The foetus, if it is still alive, will die at the point where its oxygen supply is cut off by the clamping of the maternal blood vessels leading to the tube. There is no reason why the death of the foetus, or the absence of the living foetus from the body of the mother, need be intended in such a situation.

In contrast, if the surgeon intervenes early, before the tube itself poses a threat, then the tube (or part thereof) is removed *because it contains the unborn child*. The aim is, in other words, to bring about the absence of the living foetus from the body of the mother. Alternatively, the surgeon may intend to remove the child only, if he takes the child directly from the tube, and leaves the tube in place. On my analysis, neither of these two treatment options would be morally acceptable. If there is no urgent need to intervene on the body of the woman (say, to control bleeding) it would be necessary to monitor the situation ('expectant management'[39]) until either the child miscarried – a likely event with ectopic pregnancy – or the woman's body, irrespective of the child's continued presence, needed urgent intervention.

It should, however, be noted that 'mere relocation' or 'mere refusal of bodily support' are not involved in the case of most abortions (the morning-after pill aside). Even if the aim is not to end the child's life, a lethal attack on the body of the foetus is a very common method of removing the foetus from its mother and/or withdrawing her support. Assuming the argument of this chapter regarding lethal bodily invasions is correct, such abortions will be morally proscribed, if the foetus is a human moral subject. Whatever our view of other interventions, bodily attacks must be avoided if the foetus shares the human right to respect for the boundaries between our own bodies and other parts of – or people in – the world.

Notes

I am grateful to Anthony McCarthy, Hugh Henry, and Ted Watt for their help with the writing of this chapter.

1. Double-effect reasoning applies both to moral absolutes and to choices that are merely presumptively wrong. Thus although there are cases where mild harm to innocents may be caused deliberately, in normal situations it is morally significant whether such harm is intended. Deliberately making a baby cry is not intrinsically immoral (one could do it to prevent quite a moderate harm); however, parents who deliberately upset their babies in normal situations are acting wrongly in a way that those who knowingly but unintentionally upset their babies are not.
2. Such an intention would be morally worse than killing with the mere knowledge that the victim is innocent: it seems to be more strongly opposed to the respect for innocence that the agent should have had.
3. Indeed, the victim may not even be killed *qua* human being of any kind, though this is harder to imagine. Perhaps an amoral marksman in the woods might shoot at any living target of suitable size, while he knows, but is indifferent to, the fact that the current target is a human being.
4. Of course, the victim may not be literally innocent, in the sense that he deserves no punishment (or self-defensive action) from anyone; rather, he may be 'innocent' in the sense that he is not being killed/attacked in such a context.
5. St Thomas Aquinas, *Summa Theologiae*: II–II, q. 64, art. 7.
6. By this I mean: those whose aggressive intentions are not justified by the circumstances, even if they blamelessly believe that they are. Thus a soldier

who blamelessly fights on what is, unbeknownst to him, the wrong side – or an insane person who blamelessly believes that his wife is an enemy soldier – would be 'unjust aggressors' in this sense. We could also characterise as unjust aggressors those who harmfully instrumentalise another: for example, a drowning person who climbs on top of another, threatening his life by treating him simply as a useful floating object.

7. W. Quinn, 'Actions, Intentions, and Consequences: The Doctrine of Double Effect', in W. Quinn (ed.), *Morality and Action* (Cambridge: Cambridge University Press, 1993): 184–5.

8. Ibid: 186.

9. Ibid: 190.

10. It is worth remembering that harm *as such* will not be intended in many cases where a person is deliberately affected in harmful ways. For example, an insane or otherwise misguided person may genuinely believe he is doing his victim only good by ending his life.

11. J.L.A. Garcia, 'Intentions in Medical Ethics', in D.S. Oderberg and J.A. Laing (eds), *Human Lives: Critical Essays on Consequentialist Bioethics* (London: Macmillan, 1997): 179, n. 16. Quinn (op. cit: 186–7) mentions a similar case, but concludes that the marksman is not intending anything different from what he would intend if the human shield were not there.

12. It is psychologically implausible that Cop 1 is simply intending that the bullet pass through a certain space, particularly as she may need to make calculations as to the strength of her firepower. One can, however, imagine a case – perhaps if Cop 1 was just about to shoot when Shield was seized by Crook – in which Cop 1's choice is unaffected by Shield, whose presence is barely noted. In this case, Cop 1 would, however, be acting 'inappropriately', even if not wrongly, since the bullet's passing through Shield's body is in fact necessary for her to achieve her ends, though she does not see this at the time. Similarly, if my plan, unbeknownst to me, will only succeed if your death (which I foresee, but do not intend) comes about, then my plan is morally 'lacking', at least in the weak sense that it is not the kind of plan a person would choose who was both virtuous and well-informed. Although I am not unjust or otherwise vicious in choosing this plan, justice is evident more in my just intentions than in my actually achieving a just or appropriate state of affairs.

13. Admittedly, inflicting a mortal wound (as opposed to achieving the ensuing death) does seem physically inseparable from shooting through a person's body in certain cases, though conceptually distinct.

14. See M. Moore, 'Intentions and Mens Rea', in R. Gavison (ed.), *Issues in Contemporary Legal Philosophy: The Influence of H.L.A. Hart* (Oxford: Clarendon, 1987): 260–1.

15. ' "Closeness" can matter to what an agent intends ("psychological closeness") because [...] the fact that the mind can be brought to recognise a certain distinction of possible intentional contents does not imply that, on a given occasion, it utilizes that distinction in its actual practical deliberations and decision making' (J.L.A. Garcia, op. cit: 165–6).

16. Ibid: 166.

17. Note, however, that the aim must be to remove *him*, not parts of his body. To expose him to a whirlwind which would first tear his body to pieces and then blow him off the raft would not be 'mere relocation'.

18. This principle is relevant to healthcare allocation: patients do not have an inalienable right to retain a bed in an intensive care unit (for example) if this will deprive other patients of facilities to which they have a better claim. See, for example, A. Fisher and L. Gormally (eds), *Healthcare Allocation: An Ethical Framework for Public Policy* (London: The Linacre Centre, 2001).

19. There are other moral problems here, which interestingly relate to bodily invasion: if it is wrong for the enemy to have the intention of killing the crew member, it is surely wrong to intend that they have this intention (whether or not they succeed).

20. Quinn, in contrast, lays great stress on consent on the part of those harmfully affected (op. cit: 190–3).

21. As Garcia points out, 'there is no reason to suppose that agents always intend only the bare minimum necessary to achieve their goals' (op. cit: 164).

22. John Finnis comments on a similar case (though one not involving consent): 'The surgeon intends to and does deal with the body, i.e., the very person of the patient, as his own to dispose of. Though his choice is not, precisely, to kill or even, perhaps, to impair the functioning of the patient/victim – i.e., though death and impairment of function are side-effects – the surgeon's choice is precisely to treat the bodily substance and reality of that other human person as if that person were a mere subhuman object. The moral wrong, on a precise analysis of the surgeon's intent, is a form of *knowingly death-dealing enslavement*; one who inflicts death, even as a side-effect, in order to effect such an instrumentalisation of another has, in the fullest sense, "no excuse" for thus knowingly causing death. We should not complain if both law and common moral thought treat this as murder. But nor should we distort our understanding of intention so as to bring this within the category of murder supposed, too casually, to be limited to *intent* to kill (or seriously harm)' (J. Finnis, 'Intention and Side-Effects', in R.G. Frey and C.W. Morris (eds), *Liability and Responsibility: Essays in Law and Morals* (Cambridge: Cambridge University Press, 1991): 60–1).

23. In the same way, non-lethal mutilation is immoral not just where the intention is to deprive the victim of a function that is integral to health, but where the intention is 'merely' to remove the organ in which (as it happens) this function resides.

24. It is true that this is a very 'non-invasive' invasion, closely resembling a 'location' change such as repositioning someone's limbs.

25. In other cases, the same action (making a surgical incision) that is immediately harmful is also instrumentally beneficial, in that it is part of a procedure intended to benefit the subject him- or herself.

26. On the application to a different case of conflict – the case of conjoined twins – see H. Watt, 'Conjoined Twins: Separation as Mutilation', *Medical Law Review* 4 (2001): 237–45.

27. This view is defended in H. Watt, *Life and Death in Healthcare Ethics: A Short Introduction* (London: Routledge, 2000): 57–65.

28. Absolute rights are best seen as negative, rather than positive in nature. Our right that others *not* make choices to affect us in ways that are lethally harmful defeats the interest of others in a 'positive' choice that their lives be sustained. Thus my right not to have my living body carved up for its organs will trump the interest of possible transplant beneficiaries in using those organs. Note

that my negative rights apply to the choice to affect by omitting as well by a 'positive act'. My negative right not to have my body lethally and internally affected for the benefit of others will also apply to a case where I am deliberately 'let die' to make my organs available.

29. I am thinking of a case where a doctor surgically invades a dying pregnant woman to rescue her viable child, who is threatened by the body which surrounds it. In the same way as someone who shoots through a human shield would normally intend the bullet to pass through the shield to get to the person behind, the doctor would be intending to invade the body of the woman, in a way foreseen to be fatal, in order to gain access to the foetus. This would be a deliberate and lethal bodily invasion carried out on an innocent human being, and as such would be morally unacceptable.

30. See the discussion in J. Finnis, G. Grisez, and J. Boyle, ' "Direct" and "Indirect": A Reply to Critics of Our Action Theory', *The Thomist* 65 (2001): 21–9, 32, 39–41. The authors themselves defend craniotomy, on the grounds that the child's death is not intended (but see note 22 for one author's account of wrongful homicide without this intention).

31. The case of the homicidal transplant surgeon is admittedly worse in involving 'opportunistic' rather than 'eliminative' affecting of the victim. There are, however, killings that are both 'eliminative' and 'opportunistic', as where the method of abortion is altered so that the unborn child is killed by a procedure that enables tissue from it to be used in transplantation.

32. It is true that even normal Caesarians cause long-term harm to the woman in so far as they make subsequent deliveries more difficult. However, this harm must be weighed against the potential benefits to the woman: the successful delivery of the child she is gestating, for which a Caesarian may be required, is in her immediate reproductive health interests, and possibly her wider health interests.

33. This might be compared to injuring the mouth of an infant in such a way that it could not breastfeed for several days, and would therefore die, as no other feeding method would be on offer.

34. For ethical analyses of different ways of managing ectopic pregnancies, including the use of MTX, see W. May, 'The Management of Ectopic Pregnancies: A Moral Analysis', in P. Cataldo and A. Moraczewski (eds), *The Fetal Tissue Issue* (Braintree: The Pope John XXIII Medical Ethics Research and Education Center, 1994): 121–47; A. Moraczewski, 'Managing Tubal Pregnancies: Part I', *Ethics and Medics* (June 1996): 3–4; A. Moraczewski, 'Managing Tubal Pregnancies: Part II', *Ethics and Medics* (August 1996): 3–4; G. Gleeson and C. Kaczor, 'Is the "Medical Management" of Ectopic Pregnancy by the Administration of Methotrexate Morally Acceptable?', in L. Gormally (ed.), *Issues for a Catholic Bioethic* (London: The Linacre Centre, 1999): 353–70; C. Kaczor, 'Moral Absolutism and Ectopic Pregnancy', *Journal of Medicine and Philosophy* 26 (2001): 61–74. Some have claimed that the aim in using MTX is not to attack the trophoblast's normal functions, but to stop its abnormal invasion of the tube. However, implantation, even in the tube, is an exercise of an embryonic function, in that it is a life-preserving – even if ultimately futile – activity. The activity of the embryo is rather like breathing poisoned air. It is the exercise, though in an abnormal way, of a life-preserving function of the embryo. Such functions may not be deliberately attacked,

even if, for environmental reasons, they cannot preserve life for long. In any case, it is not necessary to show that one intends to interfere with a function of the embryo to show that interference with the trophoblastic tissue is immoral. Rather, it is enough (I am arguing) to show that one intends to invade the embryo's body in a way foreseen to do the embryo only lethal harm.

35. Live births can also result from ectopic pregnancy (see note 39).

36. J.J. Thomson, 'A Defense of Abortion', *Philosophy and Public Affairs* 1 (1971): 47–66.

37. We can imagine a small country that is entirely enclosed within a larger country. The 'surrounding neighbour' relationship might impose duties on the larger country to help the smaller country and/or tolerate its harmful activities – duties which the larger country might not have to a neighbouring country it did not surround. But it might also entitle the larger country to take measures that had serious side-effects for the smaller country: side-effects more serious than it would be justified in causing for a conventional 'next-door neighbour' that was not within its general sphere of influence. Thus in the case of an environmental disaster the larger country might use a dangerous insecticide on its own territory, foreseeing serious harm to the smaller country, which would also be affected.

38. Watt, *Life and Death*: 55.

39. In the case of abdominal, as opposed to tubal ectopic pregnancy, 'expectant' management may make it possible to bring the child to viability. Surgery may then be carried out on the pregnant woman so that the child is born alive. Failing this, the child may die *in situ*, following which its body may be removed.

11
Intention, Foresight, and Success

Mark C. Murphy

1 Natural law, the intended/foreseen distinction, and double effect

My topic is the normative relevance of the intended/foreseen distinction. The normative relevance of this distinction appears most formally, and prominently, in the principle of double effect. This principle has been variously formulated, but in essentials – at least in its standard formulations – it holds that an action that foreseeably brings about evil can be permissible provided that the action is not intended to bring about that evil and that proportionate good is to be brought about through that action. Put another way: the principle of double effect proposes two distinct standards, one for intended evil and one for foreseen evil. It proposes that intentional evil is always forbidden; it proposes that foreseen evil is forbidden unless proportionate good is to be gained through the action.

A lot more would have to be said to make the principle perspicuous – particularly with respect to the very murky notion of 'proportionate' good and evil. But what is obvious about the principle is that it presupposes a morally significant, and rather severe, distinction between the moral relevance of intention and the moral relevance of foresight. It entails an absolute prohibition on intending evil. Most writers on ethics today would reject double effect in this stark formulation. But the notion that the intended/foreseen distinction is normatively relevant can be attractive not just for those who affirm a standard formulation of the principle of double effect. One might hold that the normative bar is somehow set higher for acts that intend evil than for those for which evil is merely a foreseeable, and even foreseen, result. This obviously could be true even if there were no absolute prohibition on intending evil.

I am going to offer a defense and explanation of the normative relevance of the intended/foreseen distinction. But first I want to specify the constraints of the enterprise as I plan to undertake it. I am committed to a natural law account of practical rationality. A natural law account of practical rationality holds: that the basic reasons for action have their status as such in virtue of human nature; that these basic reasons are welfare reasons, that is, aspects of agents' well-being; that the character of appropriate response to these reasons is fixed jointly by the nature of the reasons themselves and the nature of human action; and that informative general principles can be formulated that capture, at least partially, these appropriate responses to the basic reasons for action.[1] The principle of double effect, if true, would be one of these informative general principles that capture, at least partially, appropriate responses to the basic reasons for action. So would weaker principles specifying that the normative burden that must be met to justify acting with the intention of doing harm is higher than the normative burden that must be met to justify acting with the foresight of harm. So, given the initial commitment to a natural law understanding of practical rationality, the resources that I can employ to explain these normative principles consist entirely of an account of the basic reasons for action and an account of the generic features of human action.

What would violate the constraints set by this commitment to a natural law view would be, for example, to appeal to the normative difference between intention and foresight as simply a basic deontic restriction. It would also be outside of the rules simply to rely on intuitions about cases which, when neatly systematized, show that a higher normative burden is on those who propose to perform acts involving intended evil than on those who propose to perform acts involving merely foreseen evil. While the systematizing of such intuitions might offer something in the defense of the normative relevance of the intended/foreseen distinction, it would not offer anything toward the *explanation* of its relevance. Its relevance might indeed be a basic deontic relevance. But that would only be so if the natural law approach to these matters were mistaken or incomplete. I am going to proceed on the basis that it *is* complete, and I will try to show that we can in these terms provide an adequate defense and explanation of the relevance of the intended/ foreseen distinction.

I will, first, drawing for the most part on the investigations of others, report why I think it obvious that there is a distinction between intention and foresight in the sorts of cases at issue here, and that this distinction persists even in the case of fully rational agents. I will then turn to an account of three ways in which the distinction is practically relevant. While these three ways are distinct, they have as their common source the point that success in action is constitutively connected to intention but not constitutively connected to foresight. The account of the relation of success to intention is thus crucial to my argument.

2 The intended/foreseen distinction

The prominent claim that there is no real intended/foreseen distinction is not the claim that if an agent foresees that p then the agent intends that p. (I foresee that Jimmy's Old Town Tavern will be populated tonight. I do not intend that Jimmy's be populated tonight.) So there is obviously *some* conceptual difference between intention and foresight. Critics of the intended/foreseen distinction want to say, rather, that somehow, with respect to action, there is no such distinction. But we obviously cannot read this as the claim that action with foresight entails action with intention. (In writing this sentence, I foresee that Jimmy's will be populated tonight. But in writing this sentence, I do not intend that Jimmy's be populated tonight.)

What critics of the very existence of the intended/foreseen distinction want to say is, at least, that action performed with the foresight that its being the case that p will result (either logically or causally) from that action entails action performed with the intention that its being the case that p will result (either logically or causally) from my action. So Henry Sidgwick, who was extremely careful about every sentence he published, and put *The Methods of Ethics* through a half-dozen editions in his lifetime, claims in that work that 'it is best to include under the term "intention" all the consequences of an action that are foreseen as certain or probable.'[2]

It is obvious to me that the burden is on those who would fold what is foreseen as a result of one's action into the intention of the action. Once we allow that there is not even the least reason to believe that action with foresight that p entails action with the intention that p, why would we think that a special case of this – action with the foresight that its being the case that p will result from the action entails action with the intention that its being the case that p will result from the action – is true? There must be something special about this *particular* sort of foresight about the action, foresight about *what results* from the action. But no one has given any adequate account of what is special about that sort of foresight that would show that what is foreseen with respect to the results of an action is an intended result of that action.

And it is not just that this burden has never been discharged: there are strong reasons to deny the entailment. Taking the low road, that of counterexample, we can provide cases in which it is obvious that some consequences of one's action, while foreseen, are not intended. Joseph Boyle and Thomas Sullivan describe the case of a person who wishes to defend his family honor by making a speech, knowing that his speech difficulties are almost certain to make the speech come out with a serious stutter. It would be very peculiar to say that the person intends to stutter his way through his speech.[3]

Taking the high road, that of explanation, it seems clear that intention and foresight are different kinds of mental state, and thus must be conceptually distinguished. Foresight is a kind of belief: to foresee something is to believe it that it will occur. Intention is, while likely not a kind of desire, akin to it: to intend something is to seek its realization, to have it as a goal that regulates deliberation and action. But belief and desire have different 'directions of fit.' Belief aims at fitting the world: so if one believes that p, and that p is not the case, one should revise one's belief so that it fits with the world. Desire aims at fitting the world to it: so if one desires that p, and it is not the case that p, one should revise the world so that it fits with one's desire. Since foresight and intention have distinct directions of fit, there must be a difference between them.[4]

So it is possible to foresee that some state of affairs will obtain as the result of one's action without that state of affairs' obtaining being the intended result of one's action. One might say that while this is possible for agents generally, it is not possible for rational agents: that a rational agent foresees a certain result from his or her action entails that by choosing that action the agent intends, in part, that result. As Roderick Chisholm claims – he calls this the 'principle of diffusiveness of intention' – '[I]f a rational man acts with the intention of bringing about a certain state of affairs p and if he believes that by bringing about p he will bring about the conjunctive state of affairs p and q, then he does act with the intention of bringing about p and q.'[5] So, even if there is a conceptual distinction between intention and foresight, in rational agents the foreseen effects of what one intends 'flow into' one's intention, leaving the category of the foreseen-but-unintended meaningful but empty. But it seems to me that there is little warrant for this claim either.

Again – the low road. Suppose that I intend to change lanes on the highway leading into Washington, DC. I foresee that by changing lanes, even using my signal and allowing plenty of room, my action will cause the driver in the next lane to make an obscene gesture at me. According to the view that rational agents enfold the foreseen into their intentions, I must intend that I change lanes and be the recipient of the obscene gesture. This is silly enough. But suppose that the driver, feeling cheerier than usual, does not make the obscene gesture. Must I then try to provoke the driver into doing so, so that my intention will be satisfied? This is even sillier.

Again, still on the low road. The principle that rational agents enfold the foreseen into their intentions would make a solution to the paradox of happiness impossible, at least for rational, informed agents. It turns out there are some activities from which one cannot derive satisfaction – or the most satisfaction available from that activity – unless one performs the activity without attempting to derive satisfaction from it. With some activities, this is a merely contingent feature – it may just be an interesting feature of some people that they cannot derive full enjoyment from chess if they play the game while intending to get satisfaction from it. With some activities, on the other hand, the possibility of enjoyment in that activity of its very nature is excluded by the aim of enjoying it, because the activity is essentially altruistic, for example, selflessly helping others. But the principle of diffusiveness of intention would make these activities impossible for rational agents. Suppose that I intend to help others without regard to promoting my own good. Suppose that I also foresee that performing this action will lead to my enjoyment. So according to the principle, if I am rational, I will intend both to help others without regard to promoting my own good and to gain enjoyment from doing so. Since this is incoherent, if I am rational, I will never intend to help others without regard to my own good – at least so long as I believe that I might end up enjoying it.

The principle of diffusiveness of intentions is just false. The low roads clearly lead away from its acceptance. And Chisholm gives little argument for it. It is true that there is a fairly widely acknowledged principle of rational intending of the form, 'if A is rational, and A intends that p, and A believes that q, then A intends that r.' It is the necessary means principle: if A is rational, and A intends that p, and A believes that its being the case that q is a necessary means to its being the case that p, then A intends that q. But aside from the fact that the necessary means principle is not subject to the embarrassing counterexamples to which the principle of diffusiveness of intention is subject, it is clear that there is a rationale for the necessary means principle, a rationale that is absent in the case of the principle of diffusiveness of intention and explains why the latter is, on reflection, so implausible.

The necessary means principle has its plausibility in virtue of the fact that to intend an end is to set oneself to the achievement of a certain goal, and thus to commit oneself to taking a path that, so far as it is in one's power, leads to that goal. So if a rational agent comes to believe that there is only one available path to one's intended end, then that rational agent will either take that path or give up on the goal. The subordinate intention for the means is needed to guide one's conduct on the path to one's intended goal; the rational agent forms that intention because of the need to guide his or her action in pursuit of the end. But in the case of the principle of the diffusiveness of intention, there is no practical need to expand one's intention to include within it all manner of foreseen consequences of the pursuit of one's end. The point of expanding one's intention to include within it not only the goal, or the means to reach that goal, but also the further consequences, is – what? It is pointless, as the highway case shows. It requires one to include in one's intention matters in which one takes no interest.

There is, then, an important distinction between intention and foresight, and the distinction is maintained even in the case of fully rational agents.

3   Intention, foresight, and success

Put generically, the claim that there is a morally relevant intention/ foresight distinction is tantamount to the claim that acting with the intention of bringing about some intrinsically bad state of affairs S has *something* to be said against it that acting with the foresight that some intrinsically bad state of affairs S will result does not. (I am going to assume that this intrinsically bad state of affairs S is some harm to some person – that it is a state of affairs that involves evil to some person, some way in which he or she is made worse off.)

I am going to argue that there are several ways in which the distinction is morally relevant. But all of these ways will rest, at some point or another, on the connection between the intention of an action and the success of that action. The thesis is that an agent's intention in acting – both with respect to the end of the action and with respect to the means that the agent will take to achieve that end – defines the success conditions of the action, what it is for the action to be a success.[6] This is true both with respect to the intended end and with respect to the intended means. By contrast, what is merely foreseen does not at all define the success conditions of the action.

Suppose that I intend to drive from Washington, DC to Dallas, Texas, leaving at approximately a certain time and arriving at approximately a certain time. I run a route-mapping program on my computer and devise an effective route to follow to get from Washington to Dallas within these parameters. I now have a highly detailed plan of action that I mean to carry out, an ordered sequence of actions which if followed will take me from home to Dallas. I get in the car and start the engine. I proceed to follow the plan *exceedingly poorly*. I take left turns where I should take right turns. I take exits that I should not take. It is not as if I have abandoned my plan for a new one, or have decided to give up my aim to get to Dallas for the sake of a spontaneous, go-where-you-wanna-go see-America road trip: I've set my plan, and I'm screwing it up. Yet, miraculously, at approximately the time I had planned to arrive in Dallas, I end up in Dallas. I have deviated from my plan at various points. But I achieve my intended end (more on this in a moment) or, better, the end in light of which I selected my means in deliberation.

I claim that my action in getting from DC to Dallas was not successful. It was, obviously, successful in *one* sense, the most important sense: I ended up in Dallas. But it was also *not* successful in an important way: I failed to carry out the plan of action that I had set for myself. I had decided to execute a certain plan of action, and I did not execute that plan of action. So my action was unsuccessful.

One might respond: Look, you got what you ultimately cared about getting. You wanted to get to Dallas on time; you got to Dallas on time. How you got there was a mere means. But a mere means, by definition, is something you care about only insofar as it conduces to the end. Since you attained the end, your action was successful in the only sense that counts.

But this seems to me to be a bad argument. When one is deliberating between various courses of action in light of some intended end, it may well be that all that matters with respect to those courses of action is how effective and efficient each is in helping one to realize the desired end. To call a proposed action a mere means is, first and foremost, to describe what counts as a merit or demerit of that action from the point of view of deliberation. It is to say that there is no reason to choose that action except for a certain sought end or ends, and whether there is reason to choose that action depends on how well the action conduces to that end. *But: that a proposed action is a mere means in this sense does not imply that its successful execution is in itself indifferent.* For once the proposed action is decided upon, it has a feature that it previously lacked: it is now *intended*. And what I am saying is that through being intended, an action chosen merely as an effective means becomes more than a mere means: the successful execution of those means as one's route to one's sought end, along with the realization of the sought end, define the success of one's action.

I have appealed so far just directly to your judgment that my action in getting to Dallas was unsuccessful in important ways. Let me try to add some support for this. I think that, if I arrived in Dallas in the way described, I would have some reason to regret the various mistakes that I made – the turns that were not according to plan, the mile markers that went unnoticed, the lane changes that were performed late or not at all. 'I'm such an ass,' I might justly castigate myself. 'I screwed things up, not paying attention, not following the directions properly. That (and by "that" I take it to be obvious that what I am referring to is the set of concrete actions that took me from DC to Dallas) was a disaster. What a *lucky break* that I ended up here on time.' That this response is perfectly sensible suggests that I am right to think of my action as unsuccessful, though very, very lucky. I need not, and am not, claiming here that it would be reasonable for my overall attitude toward my trip to be one of regret. After all, I made it, and I'm lucky that I made it, and my enjoyment in having achieved my end and my thankfulness to divine providence for getting me there on time might swamp the reasons I have for regret about the haplessness of my attempt to execute the plan. All I claim is that I have some reason to regret my misadventures, and this reason for regret shows that the intended means define in part the success conditions for my plan of action.

Further, think of the way that direction-of-fit considerations define intention. Just as the world's being a certain way defines what makes a belief true, so the world's being a certain way defines what makes an intention satisfied. But I did not just intend the end, being in Dallas: I intended a set of means for achieving that end. Thus, even if the intention were satisfied with respect to the end, the intention is not satisfied with respect to the means. If successful belief is true belief, successful intention must be satisfied intention. So, insofar as this intention is unsatisfied, it is unsuccessful. So the unsatisfied intention with regard to the means is sufficient to make my action unsuccessful.

Again, think of the close analogy between success in coming to a true belief and success in coming to a satisfied intention. In aiming to coming to a true belief with respect to some proposition p, one's evidence with respect to the truth or falsity of p is a mere means. In looking to form an opinion about p, and knowing that the truth of q would be relevant to the truth of p, we treat the truth of q as a mere means. But if we come to form a true belief about p on the basis of screwy evidence, we do not treat our belief that p as fully successful; it falls short in some way. We (or some of us[7]) mark this falling short by denying the title of 'knowledge' to such beliefs, noting that the true belief in such cases is merely accidental or lucky. If we allow that belief, be it ever so true, can be less than fully successful on account of its evidentiary shortcomings, we should be willing to allow that action, be its end ever so realized, can be less than fully successful on account of its designated means not being properly executed.

Here is another way to criticize the view that an action in which the intended end is satisfied while the means are unaccomplished is successful: it is plausible even to deny in such cases that the intended end is satisfied. One might say: look, when an end is an object of intention, one does not simply want it, or wish for it. One aims at it as at least the partial product of the execution of these means. Think of the way that deliberation characteristically proceeds: one settles tentatively on an end to be pursued, and casts about for different ways to realize it. Only when one determines that there is an acceptable route to the end does the end become a fully-fledged intention, something that one is set on achieving. To be set on achieving an end is to cleave to it as something to be realized, in part, through one's deliberate efforts. But in the DC-to-Dallas example, I did not realize the end through my deliberate efforts: I realized it through fortuitous circumstances arising partially out of and partially in spite of my deliberate efforts. So I am not altogether confident in the case that the intended end really was achieved.

So I say that in a chosen plan of action, which involves both an intended end and means intended to realize that end, both the end and the means set the success conditions for action meant to execute that plan. By contrast: with respect to my trip to Dallas, there were a variety of things that I could foresee with some certainty. I could foresee very clearly that there would be traffic on the highway getting out of DC. I could foresee that a number of people would fail to yield in traffic, and that some of them would actually accelerate to cut me off when I signaled a lane change. I could foresee that there would be litter on the highway, and that there would be plenty of garish billboards. But if there is no traffic, everyone yields properly, there has been a recent cleanup, and all the billboards have been taken down, that would not make my action unsuccessful. The most that it would imply is either (a) that my beliefs were false, and so my beliefs about my action were unsuccessful, or (b) that my beliefs were true, and so we have decisive *evidence* that my action was unsuccessful – say, because I got lost and was not in fact driving to Dallas. (There should be no temptation to confuse the satisfaction conditions of an intention with evidence that the satisfaction conditions have been met.)

So the success conditions for an action are defined by the intention, both the intended end and the means intended to realize that end. The success conditions for an action are not defined by the merely foreseen. These theses serve as the basis for three ways that the intended/foreseen distinction is practically relevant. The first of these is based on how we are to explain the fact that the success conditions of an action include the means as well as the end. The second and third draw further implications from the fact that the success conditions include the means. We will take these in turn.

4 Intention, ends, and means

Here is a helpful way of describing the strategy that I want to pursue here. It is commonly accepted that there is something additionally shady about intending evil *as an end* rather than as just a means. Pursuing evil for its own sake is morally bad. When writers push for the irrelevance of the intended/foreseen distinction, they pair off intending evil *as a means* with foreseeing evil, and ask why there is any morally relevant distinction between those two.[8] What I want to show is that intending evil as a means is a lot more like intending evil as an end than people tend to think. I am not saying that there is no difference between pursuing some state of affairs for its own sake and pursuing it as a means to realizing some other state of affairs. Pursuing of a state of affairs for its own sake regulates the promoting of states of affairs sought as a means to it, so there must be some difference. But I think that it is important to stress the similarities between pursuing a state of affairs as an end and pursuing it as a means. Seeing the similarity between them will bring out a *prima facie* undesirability of intending evil, one that goes beyond the *prima facie* undesirability of acting in ways from which one foresees that evil will result.

When one settles on an end and grasps that some sequence of actions is an effective way to realize that end, it is not as if one is then whisked along by the motivational tug of the end into adopting the means. This is true even if the proposed means are the only ones available for achieving the end. One reason for this is the straight Kantian point that ends are revisable: when one sees that a proposed course of action is the only one available to realize an end, one nevertheless might choose to reject pursuit of the end instead of adopting those means. That means as well as ends are chosen is the reason, I think, why achievement of the means enters into the success conditions of an action, so that one has some reason for regret when the means are not carried out properly.

They are no longer mere means, in the sense that they have importance only as conducing to the end.

Here is my first argument for the extra moral badness of intended evil. When one chooses evil, even if only as a means, one sets oneself to its achievement. It is now a defining success condition of one's action: one's action is not successful unless the evil is brought about. And one has reason to regret falling short with respect to it, even if the good end that it is supposed to lead to is accomplished. But this is not the case with merely foreseen evil. When one acts with the mere foresight that evil will result, one's action is not defined in terms of it. Thus one has no reason at all for regret that the evil did not come about if one's intended aims are accomplished.

Consider the stock characters of double effect discussions – the terror bomber and the tactical bomber.[9] The terror bomber aims to bring about a good end – military victory over an unjust aggressor – through the bombing of civilian populations, which will demoralize the enemy and bring about surrender. The terror bomber intends the death of the civilians. Thus it is a success condition on his or her action that the civilians be killed. And, shockingly, if the terror bomber bungles his plan, fails to kill the civilians, yet somehow manages to cause an end to the hostilities – perhaps his bombs accidentally fall on a strategically crucial hidden weapons dump – *the terror bomber has reason to regret not causing the death of the civilians.* Again, I am not claiming that the terror bomber would be reasonable to have an overall attitude of regret toward his action: he would have to take into account the very good news that the hostilities have been ended through his action. But I do not need to claim this. All I am claiming is that the terror bomber has some reason to regret not killing the civilians. By contrast, the tactical bomber, who foresees the death of civilians living near a proper military target, does not have the success conditions of his or her action defined by the death of the civilians; and so if through chance the civilians are not killed, the action may nevertheless be fully successful, and there is no reasonable basis to regret that the civilians were not killed.

In defending the double effect principle and its presupposition that there is a morally relevant distinction between the intended and the foreseen, Thomas Nagel writes:

> The difference [between intending evil and acting with mere foresight of evil] is that action intentionally aimed at a goal is guided by that goal. Whether the goal is an end in itself or only a means, action aimed at it must follow it and be prepared to adjust its pursuit if

deflected by altered circumstances – whereas an act that merely produces an effect does not follow it, is not guided by it, even if the effect is foreseen.

But the essence of evil is that it should *repel* us. If something is evil, our actions should be guided, if they are guided by it at all, toward its elimination rather than toward its maintenance. That is what evil *means*. So when we aim at evil we are swimming against the normative current.[10]

But while Nagel thinks that this explains why, as a matter of moral psychology, intending evil exerts severe pressure on the agent, it is not clear why, as a matter of justification, intending evil is unjustifiable when carried out as a means to a greater good.[11] My argument in this section, I hope, provides some further defense: we should not, I say, overstate the difference between intending evil as an end and intending it as a means. For once intended, the evil is no longer a mere means, one among perhaps many paths that one might follow to achieve a good; it becomes something whose obtaining is definitive of one's successful action.

Here, in sum, is the argument. When one intends evil, even as a means, one gives oneself reason to regret, as such, the absence of an evil. But one has reason *not* to have reason to regret, as such, the absence of an evil. So one has reason not to intend evil, even as a means. This argument would obviously not work if 'foresees evil' were substituted for 'intends evil, even as a means'; the first premise would be false. So there is at least one clear morally relevant difference between intending and foreseeing evil.

5   Intention, aims, and agent integrity

It is sometimes held that what makes intending evil objectionable has to do with the preservation of the agent's integrity. There are two obvious retorts to this suggestion. The first is that it puts the cart before the horse. For an agent to have integrity is for that agent to cling steadfastly to what is morally right, or to what he or she conscientiously believes to be morally right. But the latter conception of integrity would not give one who does not believe there to be anything morally untoward about intending evil reason not to intend evil, and the former would simply send us back to the problem of explaining what is morally wrong about intending evil. The second is that this way of understanding the badness of intending evil is objectionably self-centered. If there is something wrong about intending evil, it should focus on how the act responds to the patient, not on what it does to the agent. So it might be thought that explaining the badness of intending evil in terms of integrity is not a very promising idea.

There is a bit more to the appeal to integrity than this, though. I think that we can explain how intending evil is in some way a rupturing of the agent's integrity without appealing to the prior moral wrongness of intending evil, and that the case can be made in a way that shows concern for integrity not to be an entirely self-centered worry.

Here is the idea. One element of an agent's good that often appears on the 'objective lists'[12] of natural law moral philosophers – and, I hasten to add, on the lists of those Kantian,[13] utilitarian,[14] and virtue-theorist Aristotelian[15] philosophers who subscribe to objective list conceptions of well-being – is that of *excellence in agency*. (It does not always go by that name – sometimes 'agency,' sometimes 'practical reasonableness,' and so forth.) Excellence in agency consists, in part, in the successful forming and executing of plans of action. So the idea is that one's own good consists, in part, in acting successfully. One's agency is not just a mechanism by which one can achieve goods; it is itself a good, the good of properly responding to and successfully pursuing goods.

That excellence in agency is a good, and is correctly described in terms of plan-formation and execution, suggests that to a limited extent the content of one's good is up to oneself. The natural law theorist (as well as the other theorists who understand well-being in terms of an objective list) tends to recognize a whole range of goods whose status and content is not determined at all by the agent's deliberation and decision – for example, physical integrity, or speculative knowledge. But excellence in agency makes possible a bit of creativity and autonomy in the determination of the agent's good. Even if my well-being includes my being an excellent agent and your well-being includes your being an excellent agent, the states of affairs that constitute my being such an agent will differ (and not just with respect to our identities) from the states of affairs that constitute your being such an agent. For we can reasonably come up with different plans of action, and thus different states of affairs will count as success with respect to those plans, and thus different states of affairs will constitute our well-being.

But if our earlier reflections on the relationship between success and intention were sound, intended means as well as intended ends define the success of action. And thus there is further reason to worry about intending evil, whether as a means or as an end. For by intending evil, *even as a means*, one makes it a constituent of one's own well-being that someone[16] is worse off. Evil has become one's good. Again, this is not the case with respect to merely foreseen evils following upon one's actions. These evils are not defining of the success of one's actions, and thus do not become constituents of one's well-being through the good of excellence in agency. By intending evil, one becomes a person who cannot be well-off except through the suffering of others; one's well-being *just is*, in part, the suffering of others. And that, I think, is justly labeled a loss of one's integrity as an agent.

6 Intending evil and the good of community

One thing that is bad about intending evil, but not bad about acting with the foresight of evil, is that it makes one a person whose good is constituted by bad. This answers the cart-before-the-horse objection: for while I need to appeal to the prior badness of suffering to explain the loss of integrity resultant on intending evil, I do not need to appeal to the prior moral wrongness of intending evil to do so. But it does not answer the self-centeredness objection. Is the only thing we can say about the way that intending evil is taken up in one's own good that it involves a loss of the agent's integrity?

No. For there is a further good that is damaged by making another's suffering into one's good, one that is irreducibly interpersonal. This is the good of community. The good of community is, positively, the good of participating in common action for the sake of common ends; it is, negatively, the good of not being at odds with one another.[17] But this good – a good that is, unlike excellence in agency, irreducibly interpersonal – is necessarily compromised when one makes one's own good to be constituted in part by another's suffering. For to make one's good to be constituted by evil is to set oneself at odds with another.[18] It is to render things such that under no logically coherent set of circumstances could both people be well-off. It is not that the limited circumstances of the world have put them at odds with one another; one has *made* the world such that they are necessarily at odds. Again, this is not the case with foreseen evil. One may recognize fully well that by pursuing some good, others will suffer. But one's good is not defined by their suffering.

7 The principle of double effect

Recall that according to the principle of double effect, one may act in a way that foreseeably causes evil provided that one's action does not intend the resultant evil and the good proposed is proportionate to the evil foreseeably caused. It is important to see how what I have said so far bears on the defense of the principle of double effect. It justifies, I think, no more than the claim that the principle of double effect is not wrong to propose distinct standards for intended and foreseen evil, where the standard against intended evil is more rigorous than the standard against foreseen evil. The notion that intended evil is always unreasonable, that it can never be right to do evil that good may come, of course requires more than only exhibiting the relevance of the intended/ foreseen distinction. My own suspicion is that the absolute character of the prohibition on intending evil for the sake of promoting the good can be defended only by appealing to specific and highly controversial claims about the nature of the good itself – in particular, that distinct instances of the good are incommensurable.[19] But we must take one step at a time. For the moment, I rest content with the claim that intending evil is *prima facie* unreasonable in a way that foreseeably causing evil is not: it involves making of an evil something whose absence is as such regrettable; it involves constructing one's good in a way that includes evil; and it involves setting one's good intrinsically at odds with another's. One should recognize that the presumption in choice is strongly against action that pursues evil, even as a 'mere means,' even if one is hesitant to endorse the view that such actions are absolutely forbidden.

Notes

Thanks to Timothy Chappell, Chris Eberle, Alfonso Gómez-Lobo, Christopher Kaczor, Alex Pruss, and Karen Stohr for commenting on earlier drafts of this chapter. I owe thanks also to audiences at the Naval Academy and the University of Texas for their critical remarks.

1. See Murphy 2001: 1–3; also Murphy 2002.
2. Sidgwick, *Methods*: 202. (Cf. the *Dictionary of Philosophy and Psychology*'s definition of intention: 'The purpose in view in any action, along with all the consequences of the action, so far as foreseen to be certain or probable' [Baldwin *et al.* 1925: 561].)
3. Boyle and Sullivan 1977: 358.
4. Cf. Aulisio 1995: 345–7, which is indebted to Anscombe 1957.
5. Chisholm 1970: 636.
6. See also Kaczor 2001.
7. To take into account the worries indicated in Weinberg, Nichols, and Stich 2001.
8. See, for example, Bennett 1995: 215.
9. Ibid: 198, 201.
10. Nagel 1986: 181–2.
11. Ibid: 182–3.

12. For an account of objective list conceptions of well-being, contrasting them with hedonist and desire-fulfillment accounts, see Parfit 1984: 493–502.
13. See, for example, Scanlon 1998: 120–3.
14. See, for example, Griffin 1986: 67.
15. See, for example, Nussbaum 1988.
16. We are likely to think of it here as being *someone else* the destruction of whose good will end up constituting part of the agent's good. But one can intend evil to oneself, and in such cases one's own being-badly-off will come to constitute one's good. (Thanks to Timothy Chappell for reminding me of this point.)
17. See Murphy 2001: 126–31.
18. At least in those cases in which one intends evil to another; but, as remarked in note 16, one can intend evil to oneself. In such cases, the good of community will not be implicated. But, first, these are not the sorts of case in which people would be worried that the account I have offered is too self-centered; and, second, it strikes me that there may be an intrapersonal correlate to the good of community – perhaps something like the good of inner peace (Murphy 2001: 118–26), though I am not confident about its categorization – that is threatened when one intends evil to oneself.
19. This would, of course, make even more pressing the provision of a gloss on the idea of 'proportionate' good in the principle of double effect, which as it stands does seem to carry with it the suggestion of commensurability between the goods and evils at stake in one's choices. For a discussion of incommensurability in the context of the principle of double effect, see Murphy 2001: 204–7. For an argument that the notion of proportionate good in the principle of double effect does not covertly appeal to considerations that presuppose commensurability, see Finnis 1991: 97–8.

References

Anscombe, G.E.M. (1957) *Intention*, Oxford: Blackwell.

Aulisio, Mark P. (1995) 'In Defense of the Intention/Foresight Distinction', *American Philosophical Quarterly* 32: 341–54.

Baldwin, James Mark *et al.* (1925) *Dictionary of Philosophy and Psychology*, Vol. I, Gloucester, MA: P. Smith.

Bennett, Jonathan (1995) *The Act Itself*, Oxford: Oxford University Press.

Boyle, Joseph and Thomas Sullivan (1977) 'The Diffusiveness of Intention Principle: A Counter-Example', *Philosophical Studies* 31: 357–60.

Chisholm, Roderick (1970) 'The Structure of Intention', *Journal of Philosophy* 67: 633–47.

Finnis, John (1991) *Moral Absolutes: Tradition, Revision, and Truth*, Washington, DC: Catholic University of America Press.

Griffin, James (1986) *Well-Being: Its Meaning, Measurement, and Moral Importance*, Oxford: Oxford University Press.

Kaczor, Christopher (2001) 'Distinguishing Intention from Foresight: What is Included in a Means to an End?', *International Philosophical Quarterly* 41: 77–89.

Murphy, Mark C. (2001) *Natural Law and Practical Rationality*, Cambridge: Cambridge University Press.

Murphy, Mark C. (2002) 'The Natural Law Tradition in Ethics', *Stanford Encyclopedia of Philosophy*, ed. Ed Zalta (http://plato.stanford.edu/entries/natural-law-ethics/).

Nagel, Thomas (1986) *The View from Nowhere*, Oxford: Oxford University Press.

Nussbaum, Martha (1988) 'Non-Relative Virtues: An Aristotelian Approach', *Midwest Studies in Philosophy* 13: 32–53.

Parfit, Derek (1984) *Reasons and Persons*, Oxford: Oxford University Press.

Scanlon, Thomas (1998) *What We Owe to Each Other*, Cambridge, MA: Harvard University Press.

Sidgwick, Henry (1981) *The Methods of Ethics*, 7th edn, Indianapolis: Hackett.

Weinberg, Jonathan, Shaun Nichols, and Stephen Stich (2001) 'Normativity and Epistemic Intuitions', *Philosophical Topics* 29: 429–60.

Index